KINGDOM GOVERNMENT
AND THE PROMISE OF SHEEP NATIONS

DANIEL DUVAL

KINGDOM GOVERNMENT

GOVERNMENT

AND

THE PROMISE OF SHEEP NATIONS

BY

DANIEL DUVAL

Kingdom Government and the Promise of Sheep Nations

BRIDE Publications

ISBN: 978-1-943843-56-5

Cover Design: Gonz Shimura

Unless otherwise noted, all Scripture quotations are taken from the King James Version of the Bible. Emphasis in bold added by the author.

Scripture quotations marked (AMP) are taken from the Amplified Bible, Copyright © 1954, 1958, 1962, 1964, 1965, 1987 by The Lockman Foundation. Used by permission.

Unless otherwise noted, all Hebrew and Greek words were taken from New Strong's Exhaustive Concordance by James Strong (Waco, TX: Thomas Nelson, 2003).

TABLE OF CONTENTS

PART 4

PART 5

PART 6

PART 7

Dedication

This book is dedicated to future leaders in the body of Christ. It is dedicated to the forerunners, and to those that dare to look over the horizon to what is coming upon the earth. I also want to give a special thank you to my friend Mike, for the many hours he spent in review of this material years before it was published.

INTRODUCTION

What is society? This may at first seem like an odd question, but the answer is very important. According to Dictionary.com, society is "an organized group of persons associated together for religious, benevolent, cultural, scientific, political, patriotic, or other purposes." Based on this definition, my question is this: how does this organization occur? Most societies are based around a charter of some form. In the United States of America, for example, this is known as the Constitution. Could it be that mere words, spoken or written, *become* the society? Or could it be deeper than words? Is it possible that there is another level of understanding hidden deep within our human nature? I believe so. Therefore, I am going to begin with a proposition. *I propose that human society is actually a program that is subconsciously instilled into its members.*

Society and culture go hand in hand. One will always come with the other. Again referencing Dictionary.com, culture is "the quality in a person or society that arises from a concern for what is regarded as excellent in arts, letters, manners, scholarly pursuits, etc." Culture is always the result of society; society does not result from culture. Culture defines the values and qualities of a society. *Therefore, I propose that while society is the program, the culture becomes the observable product of a society's set of values.*

We must understand that because society is merely a program, it can be rewritten. Where does this writing/programming/rewriting occur? It occurs within the hearts of men, which is best understood as the subconscious. In other words, society first exists within the hearts of those that comprise it, and is then expressed through culture. Without understanding how our heart dictates our reality, we cannot embrace a reality that exists outside of this dimension. This reality is the kingdom of God, and it is the program for the coming society.

The kingdom of God is a society that exists in another realm entirely. This realm is located above our dimension in a place defined in the Bible as the third heaven (2 Corinthians 12:2-4). In order to understand the society of the kingdom, our thinking has to be in line with the reality of how things work. We participate in this heavenly kingdom and society while simultaneously maintaining an existence in the world. This is because we are raised up into heavenly places the moment we experience salvation (Ephesians 2:6). This society exists for one reason, and that is to execute the agendas of its King.

This society has a culture. Its culture is an expression of the values of the society. Since the society we are partaking of is based in a government that is fashioned as a kingdom, the values of the society are intended to be extracted from the single Potentate of that kingdom. This is the King, and he is God. The purest expression of the values of the King occur as worship. Hence, the culture of God's kingdom is a culture of worship. As society and culture from the realm of God's kingdom are implemented through a mature company of people, it will shake the nations of this world. This will lead to sheep nations, which will be entire geographies that are heavily influenced by the kingdom of God reigning in and through the hearts of men.

In order to understand how to tap into the reality of this kingdom, we must understand the heart. It is through the heart that we come in contact with the mysteries of God. Therefore, before we entertain the revelation of kingdom government and sheep nations, we must address the heart.

PART 1

CHAPTER 1

Introducing the Heart

"For as he thinketh in his heart, so is he: Eat and drink, saith he to thee; but his heart is not with thee" (Proverbs 23:7).

Our experiences in life will always mirror the belief system in our heart. If we perceive ourselves as failures, we will be failures. If we perceive ourselves as successful, we will be successful. *As he thinketh in his heart, so is he*. The heart is one of the most important revelations in the Bible. Think about it. The majority of our life experiences *will* manifest according to what is in our heart. This being true, our goal should be to convince our heart, which I will introduce as the subconscious, of the things that will give us the best life possible. The question is: how do we convince our subconscious of something? The answer: convincing the subconscious is actually done via programming.

Programming the heart is not necessarily easy. Why not? It is because we do not have direct access to the thoughts of our heart. Unlike the thoughts of our mind, which we can consciously change, the thoughts of the heart go deeper than our conscious mind. The subconscious is beneath the reach of the conscious mind, hence the prefix "sub." The heart contains the underlying thought base, out of which all of our decisions are made. This is why Jesus says defilement comes from within a man.

"Not that which goeth into the mouth defileth a man; but that which cometh out of the mouth, this defileth a man" (Matthew 15:11).

Jesus said this because he knew that we speak according to what is in our heart. A true confession is based on subconscious thoughts.

UNDERSTANDING CONFESSION

"O generation of vipers, how can ye, being evil, speak good things? **for out of the abundance of the heart the mouth speaketh**" (Matthew 12:34).

Confessions are simply the words we speak concerning various aspects of our lives, such as ourselves, our finances, our families, our physical bodies, our jobs, our relationships, etc. By understanding the interaction between our words and our hearts, it gives us greater insight into just how the subconscious works, and how programming can occur. For instance, if we change our confession before our heart is changed, we contradict our subconscious. This can have several effects. For starters, it can allow the heart to question itself and change. This happens in situations where a change in confession results in a rewarding experience. Conversely, it can cause the heart to reinforce its thoughts. This happens in situations where a change in confession results in a painful experience.

For example, consider a fictional character named Steve. Steve has been told that he is a terrible cook. This has been said to him ever since he tried to make pancakes at the age of five. As one would imagine, after hearing a lifetime of putdowns, he truly believes that he is a terrible cook. If someone said they saw potential for him to be a world-class chef, his heart would be presented with a contradiction. The new information would have to be tested. If he were to try and cook with success at this point, it would be a rewarding experience. As a result, his heart would change, and his self-perception would be altered. If he tried to cook and utterly failed, his heart would reinforce its former thoughts.

This can also be true of the inverse, in that our heart can believe truth and be questioned with lies. If the lies, accompanied by a change in confession, result in a logical experience, the heart will also change. It follows that if lies accompanied by a change in confession result in an illogical experience, the heart will reinforce its thoughts.

For example, consider another fictional character named Sue. Sue has an IQ of 157. If someone were to tell her that she is an imbecile, they would be presenting her heart with a lie. According to her IQ, she is actually a genius. If she went to take a test after hearing this nonsense and scored a perfect score, her heart would dismiss the lie because of the illogical experience. She cannot be an imbecile and score a perfect score. Conversely, if she scored a terrible score on the test, her heart would be willing to embrace a lie because of the outcome. Many of us have been deceived into embracing lies about ourselves on one level or another.

The heart is an instrument that can be utilized to make us more than we ever imagined we could become. It is also our great obstacle. It can effectively establish us in truth, or destroy us with lies. How many of us, wanting to do good things, repeatedly fall short? Moreover, how many of us look at the experiences in our lives and say we can never be like Christ? Yet the Bible says that we must come to the measure of the stature of the fullness of Christ before his second coming. This must occur in our hearts.

"And he gave some, apostles; and some, prophets; and some, evangelists; and some, pastors and teachers; For the perfecting of the saints, for the work of the ministry, for the edifying of the body of Christ: **Till we all come in the unity of the faith, and of the knowledge of the Son of God, unto a perfect man, unto the measure of the stature of the fulness of Christ**" (Ephesians 4:11-13).

KINGDOM SOCIETY

The kingdom of God has been sent to cause both society and culture to be conformed to an agenda. In opposition to this, the kingdoms of men and the kingdom of darkness exert power to conform culture and society to *their* agenda. Society is designed to be controlled. *The goal, then, is to participate in a society that is conformed to the right agenda*. If there is no agenda, the purpose of a society dies, because without an agenda, there can be no vision. Where there is no vision, death reigns.

"Where there is no vision, the people perish: but he that keepeth the law, happy is he" (Proverbs 29:18).

Beginning at this point, we are going to explore the agenda of the kingdom of God as the world spirals into the countdown to the end of the age. This will reveal kingdom government: its purpose and its reality. Out of this understanding, we will have a glimpse of sheep nations. These are to express both the society and culture of the kingdom of God. Together, they will be the sustaining force that allows the people of God to overcome, in spite of what will be revealed.

CHAPTER 2

Spirit, Soul, Body & Heart

The Bible breaks us up into three main components. These components are the body, the soul, and the spirit. There is a fourth component that allows the other three to function according to God's purpose. This fourth component is the heart. This chapter will explain this interaction. Let us begin with Paul's comment in 1 Thessalonians.

"And the very God of peace sanctify you wholly; and I pray God your whole **spirit and soul and body** be preserved blameless unto the coming of our Lord Jesus Christ" (1 Thessalonians 5:23).

THE BODY

The body is composed of our mortal flesh. It is composed primarily of carbon, and it executes all of our physiological processes. It consists of our five senses, which are touch, taste, sight, smell, and hearing. Our physical body is the aspect of our being that interacts with this world. It releases certain chemicals that affect our perception of the world for both good and bad. The body is subject to sickness, disease, deterioration, and ultimately, death. It also experiences physical needs and urges that have the potential to drive us to sin. One example is the sexual urge. Another is gluttony. The Bible instructs us to not obey the lusts of our mortal body.

"Let not sin therefore reign in your mortal body, that ye should obey it in the lusts thereof" (Romans 6:12).

THE SOUL

The soul is composed of our mind, will, and emotions. The soul is our main battleground as Christians. This is the aspect of our composition that needs to be continually and progressively redeemed throughout our lives. Although we have received Jesus, our emotions are not perfect. Although we have found salvation, we still think sinful thoughts. Even when we want to repent, we may still desire things of the world. Our mind, will, and emotions must be continually placed in submission to the Holy Spirit as we move forward in our faith. Moving forward in our faith requires us to believe unto the saving of the soul. This means that our soul progressively comes under increasing control of our spirit, which is inhabited by the perfect Spirit of God.

"But we are not of them who draw back unto perdition; but of them that believe to the saving of the soul" (Hebrews 10:39).

THE SPIRIT

Our spirit is redeemed at salvation. *Our spirit is our point of contact with God and with the spirit realm.* When the Bible says we have been made the righteousness of God in Christ, it is referring to the state of our spirit (2 Corinthians 5:21). Our spirit is also made alive in Christ when we find salvation. Before salvation, our spirit is dead in sin.

Our spirit is our gateway to the heavenly dimensions. It is our spirit that has become one with the Holy Spirit (1 Corinthians 6:17). Many do not realize that when the Bible refers to the "old man" it is referring to the spirit man prior to salvation (Romans 6:6). When we are saved, our spirit man is baptized in the death of Christ and raised in new life with Christ (Romans 6:4). From this point forward, our spirit has been freed from sin (Romans 6:7). Here is a simple way to distinguish soul and spirit: our spirit can be understood as *what* we are, and our soul can be understood as *who* we are.

It is important to understand that our spirit can still become filthy, even after being joined to the Holy Spirit (2 Corinthians 7:1). We must seek to preserve it blameless, just like our soul and our body (1 Thessalonians 5:23). Although the Holy Spirit enters our spirit and becomes one with it, he does not completely replace it. The Holy Spirit comes to live inside our spirit, but our spirit always remains an individual spirit.

The Heart

The heart, being our subconscious, should be understood as the *gateway* between our soul and our spirit. It is here that the Word of God divides between what is of the soul, and what is of the spirit. Consider what is written:

"For the word of God is quick, and powerful, and sharper than any two edged sword, piercing even to the **dividing asunder of soul and spirit**, and of the joints and marrow, **and is a discerner of the thoughts and intents of the <u>heart</u> [emphasis mine]**" (Hebrews 4:12).

It is clear from this passage that the Word of God is intended to do its work in our heart. First, it divides what is spirit from what is soul. Then, it discerns the thoughts and intents of the heart. All of this occurs in the heart. The power of the Word of God extends into our mortal flesh, but even this work is rooted in the heart. The Word of God cannot begin to affect our physical body until we believe that God has this power in our heart. Again, this means that all of these works occur in the human subconscious.

This becomes the essential link between everything that God intended for us to be, and the reality that we experience. The heart, being the subconscious, becomes the seat of human intuition. It receives and processes information from multiple inputs. Input comes from a physical level, a soul level, or a spiritual level. God's will is to be our primary source of input. His Spirit communicates revelation from our spirit to our heart.

Proper understanding of the soul and the spirit leads us into greater understanding regarding how revelation actually works for the Christian. Revelation is not based on what we can figure out. It is actually based on the truth that God knows. This truth must be revealed to us through our spirit.

THE MIND OF CHRIST

"For who hath known the mind of the Lord, that he may instruct him? **but we have the mind of Christ**" (1 Corinthians 2:16).

When we are saved, we actually receive the mind of Christ. The mind of Christ does not replace our individual mind when we are saved. However, *it places in our spirit access to all that Jesus Christ knows*. This is a profound concept! Once we are saved, we are granted access to the sum total of all that the person of the Godhead, Jesus Christ, knows. As we receive revelation, the truth that is in the mind of Christ is progressively illuminated to our conscious mind. This information is funneled from the spirit, through the heart, and into the mind. We cannot have truth added to us as Christians. We have all truth in spirit once we have been made "one" with the Holy Spirit (1 Corinthians 6:17). We simply become enlightened to the truth that is already in us, and this is why we feel inner confirmation when truth is spoken.

This is also why the Bible says the Holy Spirit teaches us all things. He teaches by revelation. While men and books can only convince our subconscious of things through repetition, the Holy Spirit teaches our hearts, and changes us from within accordingly. The Bible says that the Holy Spirit will *guide* us into all truth. He takes us on a journey, illuminating to us what Jesus knows. We can choose to receive or to reject the truth. We can choose to program our heart by the truth that is in our spirit, or by the deception that has been planted in the soul.

"Howbeit when he, the Spirit of truth, is come, **he will guide you into all truth**: for he shall not speak of himself; but whatsoever he shall hear, that shall he speak: and he will shew you things to come" (John 16:13).

"But the Comforter, which is the Holy Ghost, whom the Father will send in my name, **he shall teach you all things**, and bring all things to your remembrance, whatsoever I have said unto you" (John 14:26).

Now that we understand the interaction between the body, soul, spirit, and heart, we will move into the process of programming the heart. What is involved in programming the heart? How does this relate to the kingdom of God? The answers will prove revolutionary.

CHAPTER 3

Programming the Heart

To understand how a society can be directed, or even controlled, we must understand what needs to be targeted. In order to direct society, one must assume control over the subconscious realm. This is synonymous with the heart. It is within this realm that the thoughts of the heart, meaning the compilation of carnal and spiritual knowledge, are creating a worldview. Directing a society is achieved by programming the hearts of the people in that society. Programming the heart can be defined as changing the thoughts of the heart.

There are three main ways to program the heart. The method of programming is dependent on which kingdom has created the program. There are three main types of kingdoms, but only two have the ability to take us beyond the limitations of our natural fallen state.

➤ The kingdom of God

➤ The kingdoms of men

➤ The kingdom of darkness

For clarity, keep in mind from this point forward that the terms *kingdom of God* and *kingdom of heaven* will be used interchangeably (more on this in chapter 22). The kingdoms of men will either further the agenda of the kingdom of darkness, or the agenda of the kingdom of God. Why? There are three kinds of kingdoms in operation, but only two agendas at work. The agendas are the Christ agenda, and the antichrist agenda. The Christ agenda is the redemption of the fallen race of men by the death and resurrection of Jesus. The antichrist agenda is any agenda that denies that Jesus is Lord. There is no middle ground, and there is no alternative. As mortals, we will die. There are two destinies that await those who die: eternal damnation, or eternal life in Christ. The kingdoms of men will either further the Christ agenda by submitting to it, or stand in its way by resisting it. Resisting the Christ agenda is furthering the antichrist agenda. As it is written:

"He that is not with me [Jesus] is against me; and he that gathereth not with me scattereth abroad" (Matthew 12:30).

PROGRAMMING AND OPERATIONAL PARADIGMS

The two kingdoms that have the ability to take us beyond our natural state are the kingdom of darkness and the kingdom of God. This means that when our hearts are being conformed to the thoughts given by these sources, our lives exceed that which is natural, or even considered to be possible. Each kingdom has its own method of programming when it comes to the heart.

- ➤ In the kingdom of God, our hearts are programmed through revelation

- ➤ In the kingdoms of men, our hearts are programmed through repetition

- ➤ In the kingdom of darkness, our hearts are programmed through trauma

As it follows, each form of programming leads to a different operational paradigm. When our hearts are programmed by revelation from God, we have a love-based paradigm. We think and act like God thinks and acts. It is possible for a society to reflect this—in fact, this is exactly where God wants to take us. When our hearts are programmed by repetition, we have a tradition-based paradigm. This is the difference between religion and relationship. We will think and act like our forefathers thought and acted. Most societies reflect this. When our hearts are programmed by trauma we have a fear and lie-based paradigm. We begin to think and act like Satan would think and act. The world in which Noah lived existed according to this program (Genesis 6:5), and we can expect to it recur before the second advent of Jesus (Matthew 24:37).

"Ye are of your father the devil, and the lusts of your father ye will do. He was a murderer from the beginning, and abode not in the truth, because there is no truth in him. When he speaketh a lie, he speaketh of his own: for he is a liar, and the father of it" (John 8:44).

Society is intended to be directed by a subconscious program. Whatever kingdom maintains control over the subconscious realm maintains control over that society. It is important to realize that society cannot exist without the individual. Therefore, the battle for the control of society begins with the control over the individuals that comprise it. In other words, it begins with you. How do we take this revelation from a corporate perspective to an individual perspective?

The War for the Heart

The spirit and the soul are in a perpetual war for the thoughts of the heart. For Christians, while the spirit is attempting to program the heart according to the truths of God and his kingdom, the soul is attempting to program the heart according to the experiences of life. For this reason, we must continually renew our minds with the Word of God, so that we can live according to the victory purchased by Jesus.

"And be not conformed to this world: **but be ye transformed by the renewing of your mind**, that ye may prove what is that good, and acceptable, and perfect, will of God" (Romans 12:2).

When we allow our soul to program our heart according to our experiences, we program ourselves with lies. *We were not created to live according to the realities of a fallen world*. But if we believe these realities in our heart, we will inevitably live according to them. We will serve what we yield ourselves to. What we yield ourselves to will become the primary influence upon our heart.

"Know ye not, that to whom ye yield yourselves servants to obey, his servants ye are to whom ye obey; whether of sin unto death, or of obedience unto righteousness" (Romans 6:16)?

Even after we have received Jesus, if we serve sin unto death, the heart has received its program from our soul. We have failed to move on towards the saving of the soul, and instead have chosen to serve the lie. Before we can transition from where we are as the body of Christ, we must understand that we live according to whatever our hearts believe. *Until we begin to serve the law of the kingdom of God, we will live according to earthly boundaries. We cannot live according to the heavenly dimensions until our subconscious has been programmed according to its corresponding realities.* We must reject the fallen realities of this world from the very depths of our being.

Facts and Reality

We can have better understanding with an illustration. Let's take Bob, a hypothetical middle-aged man. Bob has always been average. His family was average, he is average, and his children are expected to be average. Bob earns an average income. These are the facts of Bob's life. Thus, these facts constitute Bob's reality. Or do they?

Reality is not based on facts. Reality is actually based upon agreement. If we agree with the facts, they will always remain our reality. Bob is in agreement with the fact that he is average. However, if Bob has received Jesus, his heavenly reality makes him a king and a priest (Revelation 1:6) and more than a conqueror (Romans 8:37). Suddenly we are faced with a paradox. Two realities are in competition. Bob cannot be average and more than a conqueror at the same time. There is the reality of circumstance and fact, and there is the reality of the kingdom of God. Which reality wins? The reality that wins is whichever reality Bob is in agreement with *in his heart.* The reality of circumstance and fact is presented to his heart by his soul. The reality of the kingdom of God is presented to his heart by his spirit and confirmed through the written Word of God.

At this point we can understand that the heart becomes a gateway, or "valley of decision" between the soul and the spirit. Remember, the soul is comprised of our mind, will and emotions. Our spirit is our contact point with God. The heart compiles information according to our input and creates a program. We live according to this program. Our heart meditates on the primary source of influence that we receive on any particular issue or aspect of life. God looks upon these meditations when he judges the hearts of men. These are not conscious thoughts, but subconscious thoughts that are affecting us, even when we purpose to think differently.

"Let the words of my mouth, and **the meditation of my heart**, be acceptable in thy sight, O LORD, my strength, and my redeemer" (Psalm 19:14).

CHAPTER 4

The Gospel of Jesus Christ

At this point you, as the reader, need to ask yourself a pertinent question. What program do you want operating in your heart? Do you want the agendas of other men dictating your existence to you? If so, you may as well put this book down. Do you want the agenda of the kingdom of darkness dictating your existence to you? If so, you can also put this book down. Do you want the kingdom of God to dictate your existence to you? It all begins with Jesus Christ. There is no alternative.

In order to make a decision for Jesus, we must believe that he is the only begotten Son of the Father. When he came to earth he was born of a virgin, being entirely God and entirely man. He lived among us, being tempted in all points as we are, yet untainted by sin. In this way, he became an acceptable sacrifice for the sins of man. God sent him because he loved the world—and he still does. This means that he loves you, and he sent his Son to lay down his life so that he could restore and fulfill yours!

THE ULTIMATE SACRIFICE

God was burdened with an unquenchable love for the whole world. For this love, Jesus died an excruciating, reprehensible, and utterly denigrating death. He was beaten, and his hairs were plucked from his face. A crown of thorns was twisted around his scalp, rupturing blood vessels so that the blood poured from his head. He was beaten with a cat-o-nine tails—a whip with nine strands often containing shards of metal, bone, and glass. The stripes upon his back were not from bruised or bleeding skin. His flesh was voraciously torn from his back, muscles and bones left totally exposed. After they were finished, the skin and muscle that was still attached to his body hung in ribbons.

Upon this back they laid a cross, forcing him to carry it alone. As he dragged this cross, the weight pressed into his open body, inserting splinters of wood. When he could no longer carry it, the cross was given to another, yet Jesus was forced to walk the remaining distance to Golgotha. He was dehydrated. As he walked, the blood that continually dripped into his eyes caused severe burning, and the flesh of his back was totally exposed. He did this for you!

At Golgotha, where Jesus was crucified, they laid his body upon the cross, naked. They rolled dice amongst themselves for his garments. For all of those who have ever been raped, in this moment, Jesus felt that shame. They nailed him to that cross, placing the nails into the major nerves connecting the hands to the central nervous system. They placed a single nail through both of his feet. His legs were not allowed to hang straight down, but were fixed so that his knees were bent at forty-five degrees, causing severe and excruciating cramping in his thighs. His muscles fatigued in minutes, but he continued to live for hours.

Upon the cross, death came by asphyxiation. In the position that Jesus was nailed to the cross, it was impossible to breathe. It was not that he was gasping for air. The position of crucifixion caused his lungs to be maximally inflated with air. He had to struggle to breathe *out*. Jesus had to drag his back up and down the wooden cross for hours before breathing his final breath. In order to drag his open flesh up the cross, he had to push up on his feet, causing his hands to twist upon the nails that were driven through his nerves. Crucifixion placed the body in such a position that the joints of the arm would slowly become dislocated as the victim suffered. By the time Jesus neared death, all of his bones were out of joint, adding literal inches to the lengths of his arms. He did this for you![1]

With a face marred beyond recognition, Jesus cried out to the Father, "My God! My God! Why have you forsaken me?" He suffered the ultimate feelings of rejection, because when he became sin for us, he had to be forsaken by his Father in heaven. In the end, the internal complications resulting from crucifixion ruptured the heart of Jesus. When they pierced his side, blood and water poured out. Jesus died of a heart broken for us. He died that we might live, not only eternally, but also abundantly. He died to give us the very life of God. He is the acceptable sacrifice—the only sacrifice that God will accept for our sins.

How to have Salvation in Jesus Christ

In order to be saved, we must not only believe that Jesus died, but that he was resurrected on the third day. He later ascended to heaven, and sat down at the right hand of the Father, where he remains to this day continually making intercession for us. This is the God that I serve! This is the God of love! This is the gospel of Jesus Christ! If you believe this in your heart, then you can confess this prayer with your mouth and you will be saved:

Jesus, I come before you and acknowledge that I am a sinner. I repent. I call upon your name and I ask you to cleanse me with your blood. Forgive me of my sins. I invite you into my heart, Jesus Christ. I believe that you were born of a virgin, died, and were resurrected on the third day that I might have eternal life. I open my life to you and I ask you to come in and be my Lord and Savior. Thank you for saving me. In Jesus' name I pray. Amen.

If you just said that prayer, the next step is to find a born-again, Bible-believing church. You also need to get baptized. Welcome to your new life!

CHAPTER 5

Glory

We have defined the heart. We have tied it into the kingdom. Where do we go from here? How do we take Christianity from what it is today, and propel it into the destiny that God has ordained? A major step is unification. There is actually a strategy for uniting Christians from one end of the world to the other, and it is based upon the revealed glory of God amongst His people.

Neither pray I for these alone, but for them also which shall believe on me through their word; That they all may be one; as thou, Father, art in me, and I in thee, that they also may be one in us: that the world may believe that thou hast sent me. **And the glory which thou gavest me I have given them; that they may be one, even as we are one**: I in them, and thou in me, that they may be made perfect in one; and that the world may know that thou hast sent me, and hast loved them, as thou hast loved me. Father, I will that they also, whom thou hast given me, be with me where I am; that they may behold my glory, which thou hast given me: for thou lovedst me before the foundation of the world. O righteous Father, the world hath not known thee: but I have known thee, and these have known that thou hast sent me. And I have declared unto them thy name, and will declare it: that the love wherewith thou hast loved me may be in them, and I in them.

(John 17:20-26)

Understanding Glory

In his prayer, Jesus says that the same glory that was given to him has been granted to those who believe in him. The word "glory" used in this verse is the Greek word *doxa*. According to Vine's Expository Dictionary it means "the honor resulting from a good opinion." *Therefore, the glory of God is the honor resulting from God's manifested opinion of how things should be.* In other words, God's opinion of how things should be is intended to invade our atmosphere and become our reality. This reality results in honor being given to God. This honor is deep, and results in worship, praise and exultation.

Before God engaged in the creation, the Bible records that the Spirit of the Lord moved upon the face of the waters (Genesis 1:2). This atmosphere of earth included the tangible presence of the Spirit of God. In this atmosphere, God's opinion of reality was manifested. When God said, "Let there be light," there was light. This is the same atmosphere that the people of God are called to abide in. In this atmosphere, God's opinion becomes our reality. Heaven is our example of what the glory of God should cause in the earth. Consider what is occurring in the third heaven right now:

"And when those beasts give glory and honour and thanks to him that sat on the throne, who liveth for ever and ever, The four and twenty elders fall down before him that sat on the throne, and worship him that liveth for ever and ever, and cast their crowns before the throne, saying, Thou art worthy, O Lord, to receive glory and honour and power: for thou hast created all things, and for thy pleasure they are and were created" (Revelation 4:9-11).

The four living creatures, the heavenly angels, and the elders in heaven are compelled by the irresistible magnetic presence of God. It is so magnanimous that it literally pulls the worship out of them. They cannot help but worship him day and night. Our minds cannot comprehend this degree of majesty, and to us this force is inconceivable. However, our hearts are able to perceive information that is both spiritual and natural, and compile it to create the reality out of which we operate.

For this reason, while we are in the glory of God, our hearts implement heavenly realities into our belief systems. Heavenly realities are intended to override the other thoughts of our subconscious. When the thoughts of our hearts are in agreement with the Spirit of God, he is free to work in us and through us mightily. This enables us to live supernatural lives and attain the unity of the faith and the measure of the stature of the fullness of Christ.

FROM GLORY TO GLORY

Going back to the concept of glory, how do we gain access to the glory of God? The truth is—we already have it. We already have access; but we need to use it. Using our access involves sacrifice, worship, giving, seeking, brotherly love, fasting, and forgiveness. There is no formula, and it boils down to earnest seeking. When we ask God for it, he will show us how we can experience it and move from one glory realm to another.

"But without faith it is impossible to please him: for he that cometh to God must believe that he is, and that **he is a rewarder of them that diligently seek him**" (Hebrews 11:6).

"Ask, and it shall be given you; seek, and ye shall find; knock, and it shall be opened unto you: For every one that asketh receiveth; and he that seeketh findeth; and to him that knocketh it shall be opened" (Matthew 7:7-8).

"But we all, with open face beholding as in a glass the glory of the Lord, **are changed into the same image from glory to glory**, even as by the Spirit of the Lord" (2 Corinthians 3:18)

In moving from glory to glory, we are becoming just like Jesus. It is interesting that the apostle Paul points out that it is *all of us* moving from glory to glory. This suggests that it is something that is done corporately, not something that is intended to be reserved for spiritual superstars. This movement is by the Spirit of the Lord. We move from one glory realm to the next in partnership with the Holy Spirit. We cannot move without submitting to this relationship in progressively increasing ways. The glory is for the unity of the body. Individuals who minister in the glory realms have been granted access for the purposes of God. The radical miracles that result are not for self-promotion.

The last moves of God will take the church through radical, accelerated movement from one level of glory to the next. Those who do not cooperate will weed themselves out of God's plan. Those who do cooperate will attain the promised state of Ephesians 4:13 being the manifestation of the measure of the stature of the fullness of Christ on earth. Why? As we move into higher levels of glory, our hearts are being reprogrammed to heavenly realities more and more. The greater the glory, the less time this reprogramming takes. However, this must first begin with the heart belief that it is possible.

All of this is necessary to establish a heavenly society on earth with heavenly culture. This is central to the work Christ accomplished at Cavalry. Consider what is written:

"But ye are a chosen generation, a royal priesthood, an holy nation, a peculiar people; that ye should shew forth the praises of him who hath called you out of darkness into his marvellous light" (1 Peter 2:9).

Glory Realms

Glory realms can be understood as the degree to which the third heaven and earth intersect at any time within certain geography. The earth contains fallen realities, and the third heaven (2 Corinthians 12:2) contains God's realities. When heavenly realities win out, intersection occurs, and heavenly realities overtake fallen realities. How does this work? It is difficult to describe this with a picture, but suffice it to say that the third heaven and earth exist in different dimensions entirely. For this reason, overlap can occur at any place and any time, because space as we understand it does not separate the third heaven from earth.

Once the glory begins to manifest, there is a progression of the intensity of that glory. The intensity increases as the people who are present corporately desire increasing intimacy with the Spirit of God. In other words, our actions not only allow for overlap, but also the *degree* of overlap between the third heaven and earth. Imagine what it might look like if the heavenly temple were intersecting with earth. Of course, there would be no collision because the heavenly temple is spiritual. However, the degree of intersection can be measured by observing the atmosphere. People can stop at the gate called beautiful, the outer court, the inner court, the holy place, or the holy of holies. Once we as the people of God progress into the glory to the holy of holies (spiritually), we will find the manifestation of the unity of the Godhead and receive that impartation.

GLORY AND UNITY

This is a major aspect of how the body of Christ will be unified and the corporate heart knit together. This place is beyond miracles, and beyond description. Many things will occur on the path to this place of glory. However, in order to move into this realm, it is necessary to not get focused on the manifestations. Every level of glory will result in the occurrence and outpouring of spectacular signs and wonders. It must be the goal of the body of Christ to corporately progress through the glory realms and into the holy of holies. We are to go so deep that corporately, we are where God is. This progression occurs according to the submission and yielding of hearts corporately. People must choose in unity to submit to the increasing intensity of the presence of God, and remain in agreement to not be distracted by magnificent and indescribable miracles and manifestations.

"And the glory which thou gavest me I have given them; that they may be one, even as we are one" (John 17:22).

This glory can only be properly accessed out of a pure heart towards God. To access this glory for unity requires a new program to be written in the hearts of the people of God. This program is the kingdom of God. This happened for a moment in the first church, but God is going to bring his global church back to this point before his Son returns.

"And the multitude of them that believed were of one heart and of one soul: neither said any of them that ought of the things which he possessed was his own; but they had all things common" (Acts 4:32).

For a moment, the first church attained a degree of unity that has yet to be replicated. After two thousand years we are coming back around to this destiny. God is going to reveal his kingdom in the earth. This will manifest through a new society defined by a heavenly program. This society will have a new culture, based upon the character of Christ. It will be a culture based upon the culture of heaven—*which is a culture of worship*. Shortly after we attain this spiritual posture, Jesus will return and judge the world.

Our destiny is the unity of the faith. It is inseparable from the corporate church attaining the measure of the stature of the fullness of Christ (Ephesians 4:13). When God's glory is truly revealed amongst God's people, it affects how we experience reality. It opens us up to heavenly realities and heavenly thought patterns. When God is present, his glory is with him. His glory demands honor. If God is present, we must honor him. Spiritual thoughts are not intellectually discerned, but come into us as revelation. Revelation is immediately planted into our hearts, bypassing our conscious minds.

When our minds are bypassed, our convictions and underlying operating systems can be immediately affected. Our whole world-view can be changed without us knowing that it even happened! Suddenly, we think differently. We see things differently, and we interpret circumstances in a different light. This is the basis behind subliminal messaging. Think of revelation in the glory of God as the ultimate, infallible subliminal message. As we press into the glory as the people of God, we will find that we are in unity of the faith, individually all coming to the same conclusions. The glory of God is the highway to reprogramming the hearts within an entire geography. Our society and culture is intended to become an expression of the reality that we are drawing from. As we believe in our hearts, so will we be.

CHAPTER 6

Kingdom Government

Society can be defined as a program that produces culture. By observing a culture, we understand the program that created it. Individually, our heart creates the program that produces our lives. By observing the fruit of a person's life, their heart is clearly revealed.

"Beware of false prophets, which come to you in sheep's clothing, but inwardly they are ravening wolves. Ye shall know them by their fruits. Do men gather grapes of thorns, or figs of thistles? Even so every good tree bringeth forth good fruit; but a corrupt tree bringeth forth evil fruit. A good tree cannot bring forth evil fruit, neither can a corrupt tree bring forth good fruit. Every tree that bringeth not forth good fruit is hewn down, and cast into the fire. Wherefore by their fruits ye shall know them" (Matthew 7:15-20).

Corporately, the hearts of the masses create the program that produces the culture. *For this reason, a society must have its origins within the hearts of those who comprise it*. Only from this understanding can we move forward into kingdom government and the promise of sheep nations (Matthew 25:31-33).

What is kingdom government? Kingdom government occurs when God rules a group of people through the hearts of those who comprise the society. What are sheep nations? Sheep nations occur when a geography of people have been significantly influenced by kingdom government.

Kingdom government has two major applications that I will discuss in this work. The first is its application in governing the church. The second is its application in influencing society. In the latter, it becomes a model around which the will of God can be demonstrated in a society. It takes on literal implementation in the form of politics, education, arts, business, etc. In the former, it becomes a structure that is capable of building the will of God into his people.

A Kingdom is a Government

The first and most important thing that we must grasp is that *a kingdom is a government*. It is not a club, and it is not an ideology. It is a real government, and it exists first in the spirit, and second in this life. The kingdom of heaven has God as its King. The kingdom of heaven also has offices. These are positions of authority that have been delegated by the King to the King's constituents. Offices in the kingdom of heaven do not come by election, but by appointment.

"And God hath set [appointed] some in the church, first apostles, secondarily prophets, thirdly teachers, after that miracles, then gifts of healings, helps, governments, diversities of tongues" (1 Corinthians 12:28).

The kingdom of heaven has a divine order. This order is for the purpose of housing the glory of God as his temple upon the earth. The saints have been made into a spiritual temple for God in the earth.

"Know ye not that ye are the temple of God, and that the Spirit of God dwelleth in you" (1 Corinthians 3:16)?

"What? Know ye not that your body is the temple of the Holy Ghost which is in you, which ye have of God, and ye are not your own" (1 Corinthians 6:19)?

When we reject or attempt to override God's divine order, we are in essence creating our own kingdom, and not embracing his. We cannot expect to partake of the realities of his kingdom until we have submitted to the government of his kingdom. The government of the kingdom of God begins in heaven, and is enforced in the earth through the proper alignment of the five main offices. Working together, these offices express the fullness of the ministry of Jesus Christ to the people of God upon the earth.

Offices and the Kingdom

"And he gave some, apostles; and some, prophets; and some, evangelists; and some, pastors and teachers" (Ephesians 4:11).

There have been many outstanding books written on the roles of various offices. Since this is not the primary purpose of this book, I will give a brief overview of the functions of these offices, and how they are intended to work together.

The first thing that must be understood is that the purpose of these offices is to perfect (or equip) the saints. In other words, the five-fold ministry is instituted for the overseeing of the larger body at hand. The gifts and authority granted to these offices are not for self-glorification. God has set these ministries in his body to serve the church in a spirit of unity, and to build the church by both numbers and maturity. No one person can do this alone, and so the offices and those appointed to them must work together to accomplish the goals of God for the governing of his people. The days of solo ministry are at their end so that the days of kingdom government can begin. Only with government by appointed offices working together can the glory of God be perpetually housed and revival sustained. As revival is sustained, the work of God will begin to move his people into great degrees of influence in the earth.

"And he gave some, apostles; and some, prophets; and some, evangelists; and some, pastors and teachers; for the perfecting of the saints, for the work of the ministry, for the edifying of the body of Christ: Till we all come in the unity of the faith, and of the knowledge of the Son of God, unto a perfect man, unto the measure of the stature of the fulness of Christ: That we henceforth be no more children, tossed to and fro, and carried about with every wind of doctrine, by the sleight of men, and cunning craftiness, whereby they lie in wait to deceive; But speaking the truth in love, may grow up into him in all things, which is the head, even Christ" (Ephesians 4:11-15).

In this particular passage, the purpose of the offices are stated in a very straightforward manner. It does not leave much room for question. The offices are for the purpose of setting the body of Christ in order, according to the directives of God in heaven. This ultimately leads the body of Christ into a place that is by and large beyond understanding and comprehension. To come to the measure of the stature of the fullness Christ and to grow up into all things, even Christ, is almost unbelievable. However, since the Bible says we will arrive there, *it must be believable*. Before moving forward, I will extrapolate on this a little bit.

The kingdom of God is released from the hearts of the people of God. This place, where the body of Christ is one just like Jesus and the Father are one, is unattainable alone. To go there requires the corporate body of Christ. Drawing upon the illustration of the temple from the last chapter, once we attain the glory in the holy of holies, our conscious and subconscious will be overtaken simultaneously. It is in this place that the bride attains the measure of the stature of the fullness of Jesus Christ. This cannot be done apart from the day-in and day-out ministry and structure provided by kingdom church government.

WHEN HEAVEN AND EARTH COLLIDE

As we begin to comprehend these things, it helps to understand that there are at least two avenues through which heaven can intersect with earth. Both involve the activity of the church. The first is through individual saints. Our spirit participates in heavenly activities because we have been raised up and seated in heavenly places with Christ (Ephesians 2:6). For this reason, we become a conduit between heaven and earth. However, it is only a portion of our spirit that is joined to the Holy Spirit and to heaven (2 Corinthians 7:1). Thus there are four main boundaries that stand between the glory within our spirits and this world. These are the spirit, the heart, the soul, and the body. These boundaries will either filter the glory, or allow free passage. Attaining free passage comes by maturing to Christ-likeness in every area of life. As we allow the power of God to overtake us, the power of heaven can flow through us. People who have experienced this will say things such as "the anointing was upon me." *The anointing is simply a spiritual endowment for a particular purpose.* Jesus, when operating in this manner on earth, spoke thus of himself:

"The Spirit of the Lord is upon me, because he hath anointed me to preach the gospel to the poor; he hath sent me to heal the brokenhearted, to preach deliverance to the captives, and recovering of sight to the blind, to set at liberty them that are bruised, to preach the acceptable year of the Lord" (Luke 4:18-19).

The first avenue is insufficient to accomplish the bringing about of heavenly atmospheres, but necessary for them to occur. Heavenly atmospheres, unhindered and progressively established, will give way to heavenly societies on the earth.

There is a second avenue. The second avenue is when the corporate church actually opens a spiritual portal, or gateway, into the third heaven within certain geographies. Under these circumstances, heavenly realities will overtake our time-space. I will give two examples of how this can be accomplished. There are more, but this will serve as a foundation.

The first is by creating an atmosphere of pure worship among a holy people. There are different kinds of holiness in the Word of God. There is a holiness of the spirit, which is imputed to us upon salvation. There is also a holiness of the soul, which pertains to our lifestyle.

"Follow peace with all men, and holiness, without which no man shall see the Lord" (Hebrews 12:14).

Both forms of holiness must be in operation. When they are, worship can become spirit and truth, as the flow of glory from our spirit comes out unhindered. In this environment, God will come and actually inhabit our praises—the praises of his people.

"But the hour cometh, and now is, when the true worshippers shall worship the Father in spirit and in truth: for the Father seeketh such to worship him. God is a Spirit: and they that worship him must worship him in spirit and in truth" (John 4:23-24).

"But thou art holy, O thou that inhabitest the praises of Israel [his people]" (Psalm 22:3).

God inhabited the praises of Israel, which were his people under the Old Covenant. How much more will he inhabit our praises, the people promised as the bride of his only begotten Son? He will inhabit them to the extent that a spiritual portal will open between heaven and earth, and the glory of God's presence will enter our time-space to abide therein.

The second example involves gathering in the name of Jesus. The name of Jesus is the name of God's authority in heaven and on earth. When we gather in the name of Jesus, it means that we have gathered and purposed to reveal the authority of God in heaven and on earth. If not, we have gathered in the name of so-and-so's Bible study or so-and-so's church. In order to open a corporate portal to the third heaven, we must gather with such a cause in our hearts, inviting and not resisting the supreme power, rulership, and dominion of God in and through us. Jesus promises to reveal himself during these gatherings. When a heavenly portal is opened, God takes over. This is what we must go after!

"For where two or three are gathered together in my name, there am I in the midst of them" (Matthew 18:20).

PLURALITY AND UNITY

In our Bible translations, it is sometimes difficult to identify the promises that target individual believers versus those that target the corporate body. This is because in English, the word *you* is both singular and plural. For example, one could say, "You are in excellent physical shape," and be referring to either an individual or a group of people. If they are referring to a group of people, they may qualify their speech by saying, "You *people* are in excellent physical shape," but the form of the word *you* does not change, regardless of whether it is plural or singular.

One example of this in the Word of God regards binding and loosing. As individual believers, we have a degree of power over the forces of darkness, especially the petty demons. However, the true power of the church is revealed corporately. In the following verse, the words *you* and *ye* are actually plural.

"Verily I say unto you, whatsoever ye shall bind on earth shall be bound in heaven: and whatsoever ye shall loose on earth shall be loosed in heaven. Again I say unto you, That if two of you shall agree on earth as touching any thing that they shall ask, it shall be done for them of my Father which is in heaven" (Matthew 18:18-19).

Large-scale binding and loosing is to be done by the corporate body within their respective geographies. The powers of citywide and national strongholds can only be broken by citywide and national groups of believers. The power and glory of heaven can be loosed over entire geographies in the same way. A *decision* to unify must come before unity. Territory must be taken for the kingdom of heaven in order to allow for the proper atmosphere and societal structure necessary to release the unity of the faith into the body of Christ.

We have been made to partake of one bloodline, called out of every nation on the earth. Only together can we express the fullness of Christ, because every nation has been redeemed in Christ. God's purpose is to unite his church from one end of the world to the other. As a corporate body expressing every earthly nation, tongue, and tribe, we attain a holy nation, a royal priesthood, and a peculiar people. We are to move beyond borders and boundaries in Christ, but retain our individuality as beloved sons before him.

The Five-fold Ministry

In the next chapters I am going to present teachings on the five major offices in the body of Christ, and their intended operation according to the scriptural model. Without the five-fold ministry effectively working within the church, the second aspect of kingdom government will not be possible. Again, the second aspect of kingdom government becomes a model around which the will of God can greatly influence a society. It takes on literal implementation in the form of politics, education, arts, business, etc.

The outcome of human life results from the beliefs of the heart. Only when we understand the heart do we understand what we need to target for change. An individual's life will change when the thoughts of their heart are rewritten. When the thoughts of the hearts within an entire geography are changed, the society will transform and produce an entirely different culture. The thoughts of the hearts of God's people must be directed and ruled by God. This is the program of the kingdom of God. When this occurs, the culture will express the values of God. When God rules in and through the hearts of his people in a particular geography, and this influence shapes the very societal structures found within that particular geography, a sheep nation of the last days will have been produced.

PART 2

CHAPTER 7

Teacher

We must understand that without proper structure, the glory of God cannot be housed and sustained. The Israelites had to build a temple to house the Spirit of God. Jesus, through his work at Cavalry, has removed the need for a temple and has made the saints into his holy temple.

"Know ye not that ye are the temple of God, and that the Spirit of God dwelleth in you" (1 Corinthians 3:16)?

Without proper church government, we cannot be jointly fitted together as the body of Christ. Five-fold ministry involving the offices of apostle, prophet, evangelist, pastor and teacher is the proper church government. This is the government that Jesus gave.

"**And he [Jesus] gave** some, apostles; and some, prophets; and some, evangelists; and some, pastors and teachers; for the perfecting of the saints, for the work of the ministry, for the edifying of the body of Christ" (Ephesians 4:11-12).

The office of the teacher is absolutely essential. Even though Jesus is called the Apostle of the faith, he was only able to attain this title by teaching others what he was doing. How many people would have been saved as a result of Jesus' death and resurrection if he never taught anyone what it meant? Jesus walked in the office of teacher during his entire ministry on earth.

"The same came to Jesus by night, and said unto him, Rabbi, **we know that thou art a teacher come from God**: for no man can do these miracles that thou doest, except God be with him" (John 3:2).

UNDERSTANDING THE TEACHER

The office of the teacher is unique in that, although all of the offices comprising the five-fold ministry involve a degree of teaching, the purpose and anointing of the teaching is different. For one who stands in the office of teacher, their primary desire is that the people have knowledge and understanding.

For instance, apostolic teaching involves a large degree of impartation. It is not intended to affect the minds as much as it is the hearts and the spiritual functions of the hearers. Prophetic teaching is about revelation, focusing on what the Spirit of God is saying and the word for the season. Evangelistic teaching is usually limited to the message and gospel of Jesus Christ, giving just enough information for people to make a quality decision for Jesus. Pastoral teaching is concerned with meeting the needs of the body, and helping believers to grow and continue in the faith.

Those who stand in the office of teacher are concerned with the mind. They realize that although we can be embellished by all the revelation in heaven, if we do not know why we believe what we believe, the enemy can easily change our hearts. The teacher causes the body of Christ to move beyond emotion and ground them in factual, verifiable truth. The Bible instructs us to renew our minds.

"And be not conformed to this world: but be ye transformed by the renewing of your mind, that ye may prove what is that good, and acceptable, and perfect, will of God" (Romans 12:2).

The act of renewing the mind simply means to replace outdated information with new information. It has relatively little to do with the heart at first. It means to receive education from the Word of God. The teacher is concerned that people know what they believe, and why they believe it. The danger of deception is real, and it is deadly. Therefore, they are anointed to lay out understanding in a very clear and systematic way.

The teaching anointing is not meant to change our actions, but to change our thinking. When they are joined with the other offices as Jesus intended, it all makes sense. A teacher, as a standalone ministry, can lead to very intellectual Christianity. Other offices must balance them.

It all goes back to the heart. The heart is creating the program from which we live our lives. If our heart is receiving revelation from our spirit, it will be held against the beliefs of our soul in order to be established. Spiritual knowledge must be activated as operational knowledge in our lives. This means that it must go beyond faith and into lifestyle. In order for this to occur, the beliefs in our minds must support the revelation being granted to our hearts. For this reason, the office of teacher is absolutely essential!

Those appointed to this office are moved to teach from a burden rooted in their anointing. The word *anointing* simply means an endowment of the Holy Spirit for a particular purpose. As a result of the anointing (endowment) that is in operation, they are compelled from deep within themselves to bring solid, systematic understanding of the Bible. Their primary concern is to renew the minds of the believers. When they see passionate believers without understanding or knowledge, they are grieved. This grief moves them to establish the body in understanding.

AQUILA AND PRISCILLA

A great example of individuals moving in the office of teacher occurs in the book of Acts, when Aquila and Priscilla teach Apollos. They instructed him with additional apostolic truth of which he was unaware.

And a certain Jew named Apollos, born at Alexandria, an elo-
quent man, and mighty in the scriptures, came to Ephesus.
This man was instructed in the way of the Lord; and being fer-
vent in the spirit, he spake and taught diligently the things of
the Lord, knowing only the baptism of John. And he began
to speak boldly in the synagogue: whom when Aquila and
Priscilla had heard, they took him unto them, and expounded
unto him the way of God more perfectly. And when he was
disposed to pass into Achaia, the brethren wrote, exhorting the
disciples to receive him: who, when he was come, helped them
much which had believed through grace: For he mightily convinced the Jews, and that publicly, shewing by the scriptures
that Jesus was Christ.

(Acts 18:24-28)

Apollos went on to be listed among the apostles of the first church.
The only office in the Bible recorded as receiving input from all of the other
offices is the apostolic office. Although in many respects the apostolic office
is the foremost office, it is also the one requiring the most council, input,
and accountability from the other offices. In this passage, the input came
from those operating in the office of teacher. Aquila and Priscilla had more
knowledge and foundational truth than Apollos was operating in. They
were able to take him aside and teach him the scripture "more perfectly."
Being teachers, this couple was burdened by the lack of knowledge Apollos

exhibited, and were moved by the anointing to teach him a more perfect way.

Before closing this chapter, a brief commentary on a commonly misapplied scripture is in order. It has been said that some are anointed to teach "line upon line and precept upon precept, here a little there a little" according to the following passage:

"Whom shall he teach knowledge? And whom shall he make to understand doctrine? Them that are weaned from the milk, and drawn from the breasts. **For precept must be upon precept, precept upon precept; line upon line, line upon line; here a little, and there a little**" (Isaiah 28:9-10).

This seems to be a perfect description of the teacher's ministry until one digs a little deeper and makes further inquiry into the context of this passage. The fact of the matter is that this passage is not an exhortation to teach. Instead, it is part of a lengthier portion of prophecy that is intended to be a rebuke! If we look at the two verses that precede this passage we can glean just who the Lord is addressing.

"But they also have erred through wine, and through strong drink are out of the way; the priest and the prophet have erred through strong drink, they are swallowed up of wine, they are out of the way through strong drink; they err in vision, they stumble in judgment. For all tables are full of vomit and filthiness, so that there is no place clean" (Isaiah 28:7-8).

The group of people being addressed in this passage are priests and prophets that have erred through strong drink. In other words, God is rebuking a host of drunken leaders. They are so drunk they have filled the tables with vomit. After God explains who they are and how they act, he goes on to explain what they do. Put simply, they teach in a convoluted and complicated manner that is useless. God explains this as "line upon line, precept upon precept." This is not good—this is a rebuke.

The next three verses bring it all together, as they explain this shocking issue that Israel had during the time of Isaiah. When these drunken priests and prophets taught the Word of God in their complicated, convoluted, and nonsensical manner—the result was that the people would fall backward, become broken, find themselves in a snare, and get taken by the enemy. The reading is clear.

"For with stammering lips and another tongue will he speak to this people. To whom he said, This is the rest wherewith ye may cause the weary to rest; and this is the refreshing: yet they would not hear. But the word of the Lord was unto them precept upon precept, precept upon precept; line upon line, line upon line; here a little, and there a little; **that they might go, and fall backward, and be broken, and snared, and taken**" (Isaiah 28:11-13).

When teaching goes forth that is overly convoluted, it becomes useless to the hearers. The Word of the Lord can actually be made of no effect when it is presented in an overly complicated or nonsensical fashion. The result then will be that instead of being renewed, empowered, and transformed, people will fall away and get broken. The actual lesson that we take away from this passage is that a true teaching anointing will give the individual grace to communicate the Word of the Lord both systematically, and with extreme clarity. Instead of leaving people bored and discouraged, they will be inspired and empowered. God does not want us to teach as the drunken prophets and priests of Isaiah 28:7-13!

CHAPTER 8

Pastor

The office of pastor exemplifies the shepherding heart of God. The anointing of this office will move those appointed to it to watch and care for the flock of God's children. When true pastors teach the Word of God, their primary motivation is to lead and guide the people into "green pastures."

THE HEART OF THE PASTOR

"The LORD is my shepherd; I shall not want. He maketh me to lie down in green pastures: he leadeth me beside the still waters. He restoreth my soul: he leadeth me in the paths of righteousness for his name's sake. Yea, though I walk through the valley of the shadow of death, I will fear no evil: for thou art with me; thy rod and thy staff they comfort me. Thou preparest a table before me in the presence of mine enemies: thou anointest my head with oil; my cup runneth over. Surely goodness and mercy shall follow me all the days of my life: and I will dwell in the house of the LORD for ever" (Psalm 23).

Psalm 23 is a vivid picture of how God leads us. It begins by explaining that because we have a shepherd, our needs are being met. Pastors have a need and urgency within them to meet the needs of the people. They are the manifestation of this aspect of Jesus. They seek to meet spiritual needs, emotional needs, and to the best of their ability, physical needs, like housing and clothing. They have been given this office to strengthen the body of Christ at "ground zero." They are the counselors; they see people from beginning to end, through the good times and through the hard times. Pastors will selflessly watch over those assigned to them, and they do not give up on the people. They do not give as much concern to the corporate destiny of the church as they do to the individuals that comprise it.

Psalm 23 continues to explain that the shepherd makes us to lie down in green pastures, leading us beside still waters. Pastors will show people the way to peace and growth. Green represents growth in the Word of God, and a pasture is a safe place where sheep are nurtured. The pastor cares about keeping the flock safe, and in a place of perpetual growth. Still waters can have several symbolic implications. The most straightforward is that the water represents the Word of God (Ephesians 5:26) and the stillness represents teaching that sets us at peace. A pastor wants to bring peace and stability to the body of Christ; they want to see growth, and they want to see individuals overcome.

The pastor, simply operating out of his or her anointing, will cause restoration to come to the souls of the members of their flock. Their council and wisdom will set many free on a personal level. As individuals find freedom and growth from this ministry, they will begin to walk in paths of righteousness. To see this gives a pastor great and overwhelming satisfaction. They feel that they have accomplished great success when an individual who has been assigned to them arrives in a place of continual growth, personal freedom, and is walking in the truth of their new life that has been purchased by Christ.

CHAPTER 9

Evangelist

The evangelistic office is radically different from the pastoral and teaching offices. Without proper understanding of each other, these offices can easily clash. As a matter of fact, I am aware of several such instances. Evangelists do not have much concern for establishing people in a great depth of understanding. They do not have much compassion for the needs of the body, and quickly grow impatient with others when they are responsible to help new converts grow. Their anointing drives them ruthlessly to reach the lost.

UNDERSTANDING THE EVANGELIST

When they think of ministry, their primary concern is the fact that many people are still going to hell. When they teach, they will teach in any way necessary to reach those who are lost. They will always come back to the central message of Jesus crucified and resurrected.

As a result of their message and anointing, they will have a great degree of access to the power of God and will see incredible miracles as a result of their ministry. The evangelistic ministry is usually very exciting to watch because progress is immediately measurable. Converts can be counted, miracles can be witnessed, and memorable stories can be told. The evangelistic ministry moves fast, and never stays planted for very long. The evangelist understands that their anointing is the most necessary in the darkest areas. Once their anointing has pierced the darkness and souls have received Christ, they are ready to move on, for as far as they are concerned, their ministry has been finished.

Philip

In the book of Acts, Philip has an incredible story that grants us much of our understanding regarding the ministry of the evangelist. We find that he began his ministry by serving the apostles at the first church in Jerusalem, and ended up operating in the miraculous to the extent that God would translate him to quicken the works his ministry was accomplishing. Translation is when God removes an individual into the spirit realm and then reinserts them into the physical realm at another geographic location.

"Then the twelve called the multitude of the disciples unto them, and said, It is not reason that we should leave the word of God, and serve tables. Wherefore, brethren, look ye out among you seven men of honest report, full of the Holy Ghost and wisdom, whom we may appoint over this business. And the saying pleased the whole multitude: and they chose Stephen, a man full of faith and of the Holy Ghost, **and Philip**, and Prochorus, and Nicanor, and Timon, and Parmenas, and Nicolas a proselyte of Antioch" (Acts 6:2-3, 5).

Philip began his ministry as a deacon. It is important that those who feel a calling to any five-fold office understand that God will not typically validate us in our own ministry until we have served, or at the very least did all we could to serve others in their ministry. As time passed, the church in Jerusalem came under persecution, and the followers of Jesus were scattered from Jerusalem. In Acts chapter 8, Philip's story is continued.

Then Philip went down to the city of Samaria, and preached Christ unto them. And the people with one accord gave heed unto those things which Philip spake, hearing and seeing the miracles which he did. For unclean spirits, crying with loud voice, came out of many that were possessed with them: and many taken with palsies, and that were lame, were healed. And there was great joy in that city. But there was a certain man, called Simon, which beforetime in the same city used sorcery, and bewitched the people of Samaria, giving out that himself was some great one: To whom they all gave heed, from the least to the greatest, saying, This man is the great power of God.

And to him they had regard, because that of long time he had bewitched them with sorceries. But when they believed Philip preaching the things concerning the kingdom of God, and the name of Jesus Christ, they were baptized, both men and women. Then Simon himself believed also: and when he was baptized, he continued with Philip, and wondered, beholding the miracles and signs which were done.

(Acts 8:5-13)

EVANGELISTIC POWER

When people think of the raw power of God being revealed in the New Testament, they usually point to the apostolic ministry. Although it is true that the apostolic ministry will see radical miracles, it is just as true for the evangelistic ministry. Great signs and wonders will follow anyone who has been appointed to this office by God. *The purpose of the signs and wonders is to confirm the Word of God*. In the case of the evangelist, this confirmation is largely directed at those who have not yet been saved. Jesus healed the paralytic to confirm his word to the people that he had the power to forgive sins. As it is written:

When Jesus saw their faith, he said unto the sick of the palsy, "Son, thy sins be forgiven thee…whether is it easier to say to the sick of the palsy, Thy sins be forgiven thee; or to say, Arise, and take up thy bed, and walk? **But that ye may know that the Son of man hath power on earth to forgive sins,**" (he saith to the sick of the palsy,) "**I say unto thee, Arise, and take up thy bed, and go thy way into thine house." And immediately he arose**, took up the bed, and went forth before them all; insomuch that they were all amazed, and glorified God, saying, "We never saw it on this fashion."

(Mark 2:5, 9-12)

CHAPTER 10

Prophet

The prophetic office has a unique ability to discern to voice of God and the thoughts of God. For the prophet, communication of spiritual things takes precedence over other ministries. God is very clear with prophets about what he wants, and there is a fantastic burden within them to communicate these things. Prophets have an understanding that just as God declared his word and created heaven and earth, he continues to declare his word through his prophets, that his will may be manifested on the earth.

Prophets stand in their office to give guidance and direction to the body of Christ as a whole. Prophetic ministry is necessary from the local to the international level. Prophets give little weight to matters of political correctness. They must allow God to develop sensitivity in them. For the person standing in the office prophet, the word of the Lord comes louder and clearer than any other influence. The word of God becomes a fire in their bones as explained by Jeremiah:

"Then I said, I will not make mention of him, nor speak any more in his name. But his word was in mine heart as a burning fire shut up in my bones, and I was weary with forbearing, and I could not stay" (Jeremiah 20:9).

UNDERSTANDING THE PROPHET

For individuals that have been appointed to this office, it can become very difficult to stand by and watch as God's plans and purposes remain unspoken and hence, unaddressed. Prophets express the nature of Christ's love through their gifting and anointing, which means they love others through speaking the truth of God as revealed to them. This can cause chaos when they work amongst others who do not understand them. This can also lead to problems if they are submitted to a pastoral or teaching anointing with little understanding of the prophetic office.

Although prophets carry an incredible mantle to hear and communicate the words and thoughts of God, they often do not have the ability to make what God is saying happen. They will speak and declare, but building out of a prophetic anointing is rarely successful. This is why the Bible says the church is built upon the foundation of the apostles *and* prophets. The apostolic anointing is primarily for building and manifesting the kingdom of God on earth, while the prophetic anointing deals with direction and the identification of the works that God wants to perform.

"And are built upon the foundation of the apostles and prophets, Jesus Christ himself being the chief corner stone" (Ephesians 2:20).

AGABUS

In the New Testament, apostles or close affiliates of them wrote all of the Canon text. There is little direct text dealing with how the prophetic office is to operate. However, in the book of Acts we do find a prophet named Agabus. This is his story:

> And there stood up one of them named Agabus, and signified by the Spirit that there should be great dearth throughout all the world: which came to pass in the days of Claudius Caesar… And as we tarried there many days, there came down from Judaea a certain prophet, named Agabus. And when he was come unto us, he took Paul's girdle, and bound his own hands and feet, and said, Thus saith the Holy Ghost, So shall the Jews at Jerusalem bind the man that owneth this girdle, and shall deliver him into the hands of the Gentiles. And when we heard these things, both we, and they of that place, besought him not to go up to Jerusalem. Then Paul answered, What mean ye to weep and to break mine heart? For I am ready not to be bound only, but also to die at Jerusalem for the name of the Lord Jesus.
>
> (Acts 11:28; 21:10-13)

The first mention of the New Testament prophet Agabus was in Acts chapter 11. In this passage, he stands up and declares the future. He was operating in what Scripture refers to as the word of wisdom. It was not good news! A dearth is better known as a famine. Agabus had proclaimed that a famine was going to strike the land. Our first lesson that we can take away from Agabus is that those standing in the prophetic office do not necessarily receive good news. What they do receive is accurate and truthful news. The purpose of this particular word was to prepare the Christians to live and operate under adverse circumstances.

The Prophet and the Gift of Prophecy

There can be a misunderstanding between the gift of prophecy and the prophetic office. The gift of prophecy is merely one of three revelatory gifts, the other two being word of wisdom, and word of knowledge (1 Corinthians 12:8-10). Those who stand in the prophetic office will move strongly in all three of these gifts, the specifics of which we will discuss later. Sometimes, when people do not "enjoy" a revelatory word, they reject it on the basis of 1 Corinthians 14:3, which says, "But he that prophesieth speaketh unto men to edification, and exhortation, and comfort." Some people will argue that any revelatory word that does not bring edification, exhortation, and comfort cannot be of God, and therefore must be rejected. However, the only gift addressed in this passage is the gift of prophecy. The fact of the matter is that God will tell things to his prophets in word of wisdom and word of knowledge that do not bring comfort. This was clearly the case with Agabus.

MORE LESSONS FROM AGABUS

In his next mention, Agabus had traveled from Judea to Philip's house. When he arrived there, he again delivered the word of the Lord. Instead of prophesying about something that was going to affect the whole region, he delivered a personal prophecy to Paul. Both words and actions became prophetic expression in the delivery of this prophecy. Agabus took Paul's girdle (which is a belt) and tied himself up in it. This may seem weird, and in the course of daily life it is. Prophets are made into a sign before the people of God. This was true of Ezekiel, who also did bizarre things. For instance, he had to lie on his side for months, cut a hole through his house wall, and use cow dung as fuel to cook special bread. This was also true of Isaiah, who spent three years walking around naked!

"And the LORD said, Like as my servant Isaiah hath walked naked and barefoot three years for a sign and wonder upon Egypt and upon Ethiopia" (Isaiah 20:3).

The primary concern of Agabus was not to make people happy, but to reveal truth. Prophets are anointed to reveal truth at any price or personal cost. They care little for self, and have irrepressible passion for the word of God to be heard and acted upon. In all of this, Agabus never started a church. He didn't try to conjure up a pastoral heart to get a small crowd that would listen to his prophecies. He prophesied, and let people do with the word as they would.

RECEIVING THE PROPHETS

Even in this hour, the term ministry remains in a "box" for much of the Western church. This has been to the detriment of many of those that God has anointed to the prophetic office. Under the denominational system, many prophets have had a great deal of difficulty walking out their destiny. Even within many non-denominational movements, this pattern has remained. A prophet is not a pastor, unless they are appointed the grace to walk in both offices. A pastor may be gifted in the area of prophecy, but that does not make them a prophet. Prophets are intended to work with apostles to frame the will of God into something workable. As the church grows in maturity, and the apostolic office takes its rightful place, the functions of all other ministries will flow as they should. As a result, the body of Christ will be edified as never before.

Prophets move accurately in the gifts of word of wisdom, word of knowledge and prophecy. It is important to understand that just because one moves strongly in these gifts, they do not necessarily hold a prophetic office. A prophet is a person appointed by Jesus to hold a spiritual office in the body of Christ. The gifts are available to any believer. This is an area that has left many confused, in that it is easy to naively think that the Bible speaks about prophecy and prophets synonymously. Prophets are set apart by their anointing, spiritual mantle, and appointment. All Christians, on the other hand, should seek to prophesy.

"I would that ye all spake with tongues but rather that ye prophesied: for greater is he that prophesieth than he that speaketh with tongues, except he interpret, that the church may receive edifying" (1 Corinthians 14:5).

"For ye may <u>all</u> [emphasis mine] prophesy one by one, that all may learn, and all may be comforted" (1 Corinthians 14:31).

The Gifts of the Spirit

Before closing this chapter, it is fitting to include a brief discussion on the spiritual gifts of God for those who may be unfamiliar with them. There are many outstanding books available on this topic, and for this reason, I will not provide much depth.

The basis for our understanding comes from 1 Corinthians 12:

Now concerning spiritual gifts [charismas], brethren, I would not have you ignorant...Now there are diversities of gifts [charismas], but the same Spirit. And there are differences of administrations, but the same Lord. And there are diversities of operations, but it is the same God which worketh all in all. But the manifestation of the Spirit is given to every man to profit withal. For to one is given by the Spirit the word of wisdom; to another the word of knowledge by the same Spirit; to another faith by the same Spirit; to another the gifts of healing by the same Spirit; to another the working of miracles; to another prophecy; to another discerning of spirits; to another divers kinds of tongues; to another the interpretation of tongues: But all these worketh that one and the selfsame Spirit, dividing to every man severally [any number of gifts] as he will.

(1 Corinthians 12:1, 4-11)

In this chapter, the word translated as "gifts" is the Greek word *charisma*. This word is etymologically related to the word *charis* from which we derive our word "grace." The gifts of God are a specific manifestation of his grace working through us to edify others in a specific manner. *Grace is not only the unmerited love and favor of God, but it is also God's ability at work in and through us.* The gifts are given by his Spirit, but once given, they always reside within us, meaning that God does not take them away. We can release our faith to operate in our spiritual gifts whenever it is appropriate. This is what the Bible means when it says the gifts are given without repentance.

"For the gifts [charismas] and calling of God are without repentance" (Romans 11:29).

Spiritual gifts can also be imparted from one saint to another. Many times a person standing in the prophetic office, for example, has the ability to impart to the saints the gifts that they are fluently operating in, like prophecy, word of wisdom, or word of knowledge. This is simply one approach that the Holy Spirit uses to give gifts to the saints. It is not a requirement for receiving any spiritual gift. In the following passage, Paul clearly declares that he was actively involved in the ministry of imparting gifts to other believers.

"For I long to see you, that I may impart unto you some spiritual gift [charisma], to the end ye may be established" (Romans 1:11).

On this note I will admit that some have major issues with the impartation of spiritual gifts. They are often convinced that this can only be a work of witchcraft. How silly. Not only is the Bible clear about this issue, but the fact remains that the devil can only counterfeit what is genuine. He is not creative. Just because occultists can impart satanic gifts through rituals and the laying on of hands does not mean that God does not work the same way. The laying on of hands happens to be one of the principles of the doctrine of Christ (Hebrews 6:1-2)! It requires discernment on our part to distinguish between what is of God and what is not, but when we begin to deny the things of God out of a fear-based mentality, we quench the Spirit. This is something we should avoid at all costs!

"Quench not the Spirit" (1 Thessalonians 5:19).

What follows is a list of the nine gifts listed in 1 Corinthians 12, along with their definitions. I have compiled this abbreviated list largely from operational experience, but also from the influence of those who have gone before me.[2]

1. Word of Wisdom: Supernatural wisdom leading to knowledge of future events that are to occur, should nothing change and no one intercede.

2. Word of Knowledge: Supernatural knowledge of past or presently occurring events, along with other facts in the mind of God.

3. Faith: Supernatural ability to receive a miracle from God. This gift takes us beyond our natural abiding state of faith.

4. Gifts of healing: Any number of methods through which the Holy Spirit, working through an individual, brings supernatural healing, apart from medicine or any other form of natural healing or recovery.

5. Working of Miracles: Supernatural ability to perform a miracle (i.e., walking on water, multiplying food, materialization of missing body parts, etc.).

6. Prophecy: Supernatural ability to speak what God is saying in the present moment, specifically to bring edification, exhortation, and comfort.

7. Discerning of Spirits: Supernatural ability to interact with and obtain knowledge from the spirit realm regarding the various spirits in operation whether godly, human, or demonic.

8. Tongues: Supernatural ability to speak in our heavenly prayer language, which at times can be in human languages unknown to the speaker.

9. Interpretation of Tongues: Supernatural ability to interpret a heavenly prayer language, whether it be our own or that of another saint.

It is important to understand that although the offices are a gift to the body of Christ, they are very different from the gifts of the Holy Spirit. All believers can have access to any of the gifts, should they have faith to receive and be obedient to follow through on what God requires of them. We can now move on to the final office, which is the office of the apostle.

CHAPTER 11

Apostle

The apostolic office is the office that has been set by Jesus to bring all of the other offices together. This is why the apostolic office is set first.

"And God hath set some in the church, first apostles, secondarily prophets, thirdly teachers, after that miracles, then gifts of healings, helps, governments, diversities of tongues" (1 Corinthians 12:28).

APOSTLES ARE SET FIRST

When God set the apostles first, this did not necessarily mean that the apostles were better or more spiritual than others. This does not mean apostles are to be worshipped or idolized by the church. It most certainly does not mean that an apostle should assume authority over a pastor or any other individual in the body of Christ that has not submitted to their leadership. The apostolic office is not the elitist branch of the body of Christ!

Why did God set the apostles first? There are two relevant answers to this question. Chronologically speaking, the apostles were the first office released into the early church. The church began with the twelve apostles of the Lamb. Secondly, apostles serve as a foundational ministry to the body of Christ. Their ministry makes room for the other gifts to function properly, in order for the whole body to be edified. When building a house, you cannot adorn the second floor and the ceiling until well after you have laid the foundation. The foundation supports the whole house. Along with the prophetic office, the apostolic office is a foundational ministry. Both must be built upon the Chief Corner Stone, Jesus Christ.

"And are built upon the foundation of the apostles and prophets, Jesus Christ himself being the chief corner stone" (Ephesians 2:20).

UNDERSTANDING THE APOSTLE

The person appointed to the apostolic office can typically function in a measure of the anointing given to any other office. They can teach, pastor, evangelize, and prophesy. It is necessary to do all of these things to build an effective and proper spiritual foundation. Also, by having access to these offices, they are equipped to understand how they must operate together.

Many people who enjoy travelling around the world will comment on how drastically different some cultures can be. These differences extend to the degree that what is considered polite and acceptable in one culture is considered outrageously offensive in another. I remember watching one situation play out in which a young (twenty-something) Brazilian girl, after talking about a topic the pastor asked her about on the stage, gave him a hug and a kiss on the cheek before taking her seat. In Hispanic culture, this would have been no big deal. I am Hispanic, and we hug and kiss each other all the time. However, this pastor, and a majority of those witnessing the event, were Black. As a result, you can probably imagine the extreme awkwardness of the moment! A faint "ooohhh..." passed through the crowd as the *very* embarrassed pastor did his best to awkwardly laugh the whole thing off. The poor girl had no idea what her natural inclination (as dictated to her by her culture) would produce in the midst of an entirely different group.

Consider another example. In Greek culture it is customary to spit upon the bride and groom for good luck as they walk down the aisle. If I were to do this at an American wedding, I would probably lose a lot of friends! When bringing the American and Greek cultures together for an event, say a wedding, it is necessary to have someone organize the wedding who is familiar with both cultures. This organizer can allow for a beautiful event by recognizing differences and arranging things accordingly.

Offices in the body of Christ can be the same way. The anointing that is upon different offices can manifest like warring cultures when they try to come together apart from a proper foundation. An apostle understands their differences, and creates the structure necessary to house and multiply all the gifts. The apostolic office was given for building. As a foundation layer, those burdened with this office reside not at the top of the spiritual hierarchy, but at the bottom.

Apostolic Ministry

Apostles are the greatest of servants, but their service does not come by serving tables. Their ordained service to the body of Christ is to organize, to build, to train, to equip, and to impart. For this reason, the first apostles set seven elders. They quickly realized that they were doing a disservice to the body by doing everything.

"Then the twelve called the multitude of the disciples unto them, and said, It is not reason that we should leave the word of God, and serve tables. Wherefore, brethren, look ye out among you seven men of honest report, full of the Holy Ghost and wisdom, whom we may appoint over this business. But we will give ourselves continually to prayer, and to the ministry of the word" (Acts 6:2-4).

Apostles are anointed to build and to train. In order to accomplish this, they have been granted access to any spiritual resource and gifting necessary to accomplish the task. By observation, they can appear to be spiritually elite. This is not so. The mantle and job that they have been given demands the gifts and power that God has entrusted to them. The gifts and power of God are not for self-glorification, but for the equipping and edification of the body of Christ. This endowment is also given so that those who are yet unsaved might believe in the Lord Jesus.

> And great fear came upon all the church, and upon as many as heard these things. And by the hands of the apostles were many signs and wonders wrought among the people; (and they were all with one accord in Solomon's porch. And of the rest durst no man join himself to them: but the people magnified them. And believers were the more added to the Lord, multitudes both of men and women.) Insomuch that they brought forth the sick into the streets, and laid them on beds and couches, that at the least the shadow of Peter passing by might over-shadow some of them.
>
> (Acts 5:11-15)

By the ministry of the first apostles, great fear came upon the whole church. This means that the whole church developed a deep respect for God, bowing their hearts and acknowledging his greatness and holiness. The apostles worked many signs and wonders. This edified the body of Christ, and also led to continual numerical church growth. As an inevitable result the people magnified them, but the apostles did not give in to pride. They did not exalt themselves in the gifts, but were humble and obedient to the calling and purpose they had been given. The apostolic office comes with great spiritual power, but also great responsibility. To walk successfully in this office requires impeccable character and devotion.

ONE WHO IS SENT

The Greek word *apostolos* is the origin of our word "apostle." This word literally means one who is sent. For this reason, many have falsely assumed that in our generation, an apostle is simply a missionary who is sent to a foreign place. This is rooted in a misunderstanding of the purpose of the offices in the body of Christ. It is true that an apostle is one who is sent, but we must understand that they are sent according to the revelation that wherever the Lord puts them, they have spiritual authority to implement God's plan for that geography or people group. In other words, apostles do not simply go, but wherever they go, they have been divinely sent by God to implement his will in that place. Consider how the Holy Spirit separated Barnabas and Paul (still being called Saul) and *sent* them to do his work.

"As they ministered to the Lord, and fasted, **the Holy Ghost said, Separate me Barnabas and Saul** for the work whereunto I have called them. And when they had fasted and prayed, and laid their hands on them, **they sent them away**. So they, being sent forth by the Holy Ghost, departed unto Seleucia; and from thence they sailed to Cyprus" (Acts 13:2-4).

Jesus was not the first to use this term. It was historically used by the Phoenicians, and later by the Romans. In these kingdoms, apostles were sent with an apostolic company to invade and occupy territory in an enemy kingdom. The apostles were the lead ships in naval armadas. The ships with them were called the apostolic company. The leading admirals of the armadas were named apostles as well.[3]

When these apostolic companies would successfully invade territory in an enemy kingdom, they would not destroy the culture that was there. Instead, they would keep what was good, and build into it an infrastructure that allowed it to become part of their own kingdom. The infrastructure of the society would eventually cause the culture to change, but the idea was to occupy territory, not to destroy. When Jesus sent out his apostles, he had the same picture in mind. He sent them to take territory. This office was given to build the infrastructure of the kingdom of heaven into enemy territory and expand kingdom government on the earth.

Jesus handpicked the twelve apostles of the Lamb. After his death and resurrection, they were sent to the Jews. Paul and Barnabas were separated by the Holy Spirit and sent to the Gentiles. Wherever apostles are sent, they have authority to cause God's plan for that area or people group to manifest. This is not necessarily true of missionaries. Many missionaries are sent to serve the efforts of ministries in foreign countries. Others may go to unreached people groups as evangelists. Unfortunately, there are even some missionaries that are people who are simply looking for a "feel-good" vacation. Although missionaries are people who are sent, they are not apostles unless God has appointed them to that office.

The Pearl of Great Price

Thus we have outlined kingdom government as it pertains to the offices in the body of Christ. Other positions, like deacons and elders, are to be appointed by the five-fold ministry. This foundational understanding will allow us to frame the church into a fitting vessel capable of housing the glory of God. The end-time plans of God cannot be executed with a church that is not operating according to his divine order. Our God is a God of order; he ordered the days, the time of days, the cycles of the sun and the moon, the seasons, and every other aspect of creation that he upholds by his sovereign power. Why should he operate any differently when it comes to his "Pearl of Great Price," the bride of his Son, Jesus Christ?

"Again, the kingdom of heaven is like unto a merchant man [Jesus], seeking goodly pearls: Who, when he had found one pearl of great price [the church], went and sold all that he had [died on the cross], and bought it [purchased us by his blood]" (Matthew 13:45-46).

As already discussed, coming to the measure of the stature of the fullness of Christ is a very spiritual and supernatural event. The goal of the church is to be able to attain this place so that Jesus can return. The return of Christ is intimately tied to the church "making herself ready." The church making herself ready involves attaining a place where God considers us corporately as pure and clean, without spot or wrinkle or any such thing.

"Let us be glad and rejoice, and give honour to him: for the marriage of the Lamb is come, **and his wife [the church] hath made herself ready**" (Revelation 19:7).

"That he might present it to himself **a glorious church, not having spot, or wrinkle, or any such thing**; but that it should be holy and without blemish" (Ephesians 5:27).

Again, this cannot happen without the day-by-day work of proper church structure. Proper church structure is kingdom government. *Kingdom government within the church exists wherever God is King over the hearts of his people, and rules his people through the use of those whom he has appointed to offices of leadership. The offices are apostle, prophet, evangelist, pastor and teacher. To remove any of these offices from the people of God is to remove an aspect of the wisdom of God to build his church and set it in proper order.* This must be in place for his purposes to be achieved. All five are necessary, and only out of proper structure can revival be sustained. Revival is not the goal, but a necessary step towards moving us to our ultimate destination. *The ultimate destination of the church is dominion with Christ over all things in heaven and on earth. The rulership of the saints with Christ is what all of creation has been waiting for. When this occurs, all of creation will be delivered from the bondage of corruption!*

"For I reckon that the sufferings of this present time are not worthy to be compared with the glory which shall be revealed in us. For the earnest expectation of the creature [or creation] waiteth for the manifestation of the sons of God [the saints]… **Because the creature [or creation] itself also shall be delivered from the bondage of corruption into the glorious liberty of the children of God [the saints]**" (Romans 8:18-19, 21).

PART 3

CHAPTER 12

End-Time Framework

In order to understand the plan of God for the coming days, it is essential to approach it with the proper paradigm. For instance, if I do not believe fire exists, why would I build a fire station and fire trucks? If I do not believe that people die, why would I purchase life insurance? If I do not believe that God's Word is true, why would I receive Jesus as my personal Lord and Savior? If I do not believe that Jesus returns only once at the end of the great tribulation, why would I prepare?

The concepts of kingdom government and sheep nations have little relevance to those who refuse to believe that Jesus plans to only return once at the end of a time of great tribulation. It is a very simple issue. If people do not believe there is problem, why are they going to search for a solution? It only makes sense to spend our time solving the problems that we have. Why waste time and energy developing solutions to problems that we do not believe exist? However, when problems do exist, and we are convinced they do not exist, we are deceived. Deception leaves us, along with our families, in a compromised position.

"My people are destroyed for lack of knowledge: because thou hast rejected knowledge, I will also reject thee, that thou shalt be no priest to me: seeing thou hast forgotten the law of thy God, I will also forget thy children" (Hosea 4:6).

In my first book, *Noah's Ark and the End of Days*, I devoted nearly one hundred pages to systematically dissecting end-time events in order to bring understanding and context. This is not the purpose of this work. What will follow will be a *brief* overview of what was introduced; revised and interwoven with new material.

Daniel's Seventy Weeks Prophecy

The end-time timeline revolves around Israel and the Jews. A large portion of our understanding is based on a passage of Scripture known as Daniel's seventy weeks prophecy. In this passage, a timeline is given to Daniel regarding the future of his people—the Jewish people. The first sixty-nine "weeks" of this prophecy deal strictly with the Jewish people, much of it occurring before the birth of Jesus. Just like the first sixty-nine weeks of this prophecy, Daniel's seventieth week also deals entirely with the Jewish people. However, we will find that the second half of Daniel's seventieth week and the great tribulation occupy the same three and one-half year period. For future reference, three and one-half prophetic years are composed of forty-two months, each having exactly thirty days. What is Daniel's seventy weeks prophecy?

Seventy weeks are determined upon thy people and upon thy holy city, to finish the transgression, and to make an end of sins, and to make reconciliation for iniquity, and to bring in everlasting righteousness, and to seal up the vision and prophecy, and to anoint the most Holy. Know therefore and understand, that from the going forth of the commandment to restore and to build Jerusalem unto the Messiah the Prince shall be seven weeks, and threescore and two weeks: the street shall be built again, and the wall, even in troublous times. And after threescore and two weeks shall Messiah be cut off, but not for himself: and the people of the prince that shall come shall destroy the city and the sanctuary; and the end thereof shall be with a flood, and unto the end of the war desolations are determined. And he shall confirm the covenant with many for one week: and in the midst of the week he shall cause the sacrifice and the oblation to cease, and for the overspreading of abominations he shall make it desolate, even until the consummation, and that determined shall be poured upon the desolate.

(Daniel 9:24-27)

Briefly summarized, the word translated "weeks" is the Aramaic word *shabuwa*, which literally means "sevened" and is understood by virtually all biblical scholars to denote sets of seven years. Seventy sets of seven prophetic year periods are appointed to the Jewish people according to this passage. We know that it is referring to the Jewish people because the prophet Daniel is told that these weeks are appointed for "his people." Daniel was Jewish, so his people are the Jewish people. This also means that this prophecy is appointed for the city of Jerusalem, since that would be considered his "holy city." At that time, years were measured in three-hundred-sixty-day cycles, thus prophetic years are three hundred and sixty days. Today, we use a Gregorian calendar based on 365-day cycles, with an extra day added every four years. The passage continues with a list of qualifications that signal the end of this period of time. The fulfillment of these qualifications will lead us into the millennial rule. We will now break this down verse by verse. As you will see, I have inserted commentary in brackets to help with understanding.

"Seventy weeks [70 sevened = 490 years] are determined upon thy people [Jews] and upon thy holy city [Jerusalem], to finish the transgression, and to make an end of sins, and to make reconciliation for iniquity, and to bring in everlasting righteousness, and to seal up the vision and prophecy, and to anoint the most Holy [usher in the millennial rule]" (Daniel 9:24).

This prophecy began well after Cyrus ended the seventy-year captivity of the Jews during Daniel's lifetime. The seventy-year captivity was declared by Jeremiah the prophet (Jeremiah 25:11). This prophecy we call Daniel's seventy weeks actually came as a result of Daniel's intercession for his people because he understood by "the books" that the seventy-year captivity of the Jews was over (Daniel 9:2). Although it is not recorded by Daniel, King Cyrus ended the Jewish captivity at that time. He also commanded the rebuilding of the house of God, but there was no follow through (Ezra 6:3). The succession of world rulers was as follows: Cyrus was succeeded by Cambyses, who was succeeded by Smerdis, who was succeeded by Darius (not Darius the Mede of Daniel 5:31, but another Darius), who was succeeded by Xerxes, who was succeeded by his son Artaxerxes. The first sixty-nine sets of seven years, or 173,880 days, began on the equivalent of our March 14, 445 BC, when King Artaxerxes reaffirmed the decision of Cyrus and again commanded the rebuilding of Jerusalem (Nehemiah 2:1-8).[4] This becomes our point of reference, because at this command, the rebuilding of Jerusalem and the temple actually took place.

"Know therefore and understand, that from the going forth of the commandment to restore and to build Jerusalem [King Artaxerxes] unto the Messiah the Prince [Jesus] shall be seven weeks [7 sevened = 49 years], and threescore and two weeks [62 sevened = 434 years]: the street shall be built again, and the wall, even in troublous times [see the book of Nehemiah]" (Daniel 9:25).

The Scripture above mentions that there are seven weeks and sixty-two weeks between the rebuilding of Jerusalem and Jesus. This is where we get the sixty-nine weeks of the prophecy (62 weeks +7 weeks = 69 weeks). Due to the precise nature of this prophecy, in that the numbers are so specific, it can only be interpreted in light of actual historical events. The first sixty-nine weeks ended on the equivalent of our April 6, 32 AD. This is the very day Jesus entered Jerusalem on a donkey, being acknowledged openly as the Messiah for the first time by the Jews (Luke 19:40).[5] Thus, the first sixty-nine weeks, according to Daniel 9:25, would have seen their conclusion on this date.

The exact number of days between March 14, 445 BC and April 6, 32 AD is 173,880 days. The following equation was beautifully constructed by Chuck Missler and Mark Eastman in their book *Alien Encounters*. It takes into account 365 day Gregorian calendar days and our dates of equivalency.

$$
\begin{array}{lcr}
\text{445 BC – 32 AD (476 x 365)} & = & 173,740 \\[2mm]
\text{March 14 – April 6} & = & 24 \\[2mm]
\text{Leap Years} & = +\!\!\! & \underline{\quad 116 \quad} \\[2mm]
\textbf{Total days} & & \textbf{173,880}\,^{6}
\end{array}
$$

As we can see from this equation, the timeline of this prophecy was fulfilled to the very day! You will notice that the next verse begins with the phrase "and after threescore and two weeks." Please keep in mind that "seven weeks" precede the "threescore and two weeks." Therefore, the events it goes on to describe essentially occur after the first sixty-nine weeks. In other words, they happen after April 6, 32 AD, which is the day that Jesus is acknowledged openly as the Messiah.

"And **after** [emphasis mine] threescore and two weeks [62 sevened] shall Messiah be cut off [Jesus crucified], but not for himself: and the people of the prince that shall come shall destroy the city and the sanctuary; and the end thereof shall be with a flood [figurative of the assault on Jerusalem in 70 AD], and unto the end of the war [destruction of Jerusalem in 70 AD] desolations are determined" (Daniel 9:26).

It was *after* the first sixty-nine weeks of prophetic years (or 173,880 days) that Jesus was crucified for all flesh. He did not die for himself because he needed no savior. It was also after the first sixty-nine weeks of prophetic years that Jerusalem was destroyed. This is in response to the prophecy that "the people of the prince to come shall destroy the city and the sanctuary." This shifts our attention from Messiah to the "prince to come" (representative of an antichrist). The word "flood" in verse 26 comes from the Aramaic word *sheteph,* meaning a deluge, literally or figuratively. In this case, it was used to figuratively describe the assault on Jerusalem, and rightly so. The assault on Jerusalem was severe and devastating, and at the end of the war, the armies of Rome descended upon Jerusalem as a flood. The Roman, General Titus, not only destroyed the city in 70 AD, but also the temple. The historical accounts are graphic and sorrowing. Not one stone of the temple was left standing upon another (Mark 13:2).

Verse 27 will move us into the events surrounding the seventieth "week."

"And he [antichrist, man of sin, son of perdition] shall confirm the covenant with many for one week [seventieth sevened, 7 years]: and in the midst of the week [3½ sevened = 42 months = 1,260 days] he [antichrist] shall cause the sacrifice and the oblation to cease [possibly occurring in a third temple in Jerusalem], and for the overspreading of abominations [reference to the abomination of desolation] he shall make it desolate, even until the consummation [return of Christ], and that determined shall be poured upon the desolate [bowls of God's wrath]" (Daniel 9:27).

The beginning of the "seventieth week" occurs when the final antichrist "he" signs a covenant with "many." How do we know that the "he" in this verse refers to the final antichrist? We know this by cross-referencing passages such as: 1 John 2:18, Daniel 7:8, Daniel 8:9, Daniel 11:21-45, 2 Thessalonians 2:1-4, and Revelation 13:1-5. These passages contain overlapping information that adds to our understanding of who this is and what he will do.

Apart from cross-referencing Scripture, we have to keep in mind that the transition from messiah to "the prince that shall come" was made in the previous verse. This puts our view on an antichrist figure. In Daniel 9:27, our view of the antichrist figure is expanded beyond the parameters of what was fulfilled by Titus (or any other type of antichrist throughout history) and into qualities that can only be associate with an antichrist figure that is yet to come.

Who is the "many"? The entire passage in Daniel 9:24-27 is declared to concern Daniel's people (Israel), so it follows that this "many" is most likely the nation of Israel. It may include other nations as well. This means that the final antichrist, or beast, will already be on earth *before* the final "week" begins. This idea is important for us to grasp. The period defined as Daniel's seventieth week has no bearing on the actual amount of time the final antichrist may be present on the earth.

Understanding the seventieth "week" has admittedly caused division within the body of Christ. It seems as though there are as many timelines dealing with the events housed by this time period as there are researchers and teachers talking about it. Without attacking other perspectives, I will do my best to present a clear, simple and logical explanation of the issue.

Introducing the Gap

Let us begin by understanding the "gap" between the sixty-ninth and seventieth weeks. Some people say that those who insert a gap, or indeterminable period of time, between the sixty-ninth and seventieth weeks are unjustified in doing so, and thus a future interpretation of the seventieth week is in error. These people will typically go on to point out the destruction of the temple in 70 AD, citing this event as the final fulfillment of Daniel's seventieth week.

In my humble opinion this argument makes no sense. Cutting straight to the chase, if the seventieth week had immediately followed the sixty-ninth week, a covenant involving the antichrist would have been signed the day after Jesus entered Jerusalem on a donkey. In other words, for the seventy weeks to truly be continuous, the seventieth week would have begun before Jesus was even crucified. Since this did not occur, there is no logical reason to believe this! Therefore, there *must* be a gap between the sixty-ninth and seventieth "weeks." This remains true even if we try to conclude that the destruction of the temple in 70 AD was in fact the fulfillment of Daniel's seventieth week.

Incorporating the word *after* in the phrase "And *after* threescore and two weeks shall Messiah be cut off…" Daniel 9:26 properly explains events that were appointed to happen after the sixty-nine "weeks" end and before the seventieth "week" begins. The question is not: is there a gap? The real question becomes: how long is this gap?

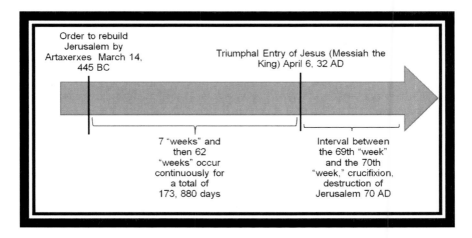

Figure 1

DEFINING THE GAP

If the seventieth week was fulfilled in 70 AD like some suggest, this scenario would require a thirty-year gap. When doing the math, a significant covenant involving the Jews would have been signed in 63 AD, which did not happen. Also, the millennial rule directly referenced in Revelation chapter 20 would have commenced in 70 AD and would have ended during the Dark Ages, in 1070 AD. When one looks at the present turmoil of the world and then studies the history of world events which took place between 70 AD and 1070 AD, it does not seem possible that this approach could make less sense. Furthermore, when was the judgment seat of Christ? When was the great white throne judgment? Can we really write these events off as symbolic allegory to make our views fit?

When I read Revelation 21 and 22, and compare it with the world I wake up to every morning, I cannot help but notice the alarming disparity! I'm sure that you as the reader can concur. Since this is not the new heaven and new earth, we can conclude that the gap between the sixty-ninth week and the seventieth week continues through this day. Even at this point, the seventieth week has not yet begun, because the referenced covenant has not yet taken place.

The Seventieth Week

"And he shall **confirm the covenant with many for one week**: and in the midst of the week he shall cause the sacrifice and the oblation to cease, and for the overspreading of abominations [abomination of desolation] he shall make it desolate, even until the consummation, and that determined shall be poured upon the desolate" (Daniel 9:27).

This verse begins by describing the covenant necessary to initiate Daniel's seventieth "week." Three and a half years after signing the covenant, the final antichrist "he" will break this covenant. At this time, the abomination of desolation will be instituted, and the final antichrist will sit down in the "temple of God"—making it his throne, according to 2 Thessalonians 2:3-4:

"Let no man deceive you by any means: for that day shall not come, except there come a falling away first, and that man of sin be revealed, the son of perdition; who opposeth and exalteth himself above all that is called God, or that is worshipped; **so that he as God sitteth in the temple of God, shewing himself that he is God.**"

During his next three and a half years, the final antichrist (also called beast, man of sin, son of perdition, wicked one) will declare war on the people of God, and the great tribulation will commence.

"And it was given unto him to **make war** with the saints, and to overcome them: and power was given him over all kindreds, and tongues, and nations" (Revelation 13:7).

In this passage, the final antichrist is clearly making war with the saints of Jesus. He is also exercising power over a large population within the world. The global impact of this leader will in no way go unnoticed. Leadership and control on this scale has never been witnessed before in the whole of human history. Even Nimrod, who united the earth to build the tower of Babel, did not command control over a relatively large population, since the world was just beginning to be repopulated after the great flood (Genesis 6:8-10, 7:1-10).

THE GREAT TRIBULATION

"And they worshipped the dragon which gave power unto the beast: and they worshipped the beast, saying, Who is like unto the beast? Who is able to make war with him? And there was given unto him a mouth speaking great things and blasphemies; and power was given unto him to continue forty and two months [three and one-half years]" (Revelation 13:4-5).

In this passage, the military ability and overall power and authority of the beast (antichrist) are praised by those that follow him. He speaks blasphemy against God, and beginning at this point in time, his power is confined to forty-two more months. This passage allows us to understand that from the point in time when he begins to make war with the saints, the last forty-two months of his power begin. These forty-two months become the great tribulation spoken of by Jesus.

> When ye therefore shall see the abomination of desolation, spoken of by Daniel the prophet, stand in the holy place, (whoso readeth, let him understand). Then let them which be in Judaea flee into the mountains. Let him which is on the housetop not come down to take any thing out of his house. Neither let him which is in the field return back to take his clothes. And woe unto them that are with child, and to them that give suck in those days! But pray ye that your flight be not in the winter, neither on the sabbath day: **For then shall be great tribulation, such as was not since the beginning of the world to this time, no, nor ever shall be**.
>
> (Matthew 24:15-21)

The abomination of desolation is placed during the middle (or forty-two months from the end) of Daniel's seventieth "week." In this passage, Jesus ties the placing of this abomination to the beginning of the war that the antichrist will conduct against the saints. He calls it the great tribulation. Thus, we find that the second half of Daniel's seventieth week overlaps with the great tribulation of the church. These forty-two months of great tribulation will continue until their consummation.

"And he shall confirm the covenant with many for one week: and in the midst of the week he shall cause the sacrifice and the oblation to cease, and for the overspreading of abominations [abomination of desolation] he shall make it desolate, **even until the consummation**, and that determined shall be poured upon the desolate" (Daniel 9:27).

THE SEVENTH TRUMPET

The consummation of all of this occurs when Jesus returns and transforms us into the immortal army of God. I firmly believe that this will occur at the seventh trumpet in the book of Revelation. Before this happens, the seven seals found in the book of Revelation chapters 6 and 8 will be opened by Jesus. These seals are upon a scroll in heaven, according to the book of Revelation chapter 5. As they are opened, their corresponding events will occur as prophesied. Additionally, all six of the first six trumpets found in the book of Revelation chapters 8 and 9 will have sounded, causing their corresponding judgments to manifest on the earth. In other words, the order of these things will be: Seal 1, Seal 2, Seal 3, Seal 4, Seal 5, Seal 6, Seal 7, Trumpet 1, Trumpet 2, Trumpet 3, Trumpet 4, Trumpet 5, Trumpet 6, and lastly Trumpet 7. Simple enough, right?

For some reason, I have encountered many students of the last days who have attempted to stagger the seals and the trumpets. In other words, it has been postulated that after the fourth or fifth seal is opened, the trumpets are all sounded prior to the sixth seal being opened. Some even say the seventh trumpet *is* the sixth seal. In my humble opinion, this has introduced endless confusion, countless arguments, and a horde of misconceptions. How this can possibly be justified is beyond me. The Bible could not be clearer on the point that the seals and trumpets happen chronologically. Why? The answer is because the seventh seal introduces the seven trumpets! Plainly stated, the first seven seals will be opened, <u>and then</u> the seven angels will be <u>given</u> seven trumpets so that the trumpets can begin to sound. How can the angels blow an instrument that they have not yet been given?

"And **when he had opened the seventh seal**, there was silence in heaven about the space of half an hour. And **I saw the seven angels** which stood before God; and **to them were given seven trumpets**" (Revelation 8:1-2).

How do we know that Jesus returns at the seventh trumpet? One reason is because Paul declares that Jesus returns at the *last* trumpet in 1 Corinthians 15:52. Since there are seven trumpets in the book of Revelation, the last trumpet must be trumpet number seven. Otherwise, Paul would have simply said "a trumpet." Why would he designate a specific trumpet if it were to be an arbitrary noise that could occur at any time? Also, the great voices in heaven (Revelation 11:15) are prophesying the victory of Jesus when the seventh trumpet is blown.

"In a moment, in the twinkling of an eye, **at the last trump**: for the trumpet shall sound, and the dead shall be raised incorruptible, and we shall be changed" (1 Corinthians 15:52).

"And the seventh angel sounded; and there were great voices in heaven, saying, The kingdoms of this world are become the kingdoms of our Lord, and of his Christ; and he shall reign for ever and ever" (Revelation 11:15).

Another reason that Jesus returns at the seventh trumpet is because the church is not caught away to the third heaven, but simply into the sky that contains the air we breathe. In the following passage, the word *air* comes from the Greek word "aer." This word literally means "the air we breathe." Why would Paul write air if he actually meant the third heaven? The fact of the matter is that we meet Jesus in the air where we are glorified, only to return to the surface of the earth and conquer with him as his immortal army.

"For the Lord himself shall descend from heaven with a shout, with the voice of the archangel, and **with the trump of God**: and the dead in Christ shall rise first: Then we which are alive and remain shall be caught up together with them in the clouds, **to meet the Lord in the air**: and so shall we ever be with the Lord" (1 Thessalonians 4:16-17).

A third reason that Jesus returns at the seventh trumpet is because it is impossible that every eye will see Jesus return if he comes to secretly sneak us away. Revelation 1:7 speaks to the fact that every eye will see Jesus.

"Behold, **he cometh with clouds [where we are gathered together to him]**; and every eye shall see him, and they also which pierced him: and all kindreds of the earth shall wail because of him. Even so, Amen" (Revelation 1:7).

A secret rapture (catching away) cannot coincide with a grand, earth-shaking entrance. Some would argue that every eye will see Jesus the *second* time that he comes again (in other words, inventing an unscriptural third coming), when his purpose is to execute judgment. However, this makes no sense, because the Bible is clear that every eye sees him when he returns in the clouds. He returns in the clouds when he returns to gather the saints. According to the famous "rapture passage" in 1 Thessalonians 4:17, these clouds are present when we are caught into the "air we breathe." In other words, every eye will see him during the time that the dead are being raised and the saints are being caught up into the sky. It only makes sense that he is returning once, at the stated time of the last, or seventh trumpet.

And the seventh angel sounded; and there were great voices in heaven, saying, The kingdoms of this world are become the kingdoms of our Lord, and of his Christ; and he shall reign for ever and ever. And the four and twenty elders, which sat before God on their seats, fell upon their faces, and worshipped God, Saying, We give thee thanks, O Lord God Almighty, which art, and wast, and art to come; because thou hast taken to thee thy great power, and hast reigned. And the nations were angry, and thy wrath is come, and **the time of the dead, that they should be judged**, and that thou shouldest give reward unto thy servants the prophets, and to the saints, and them that fear thy name, small and great; and shouldest destroy them which destroy the earth.

(Revelation 11:15-18)

Fourthly, the seventh trumpet contains a clear reference to the dead, which are destined to be judged. This judgment happens to the dead which are raised, thus making this an indirect reference to the resurrection of the dead occurring at this time. To be clear, *the dead that are to be judged are the dead saints who will be judged at the judgment seat of Christ.* All of the other dead are not judged until the great White Throne Judgment (Revelation 20:11-13). The latter event occurs after Jesus rules for one thousand years. Thus, this passage in Revelation 11:18 is clearly a reference to the resurrection of the dead that is discussed in 1 Corinthians 15:52 and 1 Thessalonians 4:15-16.

The fifth reason that the "catching away" of the church occurs at the seventh trumpet is possibly the most clear of all. At the seventh trumpet, the Bible says that the mystery of God is finished. The Greek word translated as "mystery" in the Bible is *musterion,* and according to Vine's Expository Dictionary it means "truth revealed."[7] At the seventh trumpet, Christ and his bride are revealed. His bride is "revealed" because we are changed and glorified at this time. For this reason, the angel tells John that at the seventh trumpet, the mystery of God will be finished.

"But in the days of the voice of the **seventh angel**, when he shall begin to sound, the **mystery of God should be finished**, as he hath declared to his servants the prophets" (Revelation 10:7).

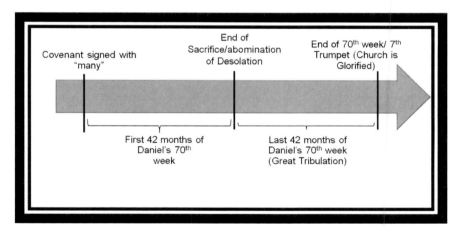

Figure 2

The evidence is further compounded when we understand that Paul actually tells us what the mystery is. "Behold, I shew you a mystery; We shall not all sleep, but we shall all be changed" (1 Corinthians 15:51). In other words, the <u>mystery</u> that Paul "shows" us is the same <u>mystery</u> that the angel speaking in Revelation 10:7 is talking about. This mystery is the glorification of the church. Paul continues on by saying, "In a moment, in the twinkling of an eye, at the *last trumpet*..." Could this be any simpler? They are talking about the same thing. The correlation is clear. It's simple! The last trumpet is, well, the last trumpet, and we are "changed" at the...drum roll, please...last trumpet!

"And the nations were angry, and **thy wrath** is come..." (Revelation 11:18a).

When the Bible says "thy wrath is come" it is referring to the bowl (or vial) judgments (Revelation 16) that are about to be poured out during the war campaign of Jesus and his army. Again, this destruction comes to the earth *after* the sounding of the seventh trumpet. For those who believe that a secret rapture is necessary for the church to escape the wrath which is to come (1 Thessalonians 1:10, 5:9) it helps to understand that the wrath of God is not poured out until the bowls of his wrath are released. The sounding of the trumpets release judgments, but the outpouring of the bowls release wrath. *There is a difference between judgment and wrath.* These bowls are poured out chronologically after the sounding of the seventh trumpet, the same trumpet that will close out Daniel's seventieth week. The outpouring of the bowls of God's wrath after the seventh trumpet happen in conjunction with other events associated with the Day of the Lord. For clarity, the Day of the Lord is a term used repeatedly (though not exclusively) in the Old Testament to refer to the coming of the conquering Messiah.

"And he shall confirm the covenant with many for one week: and in the midst of the week he shall cause the sacrifice and the oblation to cease, and for the overspreading of abominations [abomination of desolation] he shall make it desolate, even until the consummation, and **that determined shall be <u>poured</u> [emphasis mine] upon the desolate**" (Daniel 9:27).

MORE ON THE SECOND COMING

After the seventh trumpet is sounded and the catching away of the saints has occurred, we immediately proceed to conquer with Jesus, as the bowls of his wrath are poured out on the earth. This time of conquest with Jesus, paired with the outpouring of the bowls of God's wrath fulfill "that determined shall be poured upon the desolate." Again, these bowls (or vials) are discussed in the sixteenth chapter of Revelation. While the bowls are being poured out, the resurrected and glorified church will be conducting our ministry as the supernatural army of God (Isaiah 13:3, Revelation 17:14; 19:14, and possibly Joel 2:1-11). The outpouring of God's wrath and our war campaign with Jesus will likely occur as part of a brief thirty-day period also described by Daniel.

"And from the time that the daily sacrifice shall be taken away, and the abomination that maketh desolate set up, there shall be **a thousand two hundred and ninety days [1,290 days – 1,260 days = 30 days]**. Blessed is he that waiteth, and cometh to the thousand three hundred and five and thirty days [1,335 days – 1,290 days = 45 days]" (Daniel 12:11-12).

The abomination of desolation is set up during the middle of Daniel's seventieth week. When a period of 1,290 days is given, it is clearly longer than the 1,260 days necessary to reach the end of Daniel's seventieth week. It only makes sense that this thirty-day period houses certain events that occur after Jesus initially appears in the sky with his holy angels. The interesting thing about the 30-day time frame is that it seems to align perfectly with the three fall Feasts of the Lord—a prophetic necessity. Since the first four feasts were fulfilled during the first advent of Jesus Christ, it only makes sense that the last three feasts must likewise be fulfilled during his second advent. However, before I can point out this element of the issue, it helps to give a little background.

Concerning the Feasts of the Lord, some have erroneously concluded that the seven feasts are "the feasts of Israel" and thus to be attributed to the law. The same would argue that they do not hold any relevance to the present-day church. This is unfortunate. The fact of the matter is that they are not the feasts of Israel but the feasts of YHWH. They are replications of heavenly things.

"And the Lord spake unto Moses, saying, Speak unto the children of Israel, and say unto them, Concerning **the feasts of the Lord [YHWH],** which ye shall proclaim to be holy convocations, even **these are my feasts**" (Leviticus 23:1-2).

The twenty-third chapter of Leviticus describes the feasts in great detail. As this book is not intended to be an in-depth study of the feasts of YHWH, I will simply provide a brief overview of them. The purpose is to shed some light on their significance in God's prophetic timeline. There are three spring feasts (Passover, Feast of Unleavened Bread, Feast of First Fruits), one summer feast (Pentecost), and three fall feasts (Feast of Trumpets, Day of Atonement, Feast of Tabernacles). The first four feasts have been prophetically fulfilled by God. The last three feasts have yet to see their prophetic fulfillment. This will be illustrated in the following bullet points:

➢ **Passover**: This feast occurs on the fourteenth day of the month of Nissan (which is the first month of the Hebrew calendar) (Leviticus 23:5).

  o Brief explanation: This feast began when God was delivering his people from Egypt. On the night of the last plague, the plague of the firstborn children, they were to slay a spotless lamb and smear its blood on the doorposts. When the angel of death saw the blood on the doorposts, he would pass by and not kill the firstborn in that house. In like fashion, Jesus was offered up as a spotless sacrifice for our sins so that through his shed blood we could be granted forgiveness of sins (Acts 5:31, Romans 6:18, Revelation 5:11-13). He is described as the Lamb that was slain (Revelation 5:6).

- Fulfilled by Jesus at his crucifixion

➤ **Feast of Unleavened Bread**: Occurs on the fifteenth day of the month of Nissan (Leviticus 23:6-8)

- o Brief explanation: This is a seven-day period during which the Israelites were to eat only unleavened bread. Leavening is often associated with sin and false doctrine (Matthew 16:12, Luke 12:1). God sent Jesus to destroy the power of sin. Jesus was a sinless sacrifice for us (2 Corinthians 5:21), and in crucifixion his body was broken for us. Just as the Jews would break unleavened bread for this feast, Jesus was broken as the ultimate unleavened (or sinless) bread. During the Lord's Supper he made it clear that the bread represented his body (Matthew 26:26). He spent the first days of this feast in the grave (Matthew 12:40), thus fulfilling it.

  - Fulfilled by Jesus during his burial

➤ **Feast of First Fruits**: Occurs on the sixteenth day of the month of Nissan[8] (Leviticus 23:9-14)

- o Brief explanation: Just like the farmers receive the first fruits of their harvest, Jesus became the first fruit of those who would take part in the resurrection (1 Corinthians 15:20).

  - Fulfilled by Jesus at his resurrection

➢ **Feast of Pentecost (weeks)**: Occurs on the sixth day of the month of Sivan[9] (which is the third month of the Hebrew Calendar) (Leviticus 23:15-22)

  o Brief explanation: The word Pentecost means fifty, and this feast occurs fifty days after the Feast of First Fruits. When the day of Pentecost had "fully come" after the resurrection of Jesus, the disciples were in one accord in the upper room. It was at this time that the Holy Spirit came upon them as tongues of fire, causing them to be filled with the Holy Spirit and speak in new tongues (Acts 2:1-4). This signified the birth of the Church, which interestingly enough is also the birthday of the nation of Israel.

    ▪ Fulfilled by the Holy Spirit in the upper room

➢ **Feast of Trumpets**: Occurs on the first day of the month of Tishri[10] (which is the seventh month of the Hebrew Calendar) (Leviticus 23:23-25)

  o Brief Explanation: The feast of trumpets occurs over a two-day (48 hour) period during which no man knows "the day or the hour." The day and hour are distinguished by the appearing of the new moon, which is 29.5 days after the last one, meaning it might occur on the 29th or 30th day of that month. This is what Jesus referred to when saying of his coming that know man will know the day or the hour (Mark 13:32). It was a reference to this feast. This idiom reveals the parameters of our knowledge of his return, not the unscriptural notion of imminence (an anytime return of Jesus).

- Unfulfilled

➤ **The Day of Atonement**: Occurs on the tenth day of the month of Tishri[11] (Leviticus 23:26-32)

o Brief explanation: This feast is also known by the name Yom Kippur. It is a day for atonement and repentance. It is the holiest day of the year in Judaism.

- Unfulfilled

➤ **The Feast of Tabernacles (booths)**: Occurs on the fifteenth day of the month of Tishri[12] (Leviticus 23:33-44)

o Brief explanation: This is also known as Sukkot. It is a seven-day feast, although it was celebrated for eight days during the diaspora. The word *Sukkot* references the dwelling places, or coverings, that the Hebrews used during their forty years in the wilderness. According to the prophet Zechariah, this feast will continue to be celebrated annually during the millennial reign of Christ.

- Unfulfilled

Before we began discussing the Feasts of the Lord, I had explained that there are thirty days (and then a subsequent forty-five days) that extend beyond the fulfillment of Daniel's seventieth week. When it comes to the illusory thirty days of Daniel 12:11, here is how the fall feasts seem to line up. The Feast of Trumpets seems to align with the sounding of the last (or seventh) trumpet, which signifies the return of the Lord. As previously noted, the Feast of Trumpets has been historically described by the Hebrew idiom "You know neither the day nor the hour" (Matthew 25:13). The reason for this idiom is the fact that the Feast of Trumpets occurs over a two-day (48-hour) period. The day and hour are distinguished by the appearing of the new moon, which is 29.5 days after the last one, meaning it might occur on the 29th or 30th day of that month. The fact that the scripture in Matthew 25:13 has been used to justify the doctrine of imminence, which states that Jesus can come at any time, at all, right now, is laughable when placed in proper context.

When it comes to the Day of Atonement, this occurs ten days after the Feast of Trumpets. The number ten is often indicative of the perfection of Divine Order and the complete cycle of God's judgments[13]. Think of the Ten Commandments and the ten plagues of Egypt. It could make sense that this would line up with the deliverance of the Jewish Remnant (Zechariah 14:4-8; 12:10) and subsequent battle of Armageddon (Revelation 19:19). This of course is simply educated conjecture.

The Feast of Tabernacles begins five days after the Day of Atonement. This is a seven-day feast that will continue to be celebrated throughout the Millennial Reign of Christ (Zechariah 14:16). Seven days after the 15th of that month is the 22nd. Since prophetic months are thirty days, we find an interesting end to this speculative assessment. From the 22nd to the 30th there are eight days. Biblically speaking, eight is a number that is significant to "the generation of a new era or order."[14]

After these thirty days, another forty-five days is also discussed (Daniel 12:12). Remember that there are 1,260 days from the abomination of desolation to the end of Daniel's seventieth week. Then in Daniel 12:11 we are given a time-frame of 1,290 days, which is thirty days beyond the completion of Daniel's seventieth week (1,290 days – 1,260 days = 30 days). In Daniel 12:12 we are given a time-frame of 1,335 days, which adds an addition forty-five days to the thirty days of Daniel 12:11 (1,335 days – 1,290 days = 45 days). Altogether Daniel 12:11-12 adds seventy-five days to our timeline (30 days + 45 days = 75 days). Within these seventy-five days we can also expect to encounter the judgment seat of Christ (Romans 14:10; 2 Corinthians 5:10), the wedding supper of the Lamb (Revelation 19:9; Isaiah 25:6), and the organizing of the kingdom for the millennial rule. After the battle of Armageddon, Jesus sits down in the temple (in Jerusalem) and is anointed King over all the earth. The following captions of Scripture capture the transition from the battle of Armageddon and into the millennial rule of Jesus.

And the sixth angel poured out his vial upon the great river Euphrates; and the water thereof was dried up, that the way of the kings of the east might be prepared…And he gathered them together into a place called in the Hebrew tongue Armageddon…And I saw heaven opened, and behold a white horse; and he that sat upon him was called Faithful and True, and in righteousness he doth judge and make war...And I saw the beast, and the kings of the earth, and their armies, gathered together to make war against him that sat on the horse, and against his army. And the beast was taken, and with him the false prophet that wrought miracles before him, with which he deceived them that had received the mark of the beast, and them that worshipped his image. These both were cast alive into a lake of fire burning with brimstone. And the remnant were slain with the sword of him that sat upon the horse, which sword proceeded out of his mouth: and all the fowls were filled with their flesh...And I saw thrones, and they sat upon them, and judgment was given unto them: and I saw the souls of them that were beheaded for the witness of Jesus, and for the word of God, and which had not worshipped the beast, neither his image, neither had received his mark upon their foreheads, or in their hands; and they lived and reigned with Christ a thousand years.

(Revelation 16:12, 16; 19:11, 19-21; 20:4)

"At that time they shall call Jerusalem the throne of the LORD; and all the nations shall be gathered unto it, to the name of the LORD, to Jerusalem: neither shall they walk any more after the imagination of their evil heart" (Jeremiah 3:17).

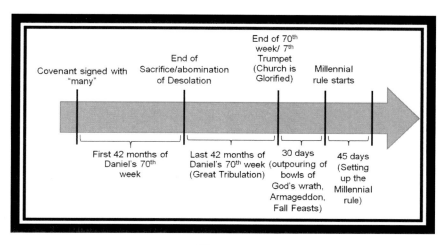

Figure 3

In Summary

To briefly summarize, Daniel's seventieth "week" is defined by events pertaining to the Jews. The second half includes the great tribulation of the church. Halfway into Daniel's seventieth "week" the final antichrist stops the sacrifice (which many assume is occurring in a rebuilt temple). He sets up the abomination of desolation, which signifies the beginning of the great tribulation for the church. From this point he is allotted 1,260 days to make war on the saints.

Prior to this, the seals of Revelation begin to be opened by Jesus in heaven. Daniel's seventieth week begins independently of the opening of these seals—it is not mandatory for the seventieth week to begin at the same time as the opening of the seals.

The seven seals and the seven trumpets of Revelation occur in chronological order. Daniel's seventieth "week" closes with the seventh trumpet signifying the return of Christ, the resurrection of the dead, and the rapture of the church. Afterwards, the church begins its ministry as the immortal army of God, and goes with Jesus into battle during the outpouring of the bowl (or vial) judgments. This ends at the battle of Armageddon, after which the judgment seat of Christ occurs and the kingdom is organized for the inception of the millennial rule.

Seven qualifications signify that these seventy "weeks" have ended, according to Daniel 9:24. These qualifications can only occur *after* the seventieth "week" has already occurred.

1. The transgression is finished.

2. There is an end of sins.

3. There is reconciliation for iniquity.

4. Everlasting righteousness is brought in.

5. The vision is sealed up.

6. The prophecy is sealed up.

7. The most Holy is anointed.

In my humble opinion, it seems clear that all of these qualifications will be fulfilled as a result of Jesus returning and destroying wickedness from the face of the earth.

CHAPTER 13

The Heavens

At this point we are going to make another transition as we progress in our study. In order to understand the way creation was ordered, and why the people of earth will see the things that will shortly come to pass, we must understand the heavens. The promise of heaven after death for the Christian is one of the best understood promises in the Bible. When we die, we *will* be in heaven with the Lord (2 Corinthians 5:8). Although the promise of heaven after death is understood, the concept of the heavens is not. Some may not have even realized that there is more than one heaven. Notice the way Paul describes where he was taken in the following passage.

"I knew a man in Christ above fourteen years ago, (whether in the body, I cannot tell; or whether out of the body, I cannot tell: God knoweth;) **such an one caught up to the third heaven.** And I knew such a man, (whether in the body, or out of the body, I cannot tell: God knoweth**;) How that he was caught up into paradise**, and heard unspeakable words, which it is not lawful for a man to utter" (2 Corinthians 12:2-4).

From this passage, we have no choice but to accept that God divided creation into at least three main realms, or "heavens," because of a direct reference to the *third* heaven. If there is a third heaven, it follows that there must also be a second heaven, as well as a first heaven.

The Third Heaven

We find in this verse that the third heaven is where paradise is currently found. Paradise is in the midst of where God resides. The same word that is translated *paradise* in 2 Corinthians 12 is also translated paradise in the following passage, and it is clearly in the midst of where God resides.

"He that hath an ear, let him hear what the Spirit saith unto the churches; To him that overcometh will I give to eat of the tree of life, which is in the midst of the paradise of God" (Revelation 2:7).

God calls himself the beginning and the end, so he must reside outside of time (Revelation 1:8). Since every place in our universe is affected by time, it is not possible for God to be confined to a location in our universe. Since God cannot be confined by our universe, he must reside in a different dimension that is outside of time. It is for this reason that I believe the third heaven exists as a realm that is a collection of higher (or the highest) dimensions, and not in a physical location in our universe, because it is not bound by the influence of time. This realm remains accessible solely through spiritual means. There is no one higher than God, so it follows that there is no realm higher than the one in which God dwells. The third heaven *is* the highest heaven.

To sum up the third heaven in a few words, it exists as a completely separate realm from the other heavens, it is only accessible through the spirit realm, and it is the highest heaven.

THE FIRST HEAVEN

Our discussion will continue with the creation account found in the book of Genesis.

"In the beginning God created the heaven and the earth. And the earth was without form, and void; and darkness was upon the face of the deep. And the Spirit of God moved upon the face of the waters" (Genesis 1:1-2).

Note that the Hebrew word translated "heaven" indicates a plurality and should be translated "heavens." The Hebrew word used here is *shamayim,* which is plural. Nearly every other biblical translation makes this distinction confirming that there is more than one heaven. This makes it adamantly clear that it is mandatory that we maintain a distinction between the different levels of heaven. What does this mean for the first heaven?

The first heaven encompasses all life that exists within earth's atmosphere. In the following passages, the fowls are spoken of as being of the heaven. Which heaven do birds fly in? Birds are residents of the earth, like the rest of creation, and fly in the space between earth's atmosphere and earth's surface, or the firmament. They fly within the first heaven. The first heaven is found in the carnal realm where people and animals dwell.

"And God said, Let the waters bring forth abundantly the moving creature that hath life, and fowl that may fly above the earth in the open firmament of heaven" (Genesis 1:20).

"I will consume man and beast; I will consume the **fowls of the heaven**, and the fishes of the sea, and the stumbling blocks with the wicked: and I will cut off man from off the land, saith the LORD" (Zephaniah 1:3).

THE SECOND HEAVEN

We have discussed the third heaven and the first heaven. This leaves the second heaven. Let's look at this verse to get insight as to what the second heaven is.

"For we wrestle not against flesh and blood, but against principalities, against powers, against the rulers of the darkness of this world, against spiritual wickedness **in high [heavenly] places**" (Ephesians 6:12).

Notice that spiritual wickedness is characteristic of the heavenly places where the powers and principalities dwell. In the third heaven, where God dwells, it is described as paradise—pointing to the conclusion that it is free from wickedness. For this reason, we know that these heavenly places are not referring to the third heaven. We also know that it is not referring to the first heaven, because it is clear that it is not talking about a physical location, but a spiritual location. The second heaven is comprised of multiple dimensions and areas where wicked spirits reside.

Regarding the wicked principalities and powers, we are in perpetual spiritual war with these beings. They are extremely powerful; some maintaining authority over multiple nations. I will add that the angels of God also conduct their ministry in the second heaven at times in their service to us (Psalm 91:11, Daniel 10:13). There is constant and significant activity occurring all of the time in the second heaven.

The second heaven is not limited to other dimensions. It also includes areas that are (or at least seem to be) part of the earth, but cannot be easily accessed. The nature of activity that occurs within them is why they are classified as part of the second heaven. The fact of the matter is that most people live their entire lives, travel to many places, and never encounter the places that I will describe.

Understanding Hell

The second heaven includes hell, which consists of Hades/*Sheol*/*Gehenna* and Tartarus. The second heaven also includes a place known as the pit. According to Scripture, these places seem to be located in deep areas of the earth. Hades is the destination of unrighteous men and women who have died. They will await the Great White Throne Judgment in this place. *Hades* is the Greek term for hell, and *Sheol* is the Hebrew term for hell. There is also the Greek word *Gehenna,* which is the term used by Jesus for an area of Hades in which torment and destruction occurs (Matthew 10:28, Luke 12:5). In the English version of the Bible, this word simply gets translated as hell, making a study of the subject solely in the English language somewhat convoluted. The word Gehenna is a historical reference to the Valley of the Son of Hinnom, a place outside of ancient Jerusalem where children were once sacrificed to the ancient god Molech. It appears as though Sheol, Hades, and Gehenna can all be used to describe the same place.

Before Jesus died, Sheol also housed paradise, which was otherwise known as Abraham's bosom. Abraham's bosom was separated from the rest of Sheol by a great divide. However, it remained close enough in proximity to permit conversation. This is revealed in the story of Lazarus.

There was a certain rich man, which was clothed in purple and fine linen, and fared sumptuously every day: And there was a certain beggar named Lazarus, which was laid at his gate, full of sores, And desiring to be fed with the crumbs which fell from the rich man's table: moreover the dogs came and licked his sores. And it came to pass, that the beggar died, and was carried by the angels into **Abraham's bosom**: the rich man also died, and was buried; And in hell he lift up his eyes, being in torments, and seeth Abraham afar off, and Lazarus in his bosom. And he cried and said, Father Abraham, have mercy on me, and send Lazarus, that he may dip the tip of his finger in water, and cool my tongue; for I am tormented in this flame. But Abraham said, Son, remember that thou in thy lifetime receivedst thy good things, and likewise Lazarus evil things: but now he is comforted, and thou art tormented. And beside all this, between us and you there is a great gulf fixed: so that they which would pass from hence to you cannot; neither can they pass to us, that would come from thence.

(Luke 16:19-26)

Jesus never said that this was a parable. Jesus was telling a story that actually occurred. Abraham's bosom was a part of Hades during the Old Covenant. However, after Jesus ascended, it was relocated to the third heaven as a result of Jesus taking "captivity captive" (Ephesians 4:8). This is confirmed by Paul, who described encountering this paradise when he related an experience of being taken to the third heaven.

"I knew a man in Christ above fourteen years ago, (whether in the body, I cannot tell; or whether out of the body, I cannot tell: God knoweth;) such an one caught **up to the third heaven**. And I knew such a man, (whether in the body, or out of the body, I cannot tell: God knoweth;) How that he was caught up **into paradise**, and heard unspeakable words, which it is not lawful for a man to utter" (2 Corinthians 12:2-4).

UNDERSTANDING TARTARUS

In addition to Sheol, Tartarus serves as another underworld location. Tartarus is the location of the fallen angels who rebelled in the days of Noah.

"For Christ also hath once suffered for sins, the just for the unjust, that he might bring us to God, being put to death in the flesh, but quickened by the Spirit: By which also he went and preached unto the **spirits** in **prison** [Tartarus]; Which sometime were disobedient [leaving their first estate], when once the longsuffering of God waited in the days of Noah, while the ark was a preparing, wherein few, that is, eight souls were saved by water" (1 Peter 3:18-20).

The word translated "prison" in this passage is the Greek word *Tartarus*. This is the only passage in the Bible where the term *Tartarus* is used, and it is significant that it is used to reference the location of the chained fallen angels. This passage is an obvious reference to the angelic rebellion that occurred in Noah's day. The English word *spirit* comes from the Greek word *pneuma*. In Greek, this word is usually classified by a noun that identifies it. For example, the Greek might read "Spirit of God" or "spirits of men." If there is no noun present to classify it, then by grammatical rule we must understand that it is referring simply to spirits. Thus we know that these are not the spirits of men, but the spirits that God bound after their offense against him. These spirits were the angels that rebelled prior to the flood of Noah, taking wives unto themselves and producing hybrid offspring—notoriously referred to as the Nephilim (or giants) (Genesis 6:1-4). In judging the "old world" God locked up these rebellious angels in chains of darkness.

"For if God spared not the angels that sinned, but cast them down to hell, and delivered them into **chains of darkness**, to be reserved unto judgment; And spared not the old world, but saved Noah the eighth person, a preacher of righteousness, bringing in the flood upon the world of the ungodly" (2 Peter 2:4-5).

These angels are again described as being in everlasting chains under darkness in the following passage.

"And the angels which kept not their first estate, but left their own habitation, he hath reserved in **everlasting chains under darkness** unto the judgment of the great day" (Jude 1:6).

The phrase "under darkness" in the previous verse is referring to Tartarus. These fallen angels are the spirits who had the gospel preached to them by Jesus during his victory campaign in the heart of the earth, according to 1 Peter 3:19. Jesus told us that he would be in the heart of the earth during the three days and three nights He would spend in the grave. Again, this meant that he would be taking a trip to the realm of the dead.

"For as Jonas [Jonah] was three days and three nights in the whale's belly; **so shall the Son of man be three days and three nights in the heart of the earth**" (Matthew 12:40).

UNDERSTANDING THE PIT

Now we will look at what the Bible tells us regarding the pit.

And the fifth angel sounded, and I saw a star [angel] fall from heaven unto the earth: and to him was given the key of the bottomless **pit**. And he opened the bottomless pit; and there arose a smoke out of the pit, as the smoke of a great furnace; and the sun and the air were darkened by reason of the smoke of the pit. And there came out of the smoke locusts upon the earth: and unto them was given power, as the scorpions of the earth have power. And it was commanded them that they should not hurt the grass of the earth, neither any green thing, neither any tree; but only those men which have not the seal of God in their foreheads. And to them it was given that they should not kill them, but that they should be tormented five months: and their torment was as the torment of a scorpion, when he striketh a man. And in those days shall men seek death, and shall not find it; and shall desire to die, and death shall flee from them. And the shapes of the locusts were like unto horses prepared unto battle; and on their heads were as it were crowns like gold, and their faces were as the faces of men. And they had hair as the hair of women, and their teeth were as the teeth of lions. And they had breastplates, as it were breastplates of iron; and the sound of their wings was as the sound of chariots of many horses running to battle. And they had tails like unto scorpions, and there were stings in their tails: and their power was to hurt men five months. **And they had a king over them, which is the angel of the bottomless pit, whose name in the Hebrew tongue is Abaddon, but in the Greek tongue hath his name Apollyon.**

(Revelation 9:1-11)

So he carried me away in the spirit into the wilderness: and I saw a woman sit upon a scarlet coloured beast, full of names of blasphemy, having seven heads and ten horns... And the angel said unto me, Wherefore didst thou marvel? I will tell thee the mystery of the woman, and of the beast that carrieth her, which hath the seven heads and ten horns… **The beast that thou sawest was, and is not; and shall ascend out of the bottomless pit, and go into perdition**: and they that dwell on the earth shall wonder, whose names were not written in the book of life from the foundation of the world, when they behold the beast that was, and is not, and yet is.

(Revelation 17:3, 7-8)

The pit is where the fallen angel Apollyon is king, and from where certain hybridized creatures will be released to torment men after another angel, alluded to as a star, has opened it. The pit is also the location out of which the beast that carries the whore of Babylon will arise.

A Workable Model

To briefly recap, the third heaven is the realm of God, the second heaven houses fallen spirits and comprises much of what we call the spirit realm, including the realms of hell, and the first heaven is contained by the earth's atmosphere. From the dimensions contained by the second and third heavens come the realities that we experience in this life. In other words, the spiritual realm is more real than the natural realm.

To illustrate this concept, imagine three boxes. The small box represents the first heaven, the medium box represents the second heaven, and the large box represents the third heaven. The size of the boxes directly corresponds with the power and authority each realm houses. In other words, the largest box holds authority over both of the other boxes, and the medium box holds authority over the smallest box. Most people view the heavens as shown in the top part of the following figure. They imagine that all of the boxes are sequential, and separated by a designated space. They believe that there is earth, and beyond earth is the cosmos, which constitutes more of heaven, and beyond the cosmos there is God. In opposition to this, the bottom part of the figure pictures a much more accurate way of looking at the heavens.

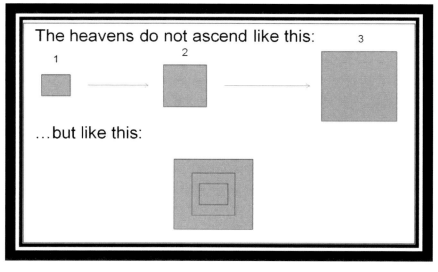

Figure 4

The heavens are not understood according to distance, but according to dimension. Everything in the first heaven is contained by both the second and third heavens. The third heaven contains all that exists. They are all overlapping. In science, there are theories based on quantum physics that argue for the existence of multiple dimensions, parallel universes, and thus a multi-verse. They are simply doing their best to explain how God ordered creation.

From these higher dimensions, potential realities exist, and are brought into manifestation through the agreement of men. Why? It is because God gave man dominion on the earth, or the first dimension (Genesis 1:28). This is why God uses men to accomplish his will on the earth, and likewise why Satan uses men as well. With this established, it becomes possible to unveil the mystery of iniquity, and the Luciferian agenda for the last days.

CHAPTER 14

The Mystery of Iniquity

The goal of the Satanic/Luciferian agenda is to bring the activity of the second heaven into manifestation in the first heaven. At any time when people are in agreement with this agenda, they can to a degree cause this to occur. In other words certain actions, rites, rituals, incantations, and other works of sorcery and witchcraft can open up lines of communication, and even portals, into the second heaven from our world.

THE RESTRAINER

"And now ye know what withholdeth that he [the final antichrist] might be revealed in his time. For the **mystery of iniquity** doth already work: **only he who now letteth will let, until he be taken out of the way**" (2 Thessalonians 2:6-7).

The creation of lines of communication and even portals between the first and second heavens is the mystery of iniquity that this passage discusses. The divisions between the three heavens are maintained by ultra-powerful forces that God has put in place. The second heaven does not have free access to the third heaven. In the same respect, the first heaven does not have free access to the second heaven. The force that maintains the division between the first and second heavens is a mysterious "restrainer." In the KJV it refers to this personage as "he who now letteth." The word translated "letteth" also means to restrain, or keep back.

The restrainer holds back the manifestation of the antichrist and the things of the end. This restrainer has a masculine gender. According to this passage, it is only after the removal of this personage that the antichrist can manifest. Only after the antichrist manifests can he sign a covenant with Israel and any other nations (Daniel 9:27). It will most certainly be some time after the antichrist arrives that this covenant will be signed, but there is no way to tell how much time.

The restrainer withholds the activity of this final age that is appointed to occur before the return of Jesus. When this restrainer is removed, the "veil"—if you will—that holds apart the first and second heavens will be lifted. *At this point, a new age will begin on the earth that will threaten to destroy all flesh.* We will be talking more about ages in the following chapter.

THE MYSTERY OF INIQUITY IN ACTION

Just what kind of present-day activity involves the mystery of iniquity? Contacting "ascended masters" is a phenomenon that is fairly well known about today. Through the use of particular occult mysteries, men and women are able to open up lines of communication with very powerful and intelligent spirit beings. These spirits can say they are whomever they want the person (usually a medium, spiritualist, etc.) to believe they are. They always promote the occult, and urge humanity to get on board with a Luciferian/Satanic agenda.

Archiometry, as I learned from Bill Schnoebelen, is another method for piercing into the second heaven. In his DVD set *Interview with an Ex-Vampire,* he describes archiometry as follows:

"Archiometry… is a very advanced branch of black magic and voodoo, which involves cultivating the ability to enter into alternate universes, and then you go into these universes and you try and energize the universe, become the god of that universe, and then draw power from that universe back into your own universe. This started out, basically, as part of the worship of the star god Sirius, which is known in Egypt as Set, which is the Egyptian version of the Devil. The idea is that because there was a black dwarf star of Sirius next to the white star Sirius, it became known as Sirius A and Sirius B. Ancient magicians realized that they could use that black star as a gateway into an alternate universe, and so that's how they discovered universe B. Then later on there was universe C and D and E and etcetera, etcetera.… The person who comes back invariably seems to have amped up their power by a whole order of magnitude.…

It's believed by these people [that] this is a very easy way of becoming a living god....The fact of the matter is [that] you're doing it by demonic power, and if you're indeed entering other universes, those are universes that are populated by extremely evil beings and extremely wise, cruel beings."[15]

This same concept appears to be referenced in the following work, although it is referred to by another name. In quoting these sources I am much less interested in the actual names assigned to these things than I am interested in the common nature of what is being said. Consider the similarities in what is being suggested.

"Transyuggothian magic is carried out in order to reach Transyuggothian Space (also known as Trans-Plutonian Space and Universe B). The existence of these dimensions are kept very secret. The ancient cult of the Star Sirius, from which supposedly we are now getting aliens, had rituals to get one into the celebrated Universe B. Sirius B (the binary twin star that exists with the actual Sirius A star) represented the god Ra Hoor Khuit. Sirius A represented the Egyptian devil."[16]

Another great example of the mystery of iniquity at work is an occult ritual performed and documented by Aleister Crowley in 1918. This overview is borrowed from the book *Nephilim Stargates*:

"In 1918, famed occultist Aleister Crowley attempted to create a dimensional vortex that would bridge the gap between the world of the seen and the unseen. The ritual was called the Amalantrah Working and according to Crowley became successful when a presence manifested itself through the rift. He called the being 'Lam' and drew a portrait of it. The startling image, detailed almost ninety years ago, bears powerful similarity with 'Alien Greys' of later pop culture."[17]

THE UNDERWORLD

Emmanuel Eni was an African witch doctor and deep occult society member who was saved and delivered by Jesus. After some time, he was able to write and publish his testimony as a book. As I read through it I learned quite a bit, including that the second heaven appears to *include* areas under water, under the earth, and above the earth's atmosphere. Remember that the second heaven is referred to as "heavenly places" in the Bible. The word "places" is plural. In this caption, Emmanuel explains how he accessed areas under the water:

"She took me to a corner of the barbeach, used something like a belt and tied [it] around us and immediately a force came from behind and pushed us into the sea. We started flying on the surface of the water and straight to the ocean. Dear reader, these happened in my physical form! At a point we sank into the sea bed and to my surprise I saw us walking along an express way. We moved into a city with a lot of people all very busy."[18]

Emmanuel goes on to reveal that the name of this being that takes him is the "Queen of the Coast." Interestingly enough, this same being (or at least this same office or title) is mentioned in an entirely separate and unrelated testimony. This testimony comes from another African man by the name of Babajika Muana Nkuba, who was also deeply involved in occult activity. From his own testimony it is written:

"I therefore went to Pointe-Noire, in the People's Republic of the Congo, to meet with the Queen of the Coast, on the shore of the Atlantic Coast. There we penetrated underneath the ocean, visiting her offices and her servants."[19]

Having two testimonies come from two unrelated sources bearing identical claims carries significant importance. The Bible says that out of the mouths of two or three witnesses will all things be established (Matthew 18:16). However, Emmanuel's testimony includes other incredible events. In this caption, Emmanuel explains how he accessed areas in space (outside of the earth's atmosphere):

"I had now become a part and parcel of the spirit world and could travel at will to any part of the world. According to the books I brought, spirit beings are living in space. Perhaps they would increase my powers, so I decided to try. I came out of my house, made some incantations and called the whirlwind and disappeared. I found myself in space and saw these spirit beings. What do you want they asked; I told them I wanted powers."[20]

Immediately after a two-week stay with these spirit beings in space, he traveled into the underworld. This is the record:

I then decided to go into [the] underworld to prove what was written in the books given to me. One day I went to a hidden place in the bush, made some incantations as stated in the books and commanded the ground to open. The ground opened and the demons created steps immediately. I stepped in and went right inside the ground. There was total darkness that can only be compared with one of the plagues that occurred in Egypt as recorded in the Bible. I saw a lot of things that are hard to explain. I saw people chained, people used for making money—their duties are to work day and night to supply money to their captors. I saw some elite society members who came in to do some sacrifices and would go back to the world with some gifts given to them by the spirits controlling the place. I saw some church leaders who came for powers, powers to say a thing that is accepted without questioning in the church. I stayed for two weeks and came back after receiving more powers."[21]

VALIDATING THE TESTIMONY

After studying Scripture, I found that there was no reason to invalidate any aspect of this testimony. In fact, I found incredible clarity come to me regarding verses that had remained by and large illusory to me. For example, why would Jesus march through the waters during his war campaign climaxing at Armageddon if there was nothing in the water to war with?

"Thou didst walk through the sea with thine horses, through the heap of great waters" (Habakkuk 3:15).

Or for that matter, how did Jonah locate Sheol (or hell) by going into the deep water in the belly of the fish? Jonah was an Old Testament prophet who was called to preach a word of repentance to the city of Nineveh. He didn't want to do this so he boarded a ship to Tarshish, attempting to run away from his calling. As they sailed, God sent a storm that threatened to break the ship to pieces. When it was discovered that Jonah was the cause of this divine storm, the men agreed to throw him overboard, and he was swallowed by a giant fish. This fish took Jonah deep under the water, and from this place Jonah spoke the following prayer:

"And said, I cried by reason of mine affliction unto the LORD, and he heard me; **out of the belly of hell [Sheol] cried I**, and thou heardest my voice. For thou hadst cast me into the deep, in the midst of the seas; and the floods compassed me about: all thy billows and thy waves passed over me" (Jonah 2:2-3).

Although it is possible that Jonah was using poetic symbolism in his prayer, *comparing* his situation to being in hell, it seems more likely that he described passing through a literal access point to Sheol from the depths of the sea. There is nothing else poetic or symbolic about his language in the prayer—the whole prayer is literal.

Below is another verse that makes a connection between Hades/Sheol and the sea. The sea actually contains certain dead that will be given up at the Great White Throne Judgment. Who are these dead?

And I saw a great white throne, and him that sat on it, from whose face the earth and the heaven fled away; and there was found no place for them. And I saw the dead, small and great, stand before God; and the books were opened: and another book was opened, which is the book of life: and the dead were judged out of those things which were written in the books, according to their works. **And the sea gave up the dead which were in it; and death and hell [Hades] delivered up the dead**

which were in them: and they were judged every man according to their works.

(Revelation 20:11-13)

Going back to Eni's testimony, does the Bible say anything about entities in space? During the war campaign of Jesus, it says that the hosts of the high ones that are on high are punished. This word "high" is from the Hebrew word *marowm*. This word literally means altitude, concretely an elevated place, or abstractly simply elevation. This is a straightforward way of describing Jesus punishing these spirit beings that abide in an elevated, high altitude location. Also, they are spoken of in the following passage as a separate category from the kings upon the earth.

"And it shall come to pass in that day, that the LORD shall punish the **host of the high ones that are on high**, and the kings of the earth upon the earth" (Isaiah 24:21).

What about under the earth? Does the Bible have say anything about wickedness there? Yes, it does. Consider that when Paul says every knee must bow to Jesus, he specifically points out that every knee *under* the earth is also included.

"That at the name of Jesus every knee should bow, of things in heaven, and things in earth, **and things under the earth**" (Philippians 2:10).

DEFINING THE MYSTERY OF INIQUITY

The testimony of Emanuel helps us to more concisely identify with what the Bible clearly explains. His recollection of occult activity models the mystery of iniquity at work. *The mystery of iniquity works to sidestep the barrier that the restrainer maintains between the first and second heavens.* These are the mysteries that are studied by mystery schools and occult adepts.

There is an old adage among the mystery schools that dates back as far as the tablets of Thoth. Legend goes that these were written by Thoth, otherwise known by some as the builder of the Great Pyramid.[22] Regardless of the legend, the writings do exist, from whatever or whoever their source may be. There is a peculiar phrase in them that translates:

As above, so below.

—Tablets of Thoth

It captures the idea that the things which are presently in the second heaven (above) are being smuggled via the mystery of iniquity into the earth realm (below). It should be noted that these writings are occult, meaning they reveal hidden wisdom that utilizes demonic assistance to carry out certain things. All things occult are based on lies, deception, and the twisting of the truth of God. This is done in order to manipulate the laws he has set in place to govern creation.

The Witch at Endor

There is an account involving Saul when the Spirit of the Lord had departed from him. When God would no longer answer him, he disguised himself and sought the counsel of a known witch who lived at Endor. She resisted him at first because she knew that the king of Israel had cut off wizards and all forms of occult practitioners from the land. When Saul swore to God that she would receive no punishment, she heeded his request and used her familiar spirit to bring up Samuel.

When she saw Samuel she cried, and knew who Saul was. This passage has caused a long-standing debate because it raises the question of whether or not it is possible to contact dead spirits. I will simply let the rest of the account speak for itself.

And when the woman saw Samuel, she cried with a loud voice: and the woman spake to Saul, saying, Why hast thou deceived me? for thou art Saul. And the king said unto her, Be not afraid: for what sawest thou? And the woman said unto Saul, I saw gods ascending out of the earth. And he said unto her, What form is he of? And she said, An old man cometh up; and he is covered with a mantle. And Saul perceived that it was Samuel, and he stooped with his face to the ground, and bowed himself. And Samuel said to Saul, Why hast thou disquieted me, to bring me up? And Saul answered, I am sore distressed; for the Philistines make war against me, and God is departed from me, and answereth me no more, neither by prophets, nor by dreams: therefore I have called thee, that thou mayest make known unto me what I shall do. Then said Samuel, Wherefore then dost thou ask of me, seeing the LORD is departed from thee, and is become thine enemy?

(1 Samuel 28:12-16)

The fact of the matter is that the Bible does not say a spirit that "looked like Samuel" came up—it says *Samuel* came up. This speaks to the fact that this woman *opened a portal* into the second heaven. This area of the second heaven would have included Sheol. Before she identified Samuel, she mentioned that "gods" (plural in the KJV) ascended out of the earth. This is unfortunately a poor translation in that the Hebrew word used here is in its singular form. She actually states that she saw a "god" or "divine being" ascending out of the earth. Why would she use this term to describe Samuel? Seeing Samuel's spirit (his true nature) was probably overwhelming, and left the witch with no other words but to describe him as a "god." While it is true that fallen spirits are repeatedly referred to as gods with a little "g" throughout the Bible (for example Deuteronomy 6:14, Jeremiah 44:8, etc.), it is also true that in this case the Bible states that it was actually

Samuel that showed up. This is similar to the account of Moses and Elijah appearing with Jesus at the transfiguration (as opposed to demons masquerading as them). It's hard to imagine Jesus accidently conversing with demons during this spectacular event!

"And His appearance underwent a change in their presence; and His face shone clear and bright like the sun, and His clothing became as white as light.And behold, there appeared to them Moses and Elijah, who kept talking with Him" (Matthew 17:2-3 AMP).

PULLING IT ALL TOGETHER

The following verse brings everything together in crystal-clear clarity. It lists all of the realms comprising the second heavens including: Sheol, heaven (speaking of higher dimensions), the top of Mount Carmel (referencing high altitudes), and the bottom of the sea.

"Though they dig into **hell [Sheol]**, thence shall mine hand take them; though they climb up to **heaven**, thence will I bring them down: And though they hide themselves in the **top of Carmel**, I will search and take them out thence; and though they be hid from my sight in the **bottom of the sea**, thence will I command the serpent, and he shall bite them" (Amos 9:2-3).

Where is this all going? The fact of the matter is that the wickedness that many only dabble with is about to have unrestrained and unlimited access to the earth. This will begin the next age that will dawn, when the restrainer is removed.

CHAPTER 15

The New Age

"Now that he [Jesus] ascended, what is it but that he also descended first into the lower parts of the earth? He that descended is the same also that ascended up far above **all heavens**, that he might fill all things" (Ephesians 4:9-10).

THE AGE OF CHRIST

Jesus has ascended into (and also somehow above) the third heaven, and he exercises his authority from this location. Now that we have established an accurate understanding of the heavens, along with an understanding of the restrainer and the mystery of iniquity, we will move into the concept of "ages." The purpose will be to lead us into an important revelation regarding the last days. Before Jesus came and died to redeem men, he was the person of the Godhead through whom the ages were made. The word translated "worlds" in the following passages comes from the Greek word *aion,* which means age: an age means perpetuity, or a Messianic period.

"[God] Hath in these last days spoken unto us by his Son, whom he hath appointed heir of all things, by whom also he made the worlds [ages]" (Hebrews 1:2).

"Through faith we understand that the worlds [ages] were framed by the word of God, so that things which are seen were not made of things which do appear" (Hebrews 11:3).

God created ages when he spoke creation into existence. Ages come and go, and with every age, things change. However, we can have confidence that there is one thing that will never change—that through every age Christians will belong to Jesus, remaining with him throughout all eternity. The age of Jesus as Messiah has been made an eternal age, and according to Ephesians, will continue throughout every generation forever.

In the following passage, the word translated "ages" actually means "generations," and the word translated "world" actually means "age." It's unfortunate that this is so awkwardly translated in the KJV, but I've inserted commentary to help with understanding.

"Unto him be glory in the church by Christ Jesus throughout all ages [generations], world [age] without end. Amen"
(Ephesians 3:21).

Overlapping Ages

The age of the glory of Jesus through the church will never end.
However, history reveals that ever since the institution of this age in 32 AD,
other ages have *overlapped* it. For instance, there were the Dark Ages, the
Renaissance period, the Industrial Age, etc. Ages continue to change on
the earth. Regardless of what age the earth is experiencing at any particular
time, Christians have continually tapped into the eternal age of the glory of
Jesus. The life of the Christian holds eternal consequence. Eventually, an age
will begin that will threaten to consume and destroy all flesh. For the sake
of the saints, God will cut these days short, and override that age to serve
his purposes.

"And except those days should be shortened, there should **no flesh
be saved**: but for the elect's sake **those days shall be shortened**" (Matthew
24:22).

At this point, the message becomes difficult. The removal of the
restrainer will allow for the rule of fallen angelic spirit beings over men to
be manifested on the earth. This is the same thing that happened in Noah's

day. When Jesus said that the end of the age would be as it was in the days of Noah, he was alluding to the fact that fallen angelic beings will become influencers and directors of things taking place in and around the earth. This also includes the open manifestation of their children, which the Bible calls Nephilim (or giants) (Genesis 6:4).

"But as the days of Noah were, so shall also the coming of the Son of man be" (Matthew 24:37).

The Nature of the Beast Kingdom

Consider this straightforward passage in Daniel 11. This passage takes place during the final antichrist's rule. We will pay special attention to the groups described in this passage. Before beginning, keep in mind that there are only four groups discussed: God, the final antichrist (referred to as the king), the gods (fallen spirit beings), and an anonymous "many."

And the king shall do according to his will; and he shall exalt himself, and magnify himself above every god, and shall speak marvellous things against the God of gods, and shall prosper till the indignation be accomplished: for that that is determined shall be done. Neither shall he regard the God of his fathers, nor the desire of women, nor regard any god: for he shall magnify himself above all. But in his estate shall he honour the God of forces: and a god whom his fathers knew not shall he honour with gold, and silver, and with precious stones, and pleasant things. Thus shall he do in the most strong holds with a strange god, whom he shall acknowledge and increase with glory: and he shall cause them to rule over many, and shall divide the land for gain.

(Daniel 11:36-39)

This passage begins by explaining that the final antichrist will exalt himself above every other fallen spirit being. It says that he will speak marvelous things (meaning incredible blasphemies) against the True God. Moreover, he will be granted the ability to prosper in these things until the indignation is accomplished. This means that God has appointed a time for him to continue, and when it's up, it's up! The final antichrist gives no regard to the God of his fathers, the desire of women, or any other fallen spirit being. The passage continues by saying that he will honor the god of forces in his estate. Who is the god of forces? At this point I am unsure. From the original language we glean that the Aramaic word translated forces is *Ma'uz*, and it literally means a fortified place, or rock.

In any case, whatever or whoever this god of forces is, it falls into the category of fallen spirit beings. Behind every idol is a fallen spirit being, otherwise called a devil.

"What say I then? that the idol is any thing, or that which is offered in sacrifice to idols is any thing? But I say, that the things which the Gentiles sacrifice, they sacrifice to devils, and not to God: and I would not that ye should have fellowship with devils. Ye cannot drink the cup of the Lord, and the cup of devils: ye cannot be partakers of the Lord's table, and of the table of devils" (1 Corinthians 10:19-21).

This god of forces will be honored with gold, silver, precious stones, and pleasant things. Thus, as we near the end of this passage, we are presented with only three parties involved in the discussion: God, the final antichrist, and the fallen spirit beings. After the passage wraps up what the antichrist "will do with the god of forces in the most strong holds," there is a peculiar phrase. It says, "And he shall cause 'them' to rule over many, and divide the land for gain." Who could this passage be discussing when it references an unnamed "them"?

"Thus shall he do in the most strong holds with a strange god, whom he shall acknowledge and increase with glory: **and he shall cause them to rule over many**, and shall divide the land for gain" (Daniel 11:39).

There are only three parties involved in the discussion when we get to the mention of the word *them*. When deciphering who this pronoun is referring to, we must limit our possibilities to God, the final antichrist, and the fallen spirit beings. The pronoun *them* cannot refer to the final antichrist because the pronoun is plural. Furthermore, it is impossible that the word *them* is referring to the Godhead because the antichrist will oppose God— he will certainly not place people under God's rulership. Thus, we can easily render this passage:

"And the final antichrist shall cause the fallen spirit beings to rule over many, and shall divide the land for gain."

THE NEPHILIM AGENDA

Not only will we be facing the issue of a strong fallen angelic presence on earth, but we will also see the actual integration of Nephilim into society. What are Nephilim? *Nephilim* is the Hebrew word that the Bible translates as giants. They indicate human hybrids. The first mention comes from the book of Genesis. In the following passage, they are the progeny that occurs from the sexual union of the daughters of men and the "sons of God." The term sons of God comes from the Hebrew *b'nei elohim*: the same b'nei elohim that worshipped God during the formation of the earth (Job 38:7) and the same b'nei elohim that accompanied Satan before the throne of God (Job 1:6; 2:1). The "sons of God" are angels.

And it came to pass, when men began to multiply on the face of the earth, and daughters were born unto them, That the sons of God [b'nei elohim] saw the daughters of men that they were fair; and they took them wives of all which they chose. And the LORD said, My spirit shall not always strive with man, for that he also is flesh: yet his days shall be an hundred and twenty years. There were giants [Nephilim] in the earth in those days; and also after that, when the sons of God came in unto the daughters of men, and they bare children to them, the same became mighty men which were of old, men of renown.

(Genesis 6:1-4)

Nephilim cannot occur unless there is a fusion between human and angelic DNA. It is recorded that this happened prior to the flood, when the sons of God took wives from the daughters of men. These women gave birth to the children of the fallen angels, and they were called Nephilim. This activity occurred as the result of angelic rebellion, and as we have already discussed, the current location of the angels that rebelled at this time is in Tartarus. They are locked up in chains under darkness awaiting judgment, and have been since the flood.

For this reason it is assumed by most that a similar angelic rebellion happened *after* the flood. The other possibility is that it occurred as the expression of a recessive gene carried into the new world by the wives of Noah's sons. While a majority of scholars do not hold this view, it certainly deserves mention.[23] Giants are recorded as occupying the Promised Land throughout the Pentateuch and the book of Joshua. With the original angels of Genesis 6:1-4 locked up and *all flesh* wiped off of the face of the earth

(Genesis 7:21), it is my strong conviction that it was by one of these two mechanisms that the Nephilim were reintroduced after the flood.

I will add that there is staggering evidence that this activity also included the manipulation of animal genetics with human and angelic genetics.[24] This activity would have led to creatures like Satyrs (half-goat, half-man), which are actually referenced to in some translations of the Bible (Isaiah 34:14).

The question is: how will it happen in the end? What will be different about the final manifestation? Should we expect giants, or is there something far more wicked waiting to be revealed? The truth is that giants *seem* to occur as a result of the natural product of sexual union between humans and angels. However, the way things occurred in the beginning will be different from the way they will occur in the end.

In the book of Daniel, Nebuchadnezzar has a dream in which a statue is shown to him. It had a head of gold, breast and arms of silver, belly and thighs of brass, legs of iron, and feet of iron and clay. Here is the interpretation:

Head of Gold: Kingdom of Babylon

Breast and Arms of Silver: Kingdom of Media-Persia

Belly and Thighs of Brass: Kingdom of Greece (under Alexander the Great)

Legs of Iron: The Roman Empire

Feet of Iron and Clay: The New World Order

These elements of the statue prophetically revealed the sequence of world powers that would dominate from the time of the vision until the return of Christ. Our interest lies in what is written of the fifth world power: the feet of iron and clay. Regarding the feet of iron and clay, all signs point to its fulfillment under a coming New World Order. This is the most unique of the five kingdoms represented by the statue. It is also the last one that will be revealed on the earth. The implications of its prophetic elements are haunting.

And whereas thou sawest the feet and toes, part of potters' clay, and part of iron, the kingdom shall be divided; but there shall be in it of the strength of the iron, forasmuch as thou sawest the iron mixed with miry clay. And as the toes of the feet were part of iron, and part of clay, so the kingdom shall be partly strong, and partly broken. **And whereas thou sawest iron mixed with miry clay, they shall mingle themselves with the seed of men**: but they shall not cleave one to another, even as iron is not mixed with clay. And in the days of these kings shall the God of heaven set up a kingdom, which shall never be destroyed: and the kingdom shall not be left to other people, but it shall break in pieces and consume all these kingdoms, and it shall stand for ever.

(Daniel 2:41-44)

Notice that it says a mysterious "they" will mingle themselves with the seed of men. Who is this mysterious "they"? In this passage, there are only two groups available for interpretation: the kings, and the men. It makes absolutely no sense to interpret the passage "men will mingle with the seed of men." If this were the intended purpose of this phrase, it wouldn't be necessary. A society has never existed apart from social institutions like marriage that allow for birth of children (the mingling of seed among men and women). In this way we are left with the interpretation "the kings will mingle with the seed of men." However, since the last kingdom will be a kingdom in which fallen spirit beings are ruling over men, angelic seed will indeed be mingled with the seed of men.[25]

The Bible goes on to describe this union as the mixing of iron with miry or brittle clay. Man was created from the dust of the earth. The word translated dust is *aphar* in the original Hebrew, which means dust, clay, earth, or mud. Keep in mind that the passage in Daniel 2 is translated from Chaldean/Aramaic texts; not Hebrew. The word translated "clay" in Daniel 2:42 is the word *chacaph,* and it straightforwardly means clay. The word *miry* used to describe this clay is the word *tiyn,* which straightforwardly means miry. Miry could be speaking to the spiritual state of people (sinful: willfully or not) that allows for the mingling activity to take place. The iron is related to the rulership within the final kingdom. This makes reference to the fallen spirit beings that will be in charge. Clearly, between these two groups, "seed" will be mingled.

Thus from "loins" of these fallen spirit beings, Nephilim (and other hybrids) will be reintroduced into the populations of the earth. However, the manner in which this occurs appears be different than in the account of Genesis 6:1-4. The passage in the book of Daniel continues on to say that "they" (now referring to the humans and fallen spirit beings) shall not cleave to one another. Interestingly, this word *cleave* is the Chaldean/Aramaic equivalent of the term used in Genesis to describe the union of marriage.

"Therefore shall a man leave his father and his mother, and shall **cleave** unto his wife: and they shall be one flesh" (Genesis 2:24).

During the first occurrence, Nephilim *seemed* to result almost unexpectedly as a result of blind angelic rebellion. The angels took women and cleaved to them, making them their wives. In the end, this mystery will be used and manipulated for a more sadistic purpose. The seed will be mingled, not within the confines of unholy marriage, but for a detestable agenda. It will move beyond mere offspring and branch into downright genetic manipulation resulting in the creation of unexplored genetic abominations. Satan plans, among other things, to defeat God and his army of saints, and his plan is to build an army by counterfeiting the glorification of the saints.

What kind of an army could be built to fight against God and his glorified saints? One example can be found in the book of Revelation.

> And the number of the army of the horsemen were two hundred thousand thousand: and I heard the number of them. And thus I saw the horses in the vision, and them that sat on them, having breastplates of fire, and of jacinth, and brimstone: and the heads of the horses were as the heads of lions; and out of their mouths issued fire and smoke and brimstone. By these three was the third part of men killed, by the fire, and by the smoke, and by the brimstone, which issued out of their mouths. For their power is in their mouth, and in their tails: for their tails were like unto serpents, and had heads, and with them they do hurt.
>
> (Revelation 9:16-19)

THE GATES OF HELL WILL NOT PREVAIL

The question may arise as to how this could all be carried out in a mere seven years, according to the length of Daniel's seventieth week. The truth is that through the mystery of iniquity, things have already been set in motion. The second heaven has been, and is perpetually being pierced and bridged, and when the restrainer is removed, all of these hidden things will be revealed. *In addition to this, the trans-human and post-human agendas taking place in our very own laboratories seek to accomplish this, not stopping only at genetic enhancement, but the integration of nanotechnology, synthetic biology, and other technologies with humans.*[26] Yet in all this, the passage in Daniel continues on to explain that during this kingdom, Jesus will set up an everlasting kingdom that will never be left to another. Jesus has the victory, and we will share in it with him. His kingdom will consume all other kingdoms. It will stand forever!

Jesus spoke directly to this when he explained the church to Peter. When he said that the gates of hell would not prevail against his church, he was explaining the power and glory of his victory. Gates represent the ability to keep things out as well as the ability to lock things in. Jesus explained that no matter what the kingdom of darkness did, the gates of hell would not be able to keep <u>his kingdom out of their territory</u>. Furthermore, the gates of hell would not be able to lock anything or anyone in that could not be taken out by the kingdom of God. The gates of hell are ultimately powerless against his glory, no matter what Satan has up his sleeve.

"And I say also unto thee, That thou art Peter, and upon this rock I will build my church; **and the gates of hell shall not prevail against it**" (Matthew 16:18).

Two Visions

In the process of understanding the way the "veil" between the first and second heavens will be torn, and other important aspects of the coming seasons, God gave me two sequential visions. I am including these visions with the expectancy that God will speak through them to bring additional clarity. Below is the record of them.

Vision 1

As I was praying, I saw Jesus walking, and he had ropes. There were children around him on these ropes. Some were walking along with him, and were under great covering, and at great peace. A powerful force was drawing to them all that they needed; destroying the works of darkness from all around them as they walked. Others ran ahead of Jesus. When they got too far, he would pull the rope and they would fling back to his side. This was painful and discomforting to them. Others would drag behind. Jesus would pull them forward. The yanking was painful and discomforting. The further behind the children were, the greater the acceleration was with which they were flung forward. As it continued, a wind like a tornado formed around the children walking with Jesus. It carried them over land and water. It sucked in everything that was necessary and utterly destroyed everything else from their path. More and more children began walking alongside Jesus as the vision continued. The more children that walked along side of him, the more powerful the force became around them. Then

Jesus began to run. It was awe-inspiring. The children who were running with him grew, and the force was indescribable.

Vision 2

I was in prayer. I heard the Lord and he said to come on a journey with him. I didn't actually go anywhere, but I experienced a vision. We began to tread over the earth, and then we took off into space. We went through the mouth of the ouroboros and I saw great evil. We took off back out through the mouth of the ouroboros and came back to earth. I saw in the sky a great angel removing the veil between the first and second heaven. Then I saw what appeared as though the sky were being peeled back, like a scroll being rolled up. I saw coming upon the earth every form of evil, from above and from below. I was with Jesus as he was running with his children like I saw in the first vision. The terrible beast that was chasing us consumed the ones that did not keep up. But we who remained alongside Jesus were protected. Spots of glory were shining forth all across the earth. They were like lights on a Christmas tree. I saw the phrase: know all, see all, and found all. We were running faster and faster towards a bright light. When we entered, it was like an explosion. The veil between the first heaven and the third heaven was torn, and again, in the sky it looked as if a scroll were being rolled back. I saw a computer and on its screen the word: Shutdown.

PART 4

CHAPTER 16

Harmony of the End Part 1

Jesus is the author and finisher of our faith. Therefore, he is an outstanding narrator of past, present, and future. In three of the four gospels: Matthew, Mark, and Luke; Jesus explains the time of the end. All three books record this same event, but each gives a slightly different perspective. Putting together these different perspectives of the same event can be daunting. For this reason, the next several chapters will attempt to do this for you.

Only in the book of Matthew is there a continuation of Jesus discussing the time of the end. This continuation is in the form of three parables and a statement that have proven elusive for many past generations. The culmination of this whole revelation is the statement of the sheep and goat nations. For this reason, it is difficult to correctly understand what Jesus was speaking about until we understand all that precedes it.

From this point forward we will take a step-by-step journey through the narrative of the end as spoken by Jesus. The climax will be at the revelation of sheep nations, because by understanding what they will mean on the day of judgment, we will understand what they will be leading up to that day. This will allow us to fully understand the revelation of kingdom government and the promise of sheep nations.

Introducing the Olivet Discourse

Shortly before Jesus was crucified, he returned to Jerusalem. During this time frame, several very important events took place, such as his triumphal entry upon the donkey, the cursing of the fig tree, the Passover and institution of the Lord's Supper, and his prayer in the garden of Gethsemane. All of these took place in less than a week. We are going to focus on his narrative of the end that took place on the Mount of Olives.

The story begins as Jesus departs from the temple. He had just witnessed a widow putting all she had into the offering, and remarked that she had given the greatest gift. He then left the temple and went toward the Mount of Olives. His disciples came up to show him the buildings of the temple and how they were adorned with beautiful stones and donations. Instead of hearing them out, Jesus prophesied the destruction of the temple, fulfilled a generation later in 70 AD.

A Difficult Approach

Bear with me as I present this story from the books of Matthew, Mark, and Luke simultaneously. I will be overlapping these three separate accounts verse by verse. The purpose is to illustrate how exhausting it can be to cross-reference this account by inserting entire verses. Although the writers repeat much of the information, each provides us with unique information at one point or another. In order to make room for unique information while maintaining the integrity of the accounts, I will thereafter present a solution to the difficulty illustrated below.

"And he looked up, and saw the rich men casting their gifts into the treasury. And he saw also a certain poor widow casting in thither two mites. And he said, Of a truth I say unto you, that this poor widow hath cast in more than they all: For all these have of their abundance cast in unto the offerings of God: but she of her penury hath cast in all the living that she had" (Luke 21:1-4).

"And Jesus sat over against the treasury, and beheld how the people cast money into the treasury: and many that were rich cast in much. And there came a certain poor widow, and she threw in two mites, which make a farthing. And he called unto him his disciples, and saith unto them, Verily I say unto you, That this poor widow hath cast more in, than all they which have cast into the treasury: For all they did cast in of their abundance; but she of her want did cast in all that she had, even all her living. And as he went out of the temple, one of his disciples saith unto him, Master, see what manner of stones and what buildings are here" (Mark 12:41-44, 13:1)!

"And Jesus went out, and departed from the temple: and his disciples came to him for to shew him the buildings of the temple" (Matthew 24:1).

"And as some spake of the temple, how it was adorned with goodly stones and gifts, he said, As for these things which ye behold, the days will come, in the which there shall not be left one stone upon another, that shall not be thrown down" (Luke 21:5-6).

"And Jesus answering said unto him, Seest thou these great buildings? there shall not be left one stone upon another, that shall not be thrown down" (Mark 13:2).

"And Jesus said unto them, See ye not all these things? verily I say unto you, There shall not be left here one stone upon another, that shall not be thrown down" (Matthew 24:2).

I want you, as the reader, to notice how much Scripture I have inserted above. The story is the same in all three gospels, yet there are differences. For example, notice that Matthew is the only one to not mention what Jesus was doing in the temple immediately before he left. However, notice also that Luke was the only gospel to not mention that Jesus left the temple before he prophesied its destruction. For our study, it would prove exceedingly strenuous to actually list out every verse in all three books one after the other, overlapping them, and reading them line-by-line, one-by-one. I am not interested in every overlapping comment, but in putting a full picture together by inserting all of the unique information of every book into a single, homologous narrative.

A More Excellent Way

What will follow will not be the rest of this passage from Matthew, Mark, or Luke, but a narrative that I have carefully constructed taking the sum total of information given. I have not integrated information that was added by Jesus to similar statements made under different circumstances. Anyone that has thoroughly studied the gospels has come to realize that Jesus was recorded as saying similar things under different circumstances. This is because he spoke about certain things more than once. For instance, when Jesus spoke that the last days would be like days of Noah in Luke 17:26, He added another allusion to the days of Lot (Luke 17:28-33). Luke 17:26 is virtually identical to Matthew 24:37. However, it was not spoken during the Olivet discourse. For this reason, this passage and others like it have not been integrated.

The following narrative should not be held or viewed as scripture, but as any other tool used for teaching the Word of God. I will not reference where each set of words comes from as I go through this, but everything that I insert outside of brackets will be directly taken from the King James Bible. After putting the whole narrative down in one place, I will begin to systematically dissect the text. We pick up the narrative as the disciples ask Jesus several questions, all of which are answered, but not necessarily in the order that they are asked.

And as he [Jesus] sat upon the Mount of Olives over against the temple, Peter and James and John and Andrew asked him privately, Tell us, when shall these things be? And what shall be the sign of thy coming, and of the end of the world [aion]? And he said, Take heed that ye be not deceived: for many shall come in my name, saying, I am Christ; and the time draweth near; and shall deceive many: go ye not therefore after them. And ye shall hear of wars and rumours of wars and commotions: see that ye be not troubled or terrified: for these things must first come to pass, but the end is not yet. For nation shall rise against nation, and kingdom against kingdom: and there shall be famines, and pestilences, and earthquakes, and troubles in diverse places; and fearful sights and great signs shall there be from heaven. All these are the beginning of sorrows. But before all these, they shall lay their hands on you, and persecute you, delivering you up to councils [and] synagogues; and in the synagogues ye shall be beaten: and into prisons, being brought before kings and rulers for my name's sake. And it shall turn to you for a testimony against them. And the gospel must first be published among all nations. Then shall they deliver you up to be afflicted, and shall kill you: and ye shall be hated by all nations for my name's sake. But when they shall lead you, and deliver you up, take no thought beforehand what ye shall speak. Settle it therefore in your hearts, not to meditate before what ye shall answer: but whatsoever shall be given you in that hour, that speak ye: for it is not ye that speak, but the Holy Ghost. For I will give you a mouth and wisdom, which all your adversaries shall not be able to gainsay nor resist. And then shall many be offended, and shall betray one another, and shall hate one another. And ye shall be betrayed both by parents, and brethren, and kinsfolks, and friends; and some of you shall they cause to be put to death. And ye shall be hated of all men for my name's sake. And many false prophets shall rise, and shall deceive many. And because iniquity shall abound, the love of many shall wax cold. But there shall not an hair of your head perish. In your patience possess ye your souls. But he that shall endure unto the end, the same shall be saved. And this gospel of the kingdom shall be preached in all the world for a witness unto all nations; and then shall the end come. And when ye shall see Jerusalem compassed with armies, then know that the desolation thereof is nigh. Then let them which are in Judaea flee to the mountains; and let them which are in the midst of it depart out; and let not them that are in the countries enter thereinto. For these be the days of vengeance, that all things which are written may be fulfilled. But woe unto them that are with child, and to them that give suck, in those days! For there shall be great distress in the land, and wrath upon this people. And they shall fall by the edge of the sword, and shall be led away captive into all nations: and Jerusalem shall be trodden down of the Gentiles, until the times of the Gentiles be fulfilled. But when ye shall see the abomination of desolation, spoken of by Daniel the prophet, standing where it ought not in the holy place (let him that readeth understand), then let them that be in Judaea flee to the mountains: And let him that is on the housetop not go down into the house, neither enter therein, to take anything out of his house: And let him that is in the field not turn back again for to take up his garment. And woe unto them that are with child, and to them that give suck in those days! But pray ye that your flight be not in the winter, neither on the Sabbath day: For then shall be great tribulation and affliction, such as was not from the beginning of the creation which God created unto this time, no, nor ever shall be. And except that the Lord had shortened those days, no flesh should be saved: but for the elect's sake, whom he hath chosen, he hath shortened the days. Then if any man shall say unto you, Lo, here is Christ, or there; believe it not.

For false Christs and false prophets shall rise, and shall shew signs and wonders, to seduce, if it were possible, even the elect. But take ye heed: behold, I have foretold you all things. Wherefore if they shall say unto you, Behold, he is in the desert; go not forth: behold, he is in the secret chambers; believe it not. For as the lightning cometh out of the east, and shineth even unto the west; so shall also the coming of the Son of man be. For wheresoever the carcass is, there will the eagles be gathered together. But in those days, immediately after that tribulation, the sun shall be darkened, and the moon shall not give her light. And the stars of heaven shall fall, and the powers that are in heaven shall be shaken. And there shall be signs in the sun, and in the moon, and in the stars; and upon the earth distress of nations, with perplexity; the sea and the waves roaring; men's hearts failing them for fear, and for looking after those things which are coming on the earth: for the powers of heaven shall be shaken. And then shall appear the sign of the Son of man in heaven: and then shall all the tribes of the earth mourn, and they shall see the Son of man coming in the clouds of heaven with great power and great glory. And when these things begin to come to pass, then look up, and lift up your heads; for your redemption draweth nigh. And he shall send his angels with a great sound of a trumpet, and they shall gather together his elect from the four winds, from the uttermost part of the earth to the uttermost part of heaven. Now learn a parable of the fig tree; when his branch is yet tender, and putteth forth leaves, ye know that summer is nigh. So likewise ye, when ye see these things come to pass, know ye that the kingdom of God is nigh at hand. Verily I say unto you, this generation shall not pass away, till all be fulfilled. Heaven and earth shall pass away, but my words shall not pass away. But of that day and that hour knoweth no man, no, not the angels which are in heaven, neither the Son, but the Father. And take heed to yourselves, lest at any time your hearts be overcharged with surfeiting, and drunkenness, and cares of this life, and so that day come upon you unawares. For as a snare shall it come on all them that dwell on the face of the whole earth. But as the days of [Noah] were, so shall also the coming of the Son of man be. For as in the days that were before the flood they were eating and drinking, marrying and giving in marriage, until the day that [Noah] entered into the ark, and knew not until the flood came, and took them all away; so shall also the coming of the Son of man be. Then shall two be in the field; the one shall be taken, and the other left. Two women shall be grinding at the mill; the one shall be taken, and the other left. Watch ye therefore, and pray always, that ye may be accounted worthy to escape all these things that shall come to pass, and to stand before the Son of man: for ye know not what hour your Lord doth come.

ANSWERING THE QUESTIONS

We will begin our study with the questions that are asked by the disciples. Four disciples ask Jesus three questions in all. The disciples are Peter, James, John and Andrew. These are the three questions:

➤ When shall these things be?

➤ What is the sign of your coming?

➤ What is the sign of the end of the age?

I have seen these questions pointed out many times, but in my experience, no one ever seems to show how they are actually answered. Here is the first question: _So when shall these things be?_ In a nutshell, most of these things begin to occur when Jesus starts opening the seals upon the scroll described in the book of Revelation chapter 5. _Jesus basically begins his lecture by telling the disciples about the opening of the first seal._ He continues to describe the seals in the sequence that they occur, interweaving additional prophetic insight. There are a few areas where his narrative refers to past events, but these are obvious. The lecture is basically a chronological narrative beginning at the opening of the first seal.

What is the sign of your coming? Regarding the sign of Jesus' coming, it is the event that immediately precedes the catching away of the church, popularly known as the rapture. As lightning strikes in one part of the sky, yet is visible in other parts of the sky, so shall his appearance be. The flash of light that lightning produces can be seen without being in the proximity of the actual lightning bolt. Similarly, the brilliant light saturating the glorified body of Jesus and the angels that accompany him will appear in the sky before he will. It will be similar to a sunrise: in the same way the sky begins to get brighter before the sun can actually be seen, the glory of Jesus will illuminate the sky before Jesus can be seen. This will be accompanied by the sounding of the seventh trumpet of the book of Revelation, and will serve as the sign of his coming. Then the dead will be resurrected with bodies that are incorruptible, and those that still remain will be changed.

What is the sign of the end of the age? When Jesus appears, *it is* the end of the age, because Jesus returns to change the age. Since the church is caught away when Jesus appears, the rapture serves as a sign of the end of the age. The fact that the world will be as it was in the days of Noah will also be a sign of the end of the age. This will involve fallen angels and their children governmentally ruling over men, meaning the integration of Nephilim (may I add, *engineered* Nephilim) into society. As we go through these passages you, as the reader, will continue to identify additional information given by Jesus that directly answers the questions posed by his disciples.

THE FIRST SEAL

With this said, let's begin to look at how Jesus responded. Keep in mind that in the compilation of unique information, the grammar becomes very awkward. After the questions were posed, this was his first comment:

> And he said, Take heed that ye be not deceived: for many shall come in my name, saying, I am Christ; and the time draweth near; and shall deceive many: go ye not therefore after them.

As I said, this narrative begins at the first seal of the book of Revelation. What are the seals in the book of Revelation? There is a scroll in heaven that only one is worthy to open. The one who is worthy is the Lamb who was slain from the foundation of the world, Jesus Christ. In order to open this scroll, seven seals must be loosed. As each seal is loosed, corresponding events occur as described in the book of Revelation. The first four seals in Revelation are highly symbolic, but can be easily understood as they are cross-referenced with the events that they describe. What follows is the first seal:

"And I saw when the Lamb opened one of the seals, and I heard, as it were the noise of thunder, one of the four beasts saying, Come and see. And

I saw, and behold a white horse: and he that sat on him had a bow; and a crown was given unto him: and he went forth conquering, and to conquer" (Revelation 6:1-2).

The rider on this horse goes forth conquering and to conquer. He will not ride and then stop riding, but once released, continues riding indefinitely. This will be true of all of the horsemen. The rider of the white horse has a bow, but neither arrows nor a quiver are mentioned. A bow often represents God's judgment (Job 16:13-14, Lamentations 3:12-13). The crown is a symbol of authority and rulership. The type of crown mentioned here is circlet, wreath, or garland that is awarded as a prize of victory or triumph. The opening of this seal indicates a judgment of God (which is why Jesus opens the seal) by giving this conquering horseman a crown of victory in the agenda for which the horseman is released.

Notice that the horse is white. In the Bible, white usually means righteousness, purity or holiness. However, there are cases where white refers to the *appearance* of righteous, purity or holiness, while concealing the true nature of those concerned. The Pharisees and scribes represented those under the antichrist spirit because they rejected Jesus as the Messiah. They went to great lengths, climaxing in murder, to stop the ministry of Jesus. This is what Jesus said to them:

"Woe unto you, scribes and Pharisees, hypocrites! for ye make clean the outside of the cup and of the platter, but within they are full of extortion and excess. Thou blind Pharisee, cleanse first that which is within the cup and platter, that the outside of them may be clean also. Woe unto you, scribes and Pharisees, hypocrites! for **ye are like unto whited sepulchers** [graves or tombs], which indeed appear beautiful outward, but are within full of dead men's bones, and of all uncleanness. Even so **ye also outwardly appear righteous** unto men, but within ye are full of hypocrisy and iniquity.

(Matthew 23:25-28)

Jesus compared them to cups and platters that are clean on the outside and filthy on the inside. He compared them to white tombs that appear to be adorned for the righteous. He said they do not contain the bones of the righteous, but contain death and uncleanness. After this, he said in a very straightforward manner, "You appear to be righteous, but you are full of hypocrisy and sin." The horse is white in the same context that Jesus called the Pharisees and scribes white sepulchers. Jesus simply says, "Do not go after them."

Once we understand the implications of the color white and the fact that this is a judgment of God, we can identify the implications of this horseman. The opening of this seal describes the reason for the false Christs that will come in the name of Jesus. In other words, it is an antichrist spirit. Those under its influence will go out to conquer and to deceive. They will represent a counterfeit solution to the world's problems. The opening of this seal is not limited to a final antichrist character. Instead, it unleashes a wave of individuals who are heavily influenced by an antichrist spirit. It is expected that these false Christs will not only show up in religious realms, but also in political realms and other key arenas of society.

It could be said that this was opened within the past century. Others believe that this is reserved for the near future. I want to add a unique possibility on the timing of this seal. Note that there have *always* been individuals under the influence of an antichrist spirit since the birth of the church. A likely option would be to say that this horse began riding across the earth shortly after Jesus ascended to heaven. Consider another relevant scripture found in 1 John.

"Little children, **it is the last time**: and as ye have heard that antichrist shall come, even now are there many antichrists; whereby we know that it is the last time. They went out from us, but they were not of us; for if they had been of us, they would no doubt have continued with us: but they went out, that they might be made manifest that they were not all of us" (1 John 2:18-19).

John tells us that it *is* the <u>last time</u>. This was written almost two thousand years ago. Of course, we know that Jesus didn't return for the first church, but we do know that in some way, it qualified as the last time. To say otherwise would force us to deny the authority of Scripture. Notice that John describes that there is a final antichrist to come, but that there were already many antichrists. He deduced: *because* there were already many antichrists it must be the "last time." John was one of the disciples that questioned Jesus on the Mount of Olives. Therefore, he saw this as the fulfillment of a sign that the end was near. Since we have established that the coming of many antichrists in the name of Jesus defines the opening of the first seal, it is highly probable that this seal was opened a long time ago, well before any of the others were opened.

This passage continues to explain that the antichrists went out from among the ranks of the first church. John says that they went out from them, but they were not of them. If these people had been partakers of the Holy Spirit, they would have been of the same Spirit as the apostles, and thus would have continued with them. These were fakes and frauds; they were against Jesus, and bent on leading others away from the faith. If we look at it like this, Jesus basically declared that the last days began shortly after he ascended on high, and are continuing through this day.

Further evidence of this is clear from the historical record. Beginning around the time of Jesus, here are some of the individuals that either claimed to be or were rumored to be the promised Messiah: Simon of Peraea, Athronges, Vespasian, Simon bar Kokhba, Simon Magus, Dositheos the Samaritan, and many more.[27] The following list of names are of people claiming to be Jesus Christ or rumored to be the Christ in just the past several hundred years: John Nichols Thom, Bahá'u'lláh, Mirza Ghulam Ahmad of Qadian, Haile Selassie I, George Ernest Roux, Krishna Venta, Sun Myung Moon, Jim Jones, Marshall Applewhite, Laszlo Toth, Ariffin Mohammed, Shoko Asahara and many more.[28] Clearly, the spirit of the antichrist has been hard at work for a very long time.

The Second Seal

The next thing that Jesus described was the second seal. Notice how similar the descriptions are between the following two passages:

And ye shall hear of wars and rumours of wars and commotions: see that ye be not troubled or terrified: for these things must first come to pass, but the end is not yet. For nation shall rise against nation, and kingdom against kingdom.

"And when he had opened the second seal, I heard the second beast say, Come and see. And there went out another horse that was red: and power was given to him that sat thereon to take peace from the earth, and that they should kill one another: and there was given unto him a great sword" (Revelation 6:3-4).

The second seal describes peace being taken from the earth. The result is wars and rumors of wars. During war, people kill one another. Notice also that unlike the first horseman, this horseman goes out with a sword. A sword is a weapon of war and it is used for killing. Jesus tells us to not be troubled, because this must first come to pass. However, by saying the end is not yet, he is really saying that things are just getting started.

THE THIRD SEAL

...and there shall be famines...

"And when he had opened the third seal, I heard the third beast say, Come and see. And I beheld, and lo a black horse; and he that sat on him had a pair of balances in his hand. And I heard a voice in the midst of the four beasts say, A measure of wheat for a penny, and three measures of barley for a penny; and see thou hurt not the oil and the wine" (Revelation 6:5-6).

The third seal of Revelation is severe economic depression, probably linked to great famine. This could very well be the obvious byproduct of wars breaking out all over the earth. The word translated in this passage as *penny* literally means "a day's wages." The pair of balances seems to hint at an absence of justice as well. As I pointed out in my first book, I believe that the phrase "hurt not the oil and the wine" can be symbolically interpreted as good news for the faithful followers of Jesus at that time. Oil is symbolic of the Holy Spirit and the anointing, and wine is symbolic of the works of the Holy Spirit and the blood of Jesus. Those involved intimately with God will not be hurt by the economic crash in the same way others will. For some, God has appointed great wealth transfer (Proverbs 13:22).

The Fourth Seal

As Jesus continues, his next comment could not align more perfectly with the fourth seal:

> ...and pestilences, and earthquakes, and troubles in diverse places; and fearful sights and great signs shall there be from heaven. All these are the beginning of sorrows.

"And when he had opened the fourth seal, I heard the voice of the fourth beast say, Come and see. And I looked, and behold a pale horse: and his name that sat on him was Death, and Hell followed with him. And power was given unto them over the fourth part of the earth, to kill with sword, and with hunger, and with death, and with the beasts of the earth" (Revelation 6:7-8).

The fourth seal describes Death and Hell being given power over a fourth of the earth. Death comes by sword, by hunger, and by the beasts of the earth. Jesus says that there will be famines and pestilences (or diseases) and troubles in various places. Jesus adds that the earth will help Death by killing people with earthquakes. Earthquakes are indirectly involved in the fourth seal because Death and Hell are given power over a fourth of the earth. This does not only mean power over people on the earth, but power over the geographies of the planet itself. In other words, their power extends into the actual matter and soil composing the earth. Considering that the earth is nearly seventy percent water, if their power were strictly limited to land masses, only five percent of livable earth will remain unscathed. Jesus adds that signs in the heavens will accompany this seal. Then, Jesus says a comment so clear-cut—so blatantly specific—that it cannot be missed. Jesus says, "These are the beginning of sorrows." In other words, by the time the fourth seal is taking place, things are still *just getting started*.

CHAPTER 17

Harmony of the End Part 2

As Jesus continues his discourse, we suddenly take a step backwards in time. He begins the next statement with the phrase, "But before all these..." This tells us two things. One, what Jesus is about to say will chronologically predate some of the things he has just told us. Two, it will not necessarily predate everything he just told us. It is to be understood as, "but before the full manifestation of everything I have already told you..." The word translated "all" comes from the Greek word *hapas* and it means absolutely all, every one, or whole. In other words, some of what we were just told *may* happen before what we are about to be told, but not necessarily.

> But before all these, they shall lay their hands on you, and persecute you, delivering you up to councils [and] synagogues; and in the synagogues ye shall be beaten: and into prisons, being brought before kings and rulers for my name's sake. And it shall turn to you for a testimony against them.

EXPECT PERSECUTION

This portion of the harmonized passage is taken from the book of Luke 21:12 and is echoed in Mark 13:9. The passage in Matthew 24 completely skips over this portion. Here, Jesus is explaining that in the days leading up to the opening of the fourth seal, the church will be persecuted. Without question, this began to be fulfilled immediately. It has continued since the Apostles of the Lamb founded the first church in Jerusalem. They were taken up to councils in synagogues, beaten, put in prison, and brought before kings and rulers for the name of Jesus. Consider this event early in the book of Acts:

> Then the high priest rose up, and all they that were with him, (which is the sect of the Sadducees,) and were filled with indignation, and **laid their hands on the apostles**, and **put them in the common prison**. But the angel of the Lord by night opened the prison doors, and brought them forth... Then came one and told them, saying, Behold, the men whom ye put in prison are standing in the temple, and teaching the people... And when they had brought them, they **set them before the council**: and the high priest asked them, Saying, Did not we straitly command you that ye should not teach in this name? and, behold, ye have filled Jerusalem with your doctrine, and intend to bring this man's blood upon us... Then stood there

up one in the council, a Pharisee, named Gamaliel, a doctor of the law, had in reputation among all the people, and commanded to put the apostles forth a little space... And to him they agreed: and when **they had called the apostles, and beaten them**, they commanded that they should not speak in the name of Jesus, and let them go.

(Acts 5:17-19, 25, 27-28, 34, 40)

Persecution is a fact that has never left the true church. According to the apostle Paul, we enter into the kingdom of heaven through much tribulation (Acts 14:22). God has never taken his people out of tribulation, but he always delivers the faithful in the midst of their persecution. For example, at one point in his ministry, Peter got locked in prison and was miraculously delivered by an angel (Acts 12). The important point is that the angel could not set him free from prison until he had already been locked up. Peter was delivered in the midst of his persecution. Nevertheless, the tribulations that we endure for a season will not compare with the glory that will be revealed in us.

"For I reckon that the sufferings of this present time are not worthy to be compared with the glory which shall be revealed in us" (Romans 8:18).

PERSECUTION AND DELIVERANCE

Peter was delivered in the midst of his persecution. In order to experience deliverance, he had to participate with the deliverance that God provided him. When it comes to God providing deliverance in our lives, we must also *participate* in his deliverance. Some Christians get confused and think that because they are miserable and in the midst of tribulation, they are somehow glorifying God. It is possible to go through tribulation as a Christian and reject God's efforts at deliverance through laziness, faithlessness, and disobedience. This is true of far too many believers. Imagine if the angel showed up and Peter replied, "Well, I don't believe in the ministry of angels, so this is certainly not of God."

The victory that Jesus purchased for us is manifested according to our heart's condition. Remember that as our heart is programmed according to heavenly realities, we begin to operate accordingly. Heavenly realities include things that result in the miraculous, but also include characteristics like the fruit of the Spirit, obedience, and the fear of the Lord. Peter was delivered because of his faithfulness towards God.

This understanding will ultimately extend into our understanding of the coming sheep nations. As the hearts of people within geographies embrace God as their King, allowing him to rule through their hearts, kingdom government will manifest. Kingdom government will lead to continual deliverance for entire nations *in the midst* of perpetual persecution. It will not keep persecution away from them. The glory is in victory, not in evasion. Jesus said that this persecution would "become a testimony for us against those who persecute us." He also said that no matter what happens, all things will continually work together for the good of those who love him.

"And we know that all things work together for good to them that love God, to them who are the called according to his purpose" (Romans 8:28).

The Gospel of Jesus Christ Must be Published

In order to properly address the next statement, we must correctly define the word *gospel.*

"And the gospel must first be published among all nations" (Mark 13:10).

This quote is only found in Mark 13:10. Both Luke and Matthew skip over this statement. However, a similar statement is made later in Matthew that appears as though it is referring to the same thing:

"And this gospel of the kingdom shall be preached in all the world for a witness unto all nations; and then shall the end come" (Matthew 24:14).

One of the primary purposes of this book is to expose the kingdom of God and what it will mean for us in the coming days. The gospel of Jesus Christ and the gospel of the kingdom are in fact two different gospels. The gospel of the kingdom *includes* the gospel of Jesus Christ, but is much more than just the death, burial, and resurrection of Jesus.

In the book of Mark, Jesus declares that the gospel will be published among all nations. This gospel that Mark refers to comes well before the preaching of the gospel of the kingdom as a witness unto all nations. Therefore I believe that Mark is alluding to the publishing of the gospel of Jesus Christ. This gospel is the message of Jesus sacrificing his life to redeem men unto God. It is the message declaring that whoever believes in their heart and confesses with their mouth that Jesus is Lord will be saved. According to this gospel, we know that we have been saved by grace through faith. This is the gospel that divides those who are going to heaven from those who are going to hell.

"In flaming fire taking vengeance on them that know not God, and that obey not the **gospel of our Lord Jesus Christ**" (2 Thessalonians 1:8).

The gospel of the kingdom is built on the foundation of the gospel of Jesus Christ, but goes far beyond it. The gospel of the kingdom is the good news that the kingdom of God is here to bring salvation to the nations, and to reclaim every pillar of society for the purpose of God. We will discuss this in further detail as we proceed. For now, suffice it to say that the gospel of Jesus Christ must at some point be published among all nations. At this point Jesus continues:

> Then shall they deliver you up to be afflicted, and shall kill you: and ye shall be hated of all nations for my name's sake. But when they shall lead you, and deliver you up, take no thought beforehand what ye shall speak. Settle it therefore in your hearts, not to meditate before what ye shall answer: but whatsoever shall be given you in that hour, that speak ye: for it is not ye that speak, but the Holy Ghost. For I will give you a mouth and wisdom, which all your adversaries shall not be able to gainsay nor resist. And then shall many be offended, and shall betray one another, and shall hate one another. And ye shall be betrayed both by parents, and brethren, and kinsfolks, and friends; and some of you shall they cause to be put to death.

At this point in the narrative, Jesus is back in the time frame where he left off, namely after the fourth seal has been opened. What is described here is absolutely terrible. Although Christians have been continually delivered up for death—beginning at the first church—this time period will be *defined* by this activity. Jesus promises special wisdom being given in the delivery of our testimony. This wisdom will deliver some, maybe even many, from the intentions of their adversaries.

Jesus also mentions that we will be hated by all nations. A question may arise as to whether this invalidates the coming existence of sheep nations. Understandably, if every nation is persecuting Christians all at once, how can sheep nations occur? However, we must remember that the word translated *nations* is the Greek word "ethnos," meaning ethnic groups. Although there will be individuals from every existing ethnic group that hate Christians, it does not mean *all* individuals from every existing ethnic group will hate Christians. I can guarantee that in every known ethnic group today, one can find members who hate Christianity. In the future, many individuals within their respective ethnics groups will choose their allegiance.

The Fifth Seal

Jesus continues by explaining that Christians will be betrayed by their families and closest friends. Offence will lead to a great slaughter, as betrayal and hatred lead to inhumanity on the earth. Of course, the primary target will be Christians, especially those who have not had the time to mature into the revelation and power granted by the gospel of the kingdom. Some will be put to death. This utterance places us at a parallel with the fifth seal of Revelation.

And when he had opened the fifth seal, I saw under the altar the souls of them that were slain for the word of God, and for the testimony which they held: And they cried with a loud voice, saying, How long, O Lord, holy and true, dost thou not judge and avenge our blood on them that dwell on the earth? And white robes were given unto every one of them; and it was said unto them, that they should rest yet for a little season, until their fellowservants also and their brethren, that should be killed as they were, should be fulfilled.

(Revelation 6:9-11)

In spite of all of the terrible things that have been discussed up to this point, Jesus has not begun to discuss Daniel's seventieth week, much less aspects of the great tribulation. As a matter of fact, most of what has been discussed thus far can be seen throughout history in some way, shape, or form. The fifth seal will no doubt involve two thousand years of Christian martyrs. When it is opened, these martyrs cry out to God for a response to the severe injustice. According to God's response, we understand that God is going to continue to forbear with the wickedness and injustice on the earth. There is yet a "little season" remaining.

At this point it may be helpful to quickly review. Thus far in his discourse, Jesus has discussed the opening of the first four seals of Revelation, taken a step back to discuss the persecution that would come upon the church beginning at its inception, discussed the publishing of the gospel of Jesus Christ among all nations, and the fifth seal. He continues with this statement:

> "And ye shall be hated of all men for my name's sake" (Luke 21:17).

In this snippet, the word translated "all" is the Greek word *pas*, and it means "any, every, the whole, as many as, whosoever," etc. In fact, the word *men* does not even appear in the original Greek manuscript. It simply says, "You will be hated of all." While it might be tempting to look at this passage and conclude "total polarization," I don't believe this is likely. The more sensible interpretation is that this quote from Luke 21:17 is intended to be interpreted in a similar light as Matthew 24:9. In other words, the phrase *"all men"* is to be understood as *"all types of men"* just like *"all nations"* is intended to be understood as *"people from every cultural background."* In Luke 21:16 the text details that Christians will be betrayed by parents and brothers and relatives and friends. In light of this, the comment is made that Christians will be hated by all. It make the most sense to understand this as pertaining to all types of men, even down to parents, siblings, and those who should be closest to us.

The Sixth Seal

"And many false prophets shall rise, and shall deceive many" (Matthew 24:11).

When Jesus first began to address the disciples, he mentioned that many false Christs would come. This did not mean that the final antichrist was coming yet, but that the antichrist spirit would cause many to rise up, intending to lead people away from the truth of Jesus Christ. The result would be both religious and political "saviors." Here, many false prophets have risen up. There is also a false prophet that will serve alongside the final antichrist. These false prophets are in addition to him, and are beginning the work of pointing men to the final antichrist, who is now coming on the scene. *I believe that this aligns with the sixth seal, which is a counterfeit second coming of Jesus Christ to create the greatest deception ever executed in all of history by the kingdom of darkness*. It will result in the revealing of the final antichrist to the world.

And I beheld when he had opened the sixth seal, and, lo, there was a great earthquake; and the sun became black as sackcloth of hair, and the moon became as blood; And the stars of heaven fell unto the earth, even as a fig tree casteth her untimely figs, when she is shaken of a mighty wind. And the heaven departed as a scroll when it is rolled together; and every mountain and island were moved out of their places. And the kings of the earth, and the great men, and the rich men, and the chief captains, and the mighty men, and every bondman, and every free man, hid themselves in the dens and in the rocks of the mountains; And said to the mountains and rocks, Fall on us, and hide us from the face of him that sitteth on the throne, and from the wrath of the Lamb: For the great day of his wrath is come; and who shall be able to stand?

(Revelation 6:12-17)

Note that the only aspect of this passage that suggests it is the day of the Lord are the comments by the <u>men</u>. This comes by way of the quote, "hide us from the face of him that sitteth upon the throne, and from the wrath of the Lamb." This is in contrast to an angel of the Lord, or Jesus himself, making this statement. This is essential to understand because if we don't, we run the risk of misinterpreting this passage. Many have falsely assumed that this describes the actual return of Jesus Christ, and have done all sorts of wacky things with their theology to make it fit. The problem when men speak in the Bible is that they don't always get it right. As a matter of fact, they are often completely wrong!

THE FALLIBILITY OF HUMAN CONCLUSIONS

One my favorite examples to illustrate this point is Job's wife. When Job is stricken with boils, his wife gives him some advice. In the following passage the Bible records this advice, as well as Job's reaction to it:

"Then said his wife unto him, Dost thou still retain thine integrity? **curse God, and die**. But he said unto her, **Thou speakest as one of the foolish women speaketh**. What? shall we receive good at the hand of God, and shall we not receive evil? In all this did not Job sin with his lips" (Job 2:9-10).

Job's wife told him to curse God and die. This is the biblical record of her utterance. This does not mean that we are intended to incorporate this into our personal prayer journal. This is the truthful record of how she responded to her husband's misfortune. What we take away from this passage is that she said the wrong thing. For this reason we find Job rebuking his wife for her false conclusion in the very next verse. He says she is speaking like a foolish woman. This is merely one example of a premise that is absolutely essential for understanding the sixth seal. The Bible records the speech of men, regardless of whether they are saying the right thing or they are deceived.

The Stars will Fall

The men speaking in the sixth seal are deceived. Taking a close look at the conditions, we are forced to admit that this deception is quite spectacular. There is a great earthquake, the sun gets dark, the moon looks like blood, the sky looks like it is being rolled up and stars are falling to the earth. "Stars," as we have already discussed, is a symbolic term repeatedly used to describe angels. One example is found in the explanation of John's first vision of Jesus in Revelation. Here, clear as day, the Bible says that stars represent angels.

"The mystery of the seven stars which thou sawest in my right hand, and the seven golden candlesticks. **The seven stars are the angels of the seven churches**: and the seven candlesticks which thou sawest are the seven churches" (Revelation 1:20).

This does not mean that every reference to stars in the Bible is a reference to angels, but we know that context helps determine interpretation. In the case of the sixth seal, or for that matter the actual return of Christ, the Bible says stars fall to earth. If these were literal stars they would consume the earth, as they are much larger than our planet. As a result, earth would cease to exist. Since this is not the result, we know that the Bible must be talking about something else, namely what it tells us that it is symbolically referring to—angels.

THE ADVENT OF THE ANTICHRIST

We have already discussed the implications of the removal of the restrainer and its involvement in revealing the antichrist. *The sixth seal appears to be the result of the removal of the restrainer.* Hence, the sixth seal would serve as the beginning of the "new age" when the second heaven opens up onto the earth. This is the age in which fallen angels and their children (Nephilim) will begin once again to rule over and corrupt men like they did in the days of Noah (Matthew 24:37). Regarding the antichrist, there is something else that is important to understand. His coming is not so much an "arrival" as it is a "return and subsequent presence with." Consider this verse:

"And then shall that Wicked be revealed, whom the Lord shall consume with the spirit of his mouth, and shall destroy with the brightness of his coming: Even him, **whose coming** is after the working of Satan with all power and signs and lying wonders" (2 Thessalonians 2:8-9).

The word translated coming is the Greek word *parousia*, which means advent, return, coming, or presence. According to Vine's Expository Dictionary (1997) it "denotes both an arrival and subsequent presence with." This is the same word that is used in every passage speaking of the return of Christ and his eternal presence with the saints. Among other places, it is used of Christ in the passage in 2 Thessalonians, "… [Jesus] shall destroy with the brightness of his **coming**." It is also used of Christ in the following passage. The second coming is a *return* of Jesus to the earth in a glorified body.

"But every man in his own order: Christ the firstfruits; afterward they that are Christ's at **his coming**" (1 Corinthians 15:23).

In the following verse, Paul uses the word *parousia* of himself. He explains that he is coming to the Philippians' church again. What does it mean to come again? It means that the person is returning.

"That your rejoicing may be more abundant in Jesus Christ for me by my **coming to you again**" (Philippians 1:26).

The counterfeit precedes the genuine. Although I am not saying that the antichrist will return in the same body he may have occupied at some indeterminable time in the past, some element of his makeup is certainly coming back. Several speculations have been made as a result of this fact. At least one author has pointed out that the antichrist may serve as a vessel for the return of the fallen angel Apollyon.[29] Another author has speculated that this might be the spirit that possessed Hitler.[30] However the process goes, on some level a return will be taking place when it comes to the arrival of the antichrist. In addition, it appears as though Satan is actually involved in the removal of the restrainer.

Paul is communicating that the "return and subsequent presence" of the antichrist on earth is after (or according to) the working of Satan, with all power and signs and lying wonders. Again, the power and signs and lying wonders are described by the account of the sixth seal. Since this is being done as a counterfeit to the actual return of Christ, we can also assume that the antichrist that will be produced and presented at this time will be a virtual mirror of the prophesied glorified messiah. He will look like God, speak like God, and wield such incredible supernatural power that many will believe he is God. When this occurs it will be obvious—there will be no room for debate. Nevertheless, many shall fall away and believe the lie (2 Thessalonians 2:3, 11).

INIQUITY SHALL ABOUND

Returning to the narrative, we are now at a point after the final antichrist has entered the scenario. Jesus continues on to describe the result:

> And because iniquity shall abound, the love of many shall wax cold. But there shall not an hair of your head perish. In your patience possess ye your souls. But he that shall endure unto the end, the same shall be saved.

The context of this portion of scripture will lead into the beginning half of Daniel's seventieth week. Under the influence of the antichrist, iniquity will abound. The result will be that love will depart from many. The word translated "love" in this passage comes from the Greek word *agape*. This is the highest love; a love that comes from God. According to the Bible, it is Christians that have access to this kind of love. For this reason, the love that grows cold is the love of the church. Of course, love will not depart from the portion of the true church that clings to Christ. Thus the word "many" is fitting.

Jesus continues to exhort his disciples by saying that in all this, "not a hair of our head would perish." No matter what is revealed against the church, whether weapon, plague, attack, torture, attempts at genetic defilement, etc., our whole body in its fullness will be preserved unto the day of our Lord Jesus Christ. In other words, there is nothing that can truly be taken from us, and against God's ability to keep his promises, the antichrist remains powerless. In the resurrection, everything will be restored in fullness and perfection, and not a hair of our head will perish.

Jesus also says, "In patience possess ye your souls." It sounds rather similar to what is written of the saints in several places of the book of Revelation:

"He that leadeth into captivity shall go into captivity: he that killeth with the sword must be killed with the sword. **Here is the patience and the faith of the saints**" (Revelation 13:10).

"And the third angel followed them, saying with a loud voice, If any man worship the beast and his image, and receive his mark in his forehead, or in his hand, The same shall drink of the wine of the wrath of God, which is poured out without mixture into the cup of his indignation; and he shall be tormented with fire and brimstone in the presence of the holy angels, and in the presence of the Lamb: And the smoke of their torment ascendeth up for ever and ever: and they have no rest day nor night, who worship the beast and his image, and whosoever receiveth the mark of his name. **Here is the patience of the saints**: here are they that keep the commandments of God, and the faith of Jesus" (Revelation 14:9-12).

THE SALVATION WAITING TO BE REVEALED

Moving forward, Jesus relates to His disciples that whoever endures to the end will be saved. There is an enduring that will be necessary in that time like no other period history has ever revealed. The gates of hell will have opened up onto the earth. This is a direct parallel to what Peter described as the salvation waiting to be revealed in the last day.

"Who are kept by the power of God through faith unto **salvation ready to be revealed in the last time**" (1 Peter 1:5).

At the time of the end our physical body will receive salvation from its fallen state. God's plan of salvation is in three parts because we are made a three-part being. Our spirit was saved, our soul is being saved, and our bodies will be saved. When Jesus finally returns, our bodies will be made perfect, and they will shine with the brilliance of the firmament. We will be transformed into the army of God and will conquer with Jesus upon white horses, becoming the most glorious and beautiful spectacle ever. We will be the very bride and queen of the King of kings, Jesus Christ!

"And they that be wise shall shine as the brightness of the firmament; and they that turn many to righteousness as the stars for ever and ever" (Daniel 12:3).

CHAPTER 18

Harmony of the End Part 3

Finally, in the context of Daniel's seventieth week and the arrival and subsequent presence of the antichrist on earth, we arrive at this comment:

> And this gospel of the kingdom shall be preached in all the world for a witness unto all nations; and then shall the end come.

THE GOSPEL OF THE KINGDOM

Not until this point do we actually come to the preaching (or heralding) of the gospel of the kingdom. This occurs when the body of Christ finally arises to the position of authority on earth that Jesus intended. This is the heralding of the good news that the kingdom of God is here. This is *not* the good news that the kingdom of God is coming. It is the point at which kingdom government—which means God ruling as King in and through the hearts of his people—has established a great deal of influence over every aspect of life and society wherever his people are located. As one can imagine, any society that has come under kingdom government will operate separately from the global satanic dictatorship that has arisen.

What will this look like? In the midst of all the evil and chaos absorbing the planet, entire geographies will be redeemed and set apart by the power and glory of God. As I briefly hinted at earlier in this book, Christians are going to manifest the kingdom on earth *before* Jesus returns. This does not mean that the whole world will come under kingdom government, but simply parts of the world where faithful saints are living. This is why the voices in heaven at the seventh trumpet declare the kingdoms of this world "are become" the kingdoms of our Lord and his Christ. This verb tense means the process started in the past and progressed into the present moment, where it has been finished.

"And the seventh angel sounded; and there were great voices in heaven, saying, The kingdoms of this world **are become** the kingdoms of our Lord, and of his Christ; and he shall reign for ever and ever" (Revelation 11:15).

THE SEVEN MOUNTAINS

Beginning in 1975 with Bill Bright and Loren Cunningham, who independently received what has come to be known as the revelation of the "seven mountains," God has been communicating to the body of Christ that there are seven major mind molders, or mountains in any given society.[31] On this note I will take the time to mention that this term has become a point of conflict within the body of Christ. Due to its association with a perspective on eschatology known as Dominionism, and its embrace by the New Apostolic Reformation, some have rejected its implications without further investigation. I believe that this is truly unfortunate. I have to thank Lance Wallnau for bringing understanding to so many regarding these things. While I do not ascribe to Dominionism as he does, I am very grateful for the wisdom and insights that the Lord has blessed him with. His famous teaching on the seven mountains has sown the seed of possibility into the minds of many. What are the seven mountains?

When Jesus went on his forty-day fast, the Holy Spirit drove him into the wilderness. While he was in the wilderness he encountered Satan, who came to tempt Him. In the book of Matthew, Satan is recorded as tempting Jesus three times, the third temptation regarding the kingdoms of the world.

Then was Jesus led up of the Spirit into the wilderness to be tempted of the devil. And when he had fasted forty days and forty nights, he was afterward an hungred. And when the tempter came to him, he said, If thou be the Son of God, command that these stones be made bread. But he answered and said, It is written, Man shall not live by bread alone, but by every word that proceedeth out of the mouth of God. Then the devil taketh him up into the holy city, and setteth him on a pinnacle of the temple, And saith unto him, If thou be the Son of God, cast thyself down: for it is written, He shall give his angels charge concerning thee: and in their hands they shall bear thee up, lest at any time thou dash thy foot against a stone. Jesus said unto him, It is written again, Thou shalt not tempt the Lord thy God. **Again, the devil taketh him up into an exceeding high mountain, and sheweth him all the kingdoms of the world**, and the glory of them; And saith unto him, **All these things will I give thee, if thou wilt fall down and worship me**. Then saith Jesus unto him, Get thee hence, Satan: for it is written, Thou shalt worship the Lord thy God, and him only shalt thou serve. Then the devil leaveth him, and, behold, angels came and ministered unto him.

(Matthew 4:1-11)

Satan was willing to offer Jesus the kingdoms of this world if only he could convince Jesus to forsake the task of bringing in the kingdom of heaven. If Jesus would have bowed, Satan would have retained the power to legally take the kingdoms of the world back from Jesus. Until the death and resurrection of Jesus, Satan had power to give the kingdoms of the world to whomever he desired. When Adam sinned and man lost fellowship with God, Satan began to pirate man's dominion, and rule over kingdoms.

"And the devil said unto him, All this power will I give thee, and the glory of them: **for that is delivered unto me**; and to whomsoever I will I give it" (Luke 4:6).

The kingdom of heaven has the power to overtake all of the kingdoms of this world and utilize them according to the power and glory of God. Jesus died to restore this power to man. In spite of this, there is a war being waged for the kingdoms of this world. Their redemption has been purchased, but Satan holds onto them illegally. The kingdoms are not simply political institutions. They are the seven basic realms of influence that govern human existence.

Lance suggests that Jesus was shown seven mountains, and upon the seven mountains that Jesus was shown were seven portals into the spirit realm. The portals upon the mountains represent the kingdoms of the world. Those who are put in control of the mountains decide what can and cannot come through from the spirit realm. In other words, the people that are put in power control how each mountain will impact society and culture. What are these mountains? According to Lance, we can look at it in the following way. These are the seven mountains which must be redeemed by the kingdom of God in order to implement kingdom culture and ultimately sheep nations:

1. Spirituality/Religion

2. Family

3. Education/Technology

4. Government

5. Media

6. Arts/Entertainment

7. Business/Economics

For those that find this teaching to be a slight stretch on Scripture, two other approaches to the same conclusion exist. One comes from Johnny Enlow in his book *The Seven Mountain Prophecy*. He arrives at this same conclusion through a study of the Canaanite tribes. His study concludes the following: Hittites represent the mountain of media, Girgashites represent the mountain of government, Amorites represent the mountain of education, Canaanites represent the mountain of economy, Perizzites represent the mountain of religion, Hivites represent the mountain of celebration (arts/entertainment), and Jebusites represent the mountain of family.[32]

A third approach looks at the seven mountains upon which the Whore of Babylon sits. This passage has been approached in various ways, often with an attempt to use the description of seven mountains as a geographic marker. In this way, some have concluded that Rome, which sits on seven hills, is where we would find the Whore of Babylon.[33] I would challenge this idea on the basis that there are nearly seventy geographies throughout the world that claim to reside upon seven hills or mountains.[34] It makes just as much sense to me to interpret this passage in light of the seven mind molders of society, which the Whore of Babylon undeniably occupies in most areas of the world. Although I do not believe this is the only or ultimate interpretation of this passage, it is certainly relevant.

"And there came one of the seven angels which had the seven vials, and talked with me, saying unto me, Come hither; I will shew unto thee the judgment of the great whore that sitteth upon many waters... So he carried me away in the spirit into the wilderness: and I saw a woman sit upon a scarlet coloured beast, full of names of blasphemy, having seven heads and ten horns... And here is the mind which hath wisdom. **The seven heads are seven mountains**, on which the woman sitteth" (Revelation 17:1, 3, 9).

This is the new paradigm that must arise: *We are not waiting for Jesus; Jesus is waiting for us*. We are to begin the process of taking the kingdoms of this world and influencing them according to the power of the kingdom of God. Jesus will not wait forever. He is going to accelerate those who will remain faithful into the destiny he has appointed for the church. Unfortunately, the realization of the gospel of the kingdom will not occur until the church is in the midst of the darkest period human history will ever record. As we move into this season of history, geographies that have come under a heavy influence of kingdom government will be known as sheep nations. On the road to this destiny, the greatest miracles ever recorded will be witnessed, and I believe the greatest revival of all time will manifest.

A Step Back in Time

And when ye shall see Jerusalem compassed with armies, then know that the desolation thereof is nigh. Then let them which are in Judaea flee to the mountains; and let them which are in the midst of it depart out; and let not them that are in the countries enter thereinto. For these be the days of vengeance, that all things which are written may be fulfilled. But woe unto them that are with child, and to them that give suck, in those days! for there shall be great distress in the land, and wrath upon this people. And they shall fall by the edge of the sword, and shall be led away captive into all nations: and Jerusalem shall be trodden down of the Gentiles, until the times of the Gentiles be fulfilled.

(Luke 21:20-24)

In my analysis, I have again made a distinction and separation between two similar passages that at first appear to be different records of the same utterance. This passage begins with the words, "And when ye shall see Jerusalem compassed with armies…" Right before Jesus began this discourse, he made this comment that sparked the disciples' questions:

"And Jesus said unto them, See ye not all these things [referring to the temple]? verily I say unto you, There shall not be left here one stone upon another, that shall not be thrown down" (Matthew 24:2)

In the record left to us by Luke, Jesus is quoted as continuing his prophecy about the destruction of the temple in Jerusalem in 70 AD. This quotation is very specific to this event. I do not believe there is any reason for this to be substituted or harmonized with a similar record in Matthew and Mark. In this passage, Jesus warns those in Jerusalem to flee to the mountains and warns those outside of Jerusalem to not enter back in. He prophesies great slaughter, and calls those days the "days of vengeance."

The quotation ends by declaring that many Jews will die, while others will be taken into captivity. He says that Jerusalem will be overtaken by the Gentiles, until the "times of the Gentiles" are fulfilled. The "times of the Gentiles" are assumed to have begun in 70 AD when Titus destroyed the temple and dispersed the Jews from Jerusalem. Many believe that the fulfillment of this prophecy (meaning the end of the times of the Gentiles) came in either in 1948 when Israel again became a nation, or in 1967 when Jerusalem was restored to the nation of Israel. I do not personally hold strong convictions either way.

THE ABOMINATION OF DESOLATION

Conversely, a similar yet distinct utterance is recorded by Matthew and Luke. Through careful harmonization, it appears as though this utterance is the very next thing Jesus says:

But when ye shall see the abomination of desolation, spoken of by Daniel the prophet, standing where it ought not in the holy place, (let him that readeth understand,) then let them that be in Judaea flee to the mountains: And let him that is on the housetop not go down into the house, neither enter therein, to take any thing out of his house: And let him that is in the field not turn back again for to take up his garment. And woe unto them that are with child, and to them that give suck in those days! But pray ye that your flight be not in the winter, neither on the Sabbath day: For then shall be great tribulation and affliction, such as was not from the beginning of the creation which God created unto this time, no, nor ever shall be.

This portion is extracted from Mark 13:14-19 and Matthew 24:15-21. Notice the article that begins this passage. It is the word "but," which is usually used to make a clarification on a former statement. This passage goes on to discuss the abomination of desolation standing where it ought not. This is very different from Jerusalem being surrounded by armies. This has no correlation whatsoever to the destruction of the temple in 70 AD. This reference places this event in the middle of Daniel's seventieth week; an event yet to come. From this passage in Daniel, which we have already discussed, we draw our parallel:

"And he [the final antichrist] shall confirm the covenant with many for one week: and in the midst [or middle] of the week he shall cause the sacrifice and the oblation to cease, and for the overspreading of abominations he shall make it desolate, even until the consummation, and that determined shall be poured upon the desolate" (Daniel 9:27).

"And from the time that the continual burnt offering is taken away and the abomination that makes desolate is set up, there shall be 1,290 days" (Daniel 12:11 AMP).

From our former discussion, we know that Jesus has just placed the timeline in the middle of Daniel's seventieth week. Prior to this, many believe that a third temple is built, and the sacrifice in Jerusalem is literally reinstituted. The fact that many prophecies in the Old Testament speak of Jerusalem and Zion in reference to the last days supports this approach.

A case can also be made that this is spiritually relevant to the temple of the body of Christ (the church) and that it is in this spiritual habitation (1 Peter 2:5) that the antichrist sets up the abomination of desolation. The fact that throughout the New Testament the body of Christ becomes the temple of God supports this approach. This interpretation would allow this passage to be fulfilled spiritually, and would not require that a temple be rebuilt on the temple mount prior to its fulfillment.

It could be that both of these interpretations go hand in hand. However it works, there is a sacrifice and oblation (offering) that the final antichrist stops. Jesus again urges those in Jerusalem to flee and not turn back (just like in Luke's account). He repeats his concern for nursing mothers. In this utterance, he adds that we should pray that this event does not happen in winter or on the Sabbath. What he says next, however, demands that this portion of his discourse be recognized as unique from the record in Luke. Jesus says, "For then shall be great tribulation and affliction, such as was not from the beginning of the creation which God created unto this time, no, nor ever shall be."

In other words, the three and one-half years of great tribulation for the church will begin at this time. No other time in history, no matter how diabolical, will come close to the measure of tribulation and affliction that will begin at that time. It will continue for the duration of Daniel's seventieth week. Luke leaves no reference to this. Thus we also find that the following prophecy from the book of Revelation, having a forty-two-month timeline, is properly paralleled to this utterance:

"And there was given unto him a mouth speaking great things and blasphemies; and power was given unto him to continue **forty and two months**. And he opened his mouth in blasphemy against God, to blaspheme his name, and his tabernacle, and them that dwell in heaven" (Revelation 13:5-6).

And except that the Lord had shortened those days, no flesh should be saved: but for the elect's sake, whom he hath chosen, he hath shortened the days.

The wickedness that will be revealed will threaten to destroy everything. The second heaven and the first heaven will have come together, and Satan will move fast to do as much damage as possible while preparing for Armageddon. Were these days not shortened, no flesh would survive. God interrupts this scenario. Jesus will cut it short when he returns and sets up his everlasting kingdom in the midst of the darkest period of human history ever revealed.

THE MARK OF THE BEAST

There are several things that are important to understand about this season. During this time, the mark of the beast will be implemented. This is what the Bible says:

"And he causeth all, both small and great, rich and poor, free and bond, to receive a mark in their right hand, or in their foreheads: And that no man might buy or sell, save he that had the mark, or the name of the beast, or the number of his name" (Revelation 13:16-17).

"And the third angel followed them, saying with a loud voice, If any man worship the beast and his image, and receive his mark in his forehead, or in his hand, The same shall drink of the wine of the wrath of God, which is poured out without mixture into the cup of his indignation; and he shall be tormented with fire and brimstone in the presence of the holy angels, and in the presence of the Lamb" (Revelation 14:9-10).

No one within the antichrist's kingdom will be able to buy, sell, or trade without the mark of the beast. Moreover, anyone who worships the beast and his image along with receiving this mark will suffer the wrath of God. There seems to be no forgiveness left for those who do this. The likelihood is that whatever this mark does, it will make it *impossible* for those people to be saved. There are several possibilities that can be considered. The first is that the mark of the beast may be a microchip capable of absolute mind control in the host. This mind-control could be the contributing factor in making salvation impossible for those who receive it. The question remains—what about those who get the chip removed? On the other hand, were this microchip administered as nanotechnology, it could make removal virtually impossible once having received it.

The second major possibility is that it may involve some form of genetic transition within those born as men. For instance, the mark could involve the insertion of foreign genetic material (DNA/RNA) that actually reconfigures the host on a genetic level—and I would add both physically and spiritually. In this way, people would no longer be covered by the blood of Jesus. They would become like Nephilim in that they would cease to retain their original human nature. When Jesus came, he came through the seed of Abraham, and did not take on the nature of angels. In doing this, Jesus died specifically for men only.

"Forasmuch then as the children are partakers of flesh and blood, he also himself likewise took part of the same; that through death he might destroy him that had the power of death, that is, the devil; And deliver them who through fear of death were all their lifetime subject to bondage. For verily **he took not on him the nature of angels; but he took on him the seed of Abraham**" (Hebrews 2:14-16).

There is a possibility that neither of the two mechanisms I have suggested will be involved in the actual mark of the beast. There is also a possibility that both may be implemented to a degree. The question that must be answered is: at what point can an action take away from us the ability to receive salvation? Jesus died for the murderers, rapists, Satanists, and pedophiles. He died for the thieves, liars, extortionists, adulterers, gang-members, drug lords, and prostitutes. However, he did not die for the Nephilim (at least first generation Nephilim), and he did not die for the angels. Jesus did not die for any life that is not after the seed of men. In the author's humble opinion, this mark will most likely cause changes to both spiritual and physical DNA in the host, permanently destroying the human nature of the entire organism: body, soul, and spirit.

GIBBORIM

There is a story in the Bible that suggests that this "directed evolution" is possible. By using the term "directed evolution," I am speaking of the alteration of human DNA with animal, plant and ultimately angelic DNA. First, consider that one of the words translated "mighty" in the Bible is the Hebrew word *gibbor*, which means powerful, warrior, *tyrant*, champion, chief, excel, *giant*, man, mighty (man, one), strong (man), and/or valiant man. This word is first used to describe the superhuman qualities of the giants of Genesis 6.

"There were giants [Nephilim] on the earth in those days—and also afterward—when the sons of God came in to the daughters of men, and they bore children to them. Those were the mighty men [gibborim] who were of old, men of renown" (Genesis 6:4 AMP).

From other books in the Bible, like Numbers, Joshua, and 2 Samuel, we learn that Nephilim were super-strong, fierce, gigantic, and struck fear into the hearts of men. Pivoting on what the Bible reveals about them, it is very fitting that gibbor is the chosen word to describe their physical attributes. The word gibbor becomes an all-sufficient adjective to describe the giants. When you think of these attributes, they seem to describe physical characteristics that are not normal, but are "superhuman." Their strength and speed, their physique, their ability to make war and fight, and quite possibly their intelligence, were superhuman. Superhuman ability is the connotation of the word.

The following passage tells us about Nimrod, the great-grandson of Noah. I have inserted brackets to help with understanding.

"And Cush begat Nimrod: he began to be a mighty one [gibbor, super-human] in the earth. He was a mighty [gibbor] hunter before the LORD:

wherefore it is said, Even as Nimrod the mighty [gibbor] hunter before the LORD. And the beginning of his kingdom was Babel, and Erech, and Accad, and Calneh, in the land of Shinar. Out of that land went forth Asshur, and builded Nineveh, and the city Rehoboth, and Calah, And Resen between Nineveh and Calah: the same is a great city" (Genesis 10:8-12).

Nimrod was a peculiar case in that he "began to become a gibbor (superhuman)." This means that when he was born he was not considered a gibbor, but at some point he was changed. When he was changed, he began to exhibit the characteristics of the giants that lived before the flood. What else can be gleaned from this passage? The name Nimrod comes from the word *marud* and literally means "rebel." Nimrod was a rebellious gibbor. The word *before* in this passage carries the interpretation of "turning the face from." It literally means that Nimrod was a rebellious hunter against God. More than that, he was a superhuman tyrant hunter. He was responsible for organizing society to begin building the tower of Babel. We must understand that by using the word *gibbor*, the Bible is creating a connection with what Nimrod became, and what the giants were.

To avoid a lopsided theology, the giants and Nimrod were not the only ones in the Bible described as gibborim. Certain men within the armies of Israel, God, and even King David are distinguished by this description. Again, the connotation of the word *gibbor* is "superhuman." It doesn't *always* mean Nephilim. For God's purposes, his Spirit elevated the capacity for war and victory within certain men of Israel. They became gibborim by the power of God, and not a demonic counterfeit. Consider these verses:

"Then answered one of the servants, and said, Behold, I have seen a son of Jesse the Bethlehemite, that is cunning in playing, and a **mighty [gibbor] valiant man**, and a man of war, and prudent in matters, and a comely person, and the LORD is with him. Wherefore Saul sent messengers unto Jesse, and said, Send me **David thy son**, which is with the sheep" (1 Samuel 16:18-19).

"Your wives, your little ones, and your cattle shall dwell in the land which Moses gave you on this side of the Jordan, but all your **mighty men [gibborim]** of valor shall pass on before your brethren armed, and help them until the LORD has given your brethren rest, as He has given you, and they also possess the land the LORD your God is giving them. Then you shall return to the land of your possession and possess it, the land Moses the LORD's servant gave you on the sunrise side of the Jordan" (Joshua 1:14-15, AMP).

When Joshua is quoting God's promise to the people in this pre-invasion pep talk, he uses the word *gibborim* to describe the armies of Israel. Why? Have you ever wondered how Israelites being mere men took on armies of giants with spears, arrows, and swords—and won? They did not have artillery, tanks, B-52 bombers, exploding bullets, etc. Yet they defeated giants (Nephilim). In this passage and others scattered throughout the Bible, we find that the armies of Israel actually had gibborim. Moreover, consider this passage:

"Who is this King of glory? The LORD strong and mighty [gibbor], the LORD mighty [gibbor] in battle" (Psalm 24:8).

God actually uses the term *gibbor* to describe himself in battle. This is a reference to the day of the Lord. As we know, God is not a nephil, and therefore this term is not strictly used to describe Nephilim. However, it still means mighty, giant, warrior, to excel, etc. Again, it basically describes the presence of superhuman characteristics, particularly pertaining to the ability to make war. It is a term referring to physiological capacity. *In other words, it is an ancient term depicting super-soldiers.*

Going back to Israel, we must realize that God changed their very physiology to make them into super-soldiers with superhuman capacity to make war. They were able to fight as if they were more than human by God's power. They were able to run faster, hit harder, take more pain, fight without tiring, excel in strength, etc. They fought with more fierceness than giants by a change in physiology according to the power of God infusing them with this ability. Consider this illustration in the men of Gad that fought with David.

"And of the Gadites there separated themselves unto David into the hold to the wilderness men of might [gibbor], and men of war fit for the battle, that could handle shield and buckler, whose faces were like the faces of lions, and were as swift as the roes upon the mountains…These were of the sons of Gad, captains of the host: one of the least was over an hundred, and the greatest over a thousand" (1 Chronicles 12:8, 14).

We begin by noting the use of the word *gibbor* to describe them as having superhuman characteristics. A change in physiology results, as their faces are compared with the faces of lions. It also says that they were swift as roes in the mountains. Roes are deer. No regular person can run this fast because it is physiologically impossible. Yet they did, because the Holy Spirit changed their physiology for his purposes. In the phrase, "one of the least was over an hundred," it does not mean that they were simply captains over a company of one hundred men. This old English actually speaks to the fact that the least was equal to having one hundred men; the least could take on one hundred men in battle and win. It follows that the greatest of these warriors was equal to an army of one thousand.

THE SEAL OF THE LIVING GOD

Is it any wonder that following the sixth seal, the Lord distributes the seal of the Living God? It may not be immediate, but it will certainly be before the seven trumpets begin to sound.

And after these things I saw four angels standing on the four corners of the earth, holding the four winds of the earth, that the wind should not blow on the earth, nor on the sea, nor on any tree. And I saw another angel ascending from the east, having the seal of the living God: and he cried with a loud voice to the four angels, to whom it was given to hurt the earth and the sea, Saying, Hurt not the earth, neither the sea, nor the trees, **till we have sealed the servants of our God in their foreheads**.

(Revelation 7:1-3)

The seal of God will be administered by an angel and placed into our foreheads. It is at this point that every person who has received Jesus as their personal Lord and Savior will be sealed. The necessity will be obvious, considering that at this point the gates of hell have literally opened up onto the earth. This will be a literal event and from this point forward; everything about what we know and understand will be radically different. The end times are very supernatural, and on this the Bible is clear. Regarding the impact of the seal of God, it will at the very least provide protection from upcoming judgments (Revelation 9:4).

The account of the administering of the seal of God goes on to give the number of Israelites from every tribe that are counted among the saints at that time (Revelation 7:4-8). The total given is 144,000—twelve thousand come from each of the tribes of Israel, excluding the tribe of Dan. Instead, the tribes of Manasseh and Joseph are listed separately, even though Manasseh was actually one of Joseph's sons (Genesis 48:1). It is important to understand that *all* of the saints are sealed at this time, and not just the Israeli saints.

THE FIFTH TRUMPET

Having addressed this, let us transition back to our original thought. Strictly considering the case involving Nimrod, could the mark of the beast be the final implementation of an ancient mystery meant to destroy humanity from men? Could the mark of the beast involve technology to counterfeit the creation of gibborim through demonic wisdom? Considering everything that the Bible has revealed thus far, I am confident that the answer is a resounding yes. Considering the current trans-humanist agenda, *I would actually be surprised to find out otherwise.*

One last thought arises from the following passage about the fifth trumpet. At the fifth trumpet, genetic monstrosities are released from the pit. They are described as locusts having bodies like horses, faces like men, teeth like lions, tails with stingers like scorpions, hair like women and breastplates like iron. This description is not symbolic, but describes their actual anatomy. Look at what it says of the men they persecute:

"And in those days shall men seek death, and shall not find it; and shall desire to die, and **death shall flee from them**" (Revelation 9:6).

Could this mean that genetic manipulation makes it much more difficult for these people to die? Again, based on what the Bible has revealed thus far, I believe the answer is yes. Going one step further, this transition may even make it impossible for men to die apart from supernatural intervention. What I do know is that death does not flee from them because they are under the power of God. These abominations cannot harm those that have the seal of the living God (Revelation 9:4). The only ones that can desire death as a result of this plague are the members of the antichrist's kingdom.

In order to be involved with this global satanic society, men will need to receive this mark. As it is written, no one can buy, sell, or trade in that society without it. The interesting thing about the mark of the beast is that the Bible seemingly places more emphasis on this mark than its anti-type, which is the seal of God upon the saints. The mark of the beast, like every-thing else Satan does, is nothing more than a counterfeit of what God is doing. For this reason, if the mark of the beast qualifies people as members of the beast kingdom, the seal of God may have something to do with sheep nations. I cannot prove it, but the implementation of the seal of God may be the very trigger that allows the church to attain the seemingly impossi-ble destiny that Christ has appointed. If nothing else, the seal of the Living God will protect us from the abominations that are released during the fifth trumpet:

"And it was commanded them that they [the judgment of the fifth trumpet] should not hurt the grass of the earth, neither any green thing, neither any tree; but only those men which have not the seal of God in their foreheads" (Revelation 9:4).

Lying Signs and Wonders

> Then if any man shall say unto you, Lo, here is Christ, or there; believe it not. For false Christs and false prophets shall rise, and shall shew signs and wonders, to seduce, if it were possible, even the elect. But take ye heed: behold, I have foretold you all things.

At this point Jesus reiterates that there will be false Christs and false prophets. These individuals will continue to rise up, even at this point in human history. He says they will show signs and wonders. This is not new; the Bible records miracles that were performed by magicians and sorcerers. One such example was when Moses and Aaron encountered Pharaoh to demand the freedom of their people.

"And Moses and Aaron went in unto Pharaoh, and they did so as the LORD had commanded: and Aaron cast down his rod before Pharaoh, and before his servants, and it became a serpent. Then Pharaoh also called the wise men and the sorcerers: now the magicians of Egypt, they also did in like manner with their enchantments. For they cast down every man his rod, and they became serpents: but Aaron's rod swallowed up their rods. And he hardened Pharaoh's heart, that he hearkened not unto them; as the LORD had said" (Exodus 7:10-13).

THE FALSE PROPHET

Often, we only consider the fact that Aaron's serpent swallowed up the serpents that emerged from the rods cast down by the magicians. Make no mistake; the magician's rods still became serpents, and that is a miracle. The final false prophet that serves alongside the antichrist will perform great and spectacular miracles. He is referred to as a second beast in the book of Revelation. The miracles attributed to his sorcery are definitely in the category of those that will, if possible, seduce even the elect.

And I beheld another beast coming up out of the earth; and he had two horns like a lamb, and he spake as a dragon. And he exerciseth all the power of the first beast before him, and causeth the earth and them which dwell therein to worship the first beast, whose deadly wound was healed. And **he doeth great wonders**, so that **he maketh fire come down from heaven** on the earth in the sight of men, **And deceiveth them that dwell on the earth by the means of those miracles which he had power to do in the sight of the beast**; saying to them that dwell on the earth, that they should make an image to the beast, which had the wound by a sword, and did live. **And he had power to give life unto the image of the beast**, that the image of the beast should both speak, and cause that as many as would not worship the image of the beast should be killed.

(Revelation 13:11-15)

From this single passage, the Bible says that this particular false prophet will:

> ➤ Exercise all the power of the antichrist

> ➤ Cause men to worship the antichrist

> ➤ Do great wonders

> ➤ Make fire come down from heaven onto the earth

> ➤ Deceive men by the miracles he performs

> ➤ Give life to an image of the antichrist made by the hands of men

Jesus leaves his bride absolutely no excuse for getting deceived by these deceptions that will be revealed in the last days. Jesus basically tells us to, "Expect these things to happen before I come, because it will be *very bad*, and you who do not endure are without excuse because I have told you beforehand."

THE SIGN OF HIS COMING

Wherefore if they shall say unto you, Behold, he is in the desert; go not forth: behold, he is in the secret chambers; believe it not. For as the lightning cometh out of the east, and shineth even unto the west; so shall also the coming of the Son of man be. For wheresoever the carcass is, there will the eagles be gathered together.

We have now arrived at the sign of the coming of Jesus. As the lightning comes out of the east and shines in the west, so also will be the appearing of the Son of man. This means that the glory resounding out of Jesus and surrounding his glorious angels will be visible throughout the sky before they come into view. The next statement says "wheresoever the carcass is, there will the eagles be gathered together." Eagles eat dead flesh, otherwise known as carrion. There will be many carcasses lying out in the open all over the world. Why? This has just alluded to the savage brutality of the sixth trumpet.

And the sixth angel sounded, and I heard a voice from the four horns of the golden altar which is before God, Saying to the sixth angel which had the trumpet, Loose the four angels which are bound in the great river Euphrates. And the four angels were loosed, which were prepared for an hour, and a day, and a month, and a year, for to slay the third part of men. And the number of the army of the horsemen were two hundred thousand thousand [200,000,000]: and I heard the number of them. And thus I saw the horses in the vision, and them that sat on them, having breastplates of fire, and of jacinth, and brimstone: and the heads of the horses were as the heads of lions; and out of their mouths issued fire and smoke and brimstone. By these three was the third part of men killed, by the fire, and by the smoke, and by the brimstone, which issued out of their mouths. For their power is in their mouth, and in their tails: for their tails were like unto serpents, and had heads, and with them they do hurt. And the rest of the men which were not killed by these plagues yet repented not of the works of their hands, that they should not worship devils, and idols of gold, and silver, and brass, and stone, and of wood: which neither can see, nor hear, nor walk: Neither repented they of their murders, nor of their sorceries, nor of their fornication, nor of their thefts.

(Revelation 9:13-21)

Thus this narrative leaves us off right after the end of the sixth trumpet, as the seventh trumpet is sounding. We must understand that this means all of the other five trumpets have already sounded, even though they haven't been specifically referenced by this narrative. These trumpet judgments are discussed in Revelation chapters 8 and 9.

But in those days, immediately after that tribulation, the sun shall be darkened, and the moon shall not give her light, And the stars of heaven shall fall, and the powers that are in heaven shall be shaken. And there shall be signs in the sun, and in the moon, and in the stars; and upon the earth distress of nations, with perplexity; the sea and the waves roaring; Men's hearts failing them for fear, and for looking after those things which are coming on the earth: for the powers of heaven shall be shaken. And then shall appear the sign of the Son of man in heaven: and then shall all the tribes of the earth mourn, and they shall see the Son of man coming in the clouds of heaven with great power and great glory.

The next statement begins with the phrase, "After the tribulation of those days…" What "days" is Jesus referring to? He is, of course, referring to the forty-two months of great tribulation. He told us that these would begin when the abomination of desolation was placed in the holy place. This is the time frame that we have been discussing for some time now.

"For then shall be **great tribulation**, such as was not since the beginning of the world to this time, no, nor ever shall be" (Matthew 24:21).

As Jesus is returning, the sun will be darkened and the moon will not give its light. In addition, more stars will fall. Again, these stars are not the actual balls of fire and gas that comprise the constellations, just like they weren't during the sixth seal. Stars takes on a symbolic meaning in this utterance, and Jesus describes that even at his coming there seems to be one last angelic rebellion occurring.

ANGELIC REBELLIONS

Regarding angelic rebellion, many people seem to believe that only one angelic rebellion occurred. They would say that it occurred before God created man, when Lucifer fell from heaven. I personally believe that this could not be further from the truth. As far as I have concluded, angelic rebellions have occurred repeatedly throughout all of history, and may continue to occur up and into the actual second coming of Jesus Christ. You are free to disagree with me on this point, but at least consider my evidence. I believe that there may be as many as ten separate angelic rebellions discussed in the Bible. By saying "as many as," I admit that not all of these instances may involve newly rebelling angels. I will list them below and leave you, as the reader, to consider the evidence:

➤ Lucifer, who is also called Satan, was cast from heaven, chronologically becoming the first fallen angel. Reference Genesis 3, Isaiah 14:12-17, Ezekiel 28:13-18, Luke 10:18, Revelation 20:2.

➤ The second fall of angels, according to biblical chronology, would be the "sons of God" of Genesis 6:1-4 that took wives and fathered the original Nephilim. Reference also Jude 1:6, 1 Peter 3:19, and 2 Peter 2:4. According to Jude, these particular angels were locked up in everlasting chains under darkness. This means that Lucifer himself was not a part of this rebellion, since he is still roaming the earth like a lion (1 Peter 5:8).

➤ Giants recurred on the earth after the days of Noah. The Jews had to expel giants from the Promised Land (see the book of Joshua). The book of Genesis lists tribes of giants (Genesis 14:5). Genesis 6:1-4 declares that giants were born when women had sex with angels. In order for giants to arise, either more angels had to rebel and have offspring with women, the wives of Noah's sons had to carry over the genetic capacity for this phenomenon, or some other even more radical explanation is required. Thus, there *may* have been a smaller third rebellion after the flood.

➤ There is also the question of the heavenly divine council. According to the book of Deuteronomy 32:8 it reads, "When the Most High divided to the nations their inheritance, when he separated the sons of Adam, he set the bounds of the people according to the number of the children of Israel." The number of the children of Israel was 70. This is significant in that according to the extra-biblical book of Jasher, it is suggested that this separation into seventy groups hap-pened because there were seventy angels that helped God to confuse the languages at the tower of Babel. It reads, "And God said to the seventy angels who stood foremost before him, to those who were near to him, saying, Come let us descend and confuse their tongues, that one man shall not understand the language of his neighbor, and they did so unto them."[35] It seems as though these angels that were originally allies of God became corrupted and began to receive the worship of men. According to Deuteronomy 4:19, "And lest thou lift up thine eyes unto heaven, and when thou seest the sun, and the moon, and the stars, even all the host of heaven, shouldest be driven to worship them, and serve them, **which the Lord thy God hath divided unto all nations under the whole heaven**." In other words, the Gentile nations were driven to worship the host of heaven, which can otherwise be understood as the heavenly divine council of angels that were once allied with God. As a matter of fact, it seems that things got so bad with this group that God addressed Psalm 82 directly to them. It reads, "God standeth in the congregation of the mighty; he judgeth among the gods. How long will ye judge unjustly, and accept the persons of the wicked? Selah....I have said, Ye are gods; and all of you are children of the most High. But ye shall die like men, and fall like one of the princes" (Psalm 82:1-2, 6-7). What would cause God to tell angels in his congregation (or council) that they are judging unjustly, shall die like men, and fall like one of the princes? Could this be yet another group of rebel angels?

➢ In Revelation 12, after the sign of the woman appears, the dragon draws a third of the stars of heaven to earth. Regarding the sign of the woman, the interpretation of this symbolism is based on Joseph's dream in Genesis 37:9-10. The sun and the moon represent the father and mother of sons of Israel, the stars are the tribes of Israel, and the woman represents the nation of Israel. After the sign of the woman is described, we read of another wonder in heaven: the dragon. His tail draws a third of the "stars" of heaven (angelic host) and casts them to earth. This is another rebellion. Many assume this is the only rebellion, and that it happened before Adam was created. While it is possible that this happened before Adam was created, there is another possibility. In the chronology of the passage (Revelation 12), this rebellion doesn't happen until *after* the sons of Jacob are born, possibly being closer to the birth of Jesus by context. It says in verse 4 that the dragon (Satan) stood before the woman (Israel) who was *ready* to give birth to devour the child (Jesus) *as soon as it was born*. Because the Nephilim tribes are mentioned *before* the birth of Abraham, who is the grandfather of Jacob, I believe that this could possibly have been another rebellion. Again, the sun in Revelation 12 represents Jacob.

➢ The sixth seal could be another rebellion (Revelation 6:12-17), if the angels who "fall" to earth are not entirely comprised of those that are already fallen and residing in the second heaven. Keep in mind that we are referencing the "stars" that fall from heaven to earth according to the wording of the passage.

➢ Once the antichrist is in power, additional angels (stars) may fall, as he will ascend into heaven and "stomp upon" them (Daniel 8:8-10). This is the antichrist's way of counterfeiting the work of Jesus having "spoiled principalities and powers" (Colossians 2:15). Of course, this may depend on what heaven (second or third) the antichrist is ascending into. Considering that the second heaven will have opened up onto the earth at this point, it is most logical to conclude that this is a reference to the some area of the third heaven—else why would he be described as "ascending" back to where he came from? It could also be a reference to angels of God that are engaged in war in the second heaven switching sides. The 2,300 days of Daniel 8:13-14 forces us to understand this activity may be causing another round of rebellion. The antichrist can be on earth no less than seven years, and 2,300 days is around 6.4 years. Clearly, during this time angels will be "stomped upon." "And it waxed great, even to the host of heaven; **and it cast down some of the host and of the stars to the ground, and stamped upon them**... Then I heard one saint speaking, and another saint said unto that certain saint which spake, How long shall be the vision concerning the daily sacrifice, and the transgression of desolation, to give both the sanctuary **and the host to be trodden under foot?** And he said unto me, Unto two thousand and three hundred days; then shall the sanctuary be cleansed" (Daniel 8:10, 13-14).

➢ During the third trumpet (Revelation 8:10-11) the Bible says that a great "star" named Wormwood falls upon one third of the rivers and fountains of waters. This causes men to die as a result. This "star" is described as falling from heaven, and could speak to the rebellion of yet another angel.

➢ During the fifth trumpet, the Bible says an angel falls from heaven with the key to the bottomless pit (Revelation 9:1). If this angel was not fallen beforehand, this could be a ninth rebellion.

➢ The last rebellion of angels may be occurring as Jesus is returning. Again, this would depend on whether the stars are falling from the second heaven or the third heaven (Reference Isaiah 34:4, Matthew 24:29-30). Note that the reference in Isaiah 34 sounds almost identical to that of the sixth seal (Revelation 6:13). However, the sixth seal is a counterfeit, and Isaiah 34 (along with Isaiah 2:10-21) is clearly describing the day of the Lord. Once we understand this, we must accept that they are not the same event.

The Holy Scriptures never cease to amaze me. The more we seek, the deeper the Holy Spirit will take us. The rest of this utterance describes how men's hearts will fail them for fear of the return of Jesus. It describes signs in the heavens, trouble in the sea with waves roaring—probably resulting from earthquakes—and finally the actual appearance of Jesus upon a white horse riding on the clouds of heaven!

CHAPTER 19

Harmony of the End Part 4

And when these things begin to come to pass, then look up, and lift up your heads; for your redemption draweth nigh. And he shall send his angels with a great sound of a trumpet, and they shall gather together his elect from the four winds, from the uttermost part of the earth to the uttermost part of heaven.

Here, we find ourselves at the sounding of the seventh trumpet. When the Bible discusses the elect being gathered, it is referring to the supernatural assembly of the army of God. First, the dead will be raised. The bodies of dead saints will be reassembled and joined to the spirits that once inhabited them. Then, the saints who are alive and remain will be gathered as well. No matter where any particle or aspect of our original body was, from one part of heaven to the other, it will be restored to us and glorified. Our once-corruptible soul will also put on incorruption.

THE SALVATION WAITING TO BE REVEALED

"For this corruptible [soul] must put on incorruption, and this mortal [body] must put on immortality. So when this corruptible [soul] shall have put on incorruption, and this mortal [body] shall have put on immortality, then shall be brought to pass the saying that is written, Death is swallowed up in victory" (1 Corinthians 15:53-54).

This is the salvation waiting to be revealed at the last day. This is the manifestation of the sons of God, and this is the revelation of the mystery of Christ in us, the hope of glory! Jesus says to those who are alive at that time, that as they begin to see the dead caught up, their own redemption draws near. The dead are raised first. They are gathered and assembled by the angels that come with Jesus at the end of the age. After the dead are raised, the saints that are still alive are also gathered together and glorified in the air.

"For the Lord himself shall descend from heaven with a shout, with the voice of the archangel, and with the trump of God: **and the dead in Christ shall rise first**" (1 Thessalonians 4:16).

"Behold, I shew you a mystery; We shall not all sleep, but we shall all be changed, In a moment, in the twinkling of an eye, at the last trump: for the trumpet shall sound, and the dead shall be raised incorruptible, and we shall be changed" (1 Corinthians 15:51-52).

THE KINGDOM AT THE END OF THE AGE

There is a lot involved in the reaping performed by these angels at the end of the age. On this issue, many passages converge to give us a full picture. The first thing that we must understand is that the definition of the kingdom changes at the end of the age. At the sounding of the seventh trumpet, the kingdoms of this world fully become the kingdoms of our Lord and his Christ. The seventh trumpet finishes this process. Everything that occurs afterwards, including the battle of Armageddon, are formalities.

"And the seventh angel sounded; and there were great voices in heaven, saying, **The kingdoms of this world are become the kingdoms of our Lord, and of his Christ**; and he shall reign for ever and ever" (Revelation 11:15).

Prior to the seventh trumpet, the only ones who can access the kingdom of God are those who are saved. Right now, the kingdom of God only exists in the spirit. In order to be established on the earth, it must come through the hearts of the people of God. When the seventh trumpet is sounded, this suddenly changes. This is extremely important, because if we do not understand this, it can lead to great confusion. Below is a graphic representation of what I'm talking about:

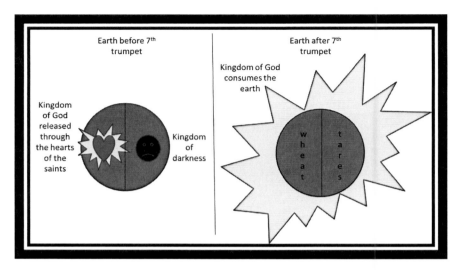

Figure 5

When we do not grasp this concept, we can conclude that Jesus will send some of the saints directly to hell when he returns! If we do not understand that the kingdom at the end of the world includes all of the earth, our view of God can easily become twisted. The following passage includes a reference to the angels that harvest at the end of the world. Notice that the tares that are sent to the furnace of fire are gathered "out of the kingdom of Jesus."

EXPLAINING THE TARES AND THE WHEAT

He answered and said unto them, He that soweth the good seed is the Son of man; The field is the world; the good seed are the children of the kingdom; but the tares are the children of the wicked one; The enemy that sowed them is the devil; **the har-vest is the end of the world; and the reapers are the angels**. As therefore the tares are gathered and burned in the fire; so shall it be in the end of this world. The Son of man shall send forth his angels, and **they shall gather out of his kingdom all things that offend**, and them which do iniquity; And shall cast them into a furnace of fire: there shall be wailing and gnashing of teeth. Then shall the righteous shine forth as the sun in the kingdom of their Father. Who hath ears to hear, let him hear.

(Matthew 13:37-43)

This passage is the explanation of a parable about "the tares among the wheat." What are the important points? The harvest is at the end of the world, and the reapers are the angels. The angels will gather out of the kingdom those who are considered "tares." The kingdom is the kingdom of heaven. Tares are defined as the spiritual offspring of the wicked one. The tares will be thrown into the "furnace of fire" and burned. The furnace of fire is a reference to eternal damnation. Then the righteous will shine forth like the sun in the kingdom of their Father. The shining is another reference to the glory of our perfected bodies.

Will Christians be gathered out of the kingdom and burned? No, because according to Revelation 11:15, the kingdoms of the world are trans-ferred into the kingdom of God. The wicked on the earth must be removed from the kingdom of God (which contains the world) at this point. In other words, tares are not false converts as some have speculated—they are individuals who blatantly reject Jesus Christ and are unfortunate enough to be present at his coming. We will dive deeper into this parable later on, but suffice it to say that this is a perfect parallel to what Jesus is currently discussing.

The Severing of the Wicked and the Just

Our next parallel also comes out of Matthew 13. It is the parable of the net.

"Again, the kingdom of heaven is like unto a net, that was cast into the sea, and gathered of every kind: Which, when it was full, they drew to shore, and sat down, and gathered the good into vessels, but cast the bad away. **So shall it be at the end of the world: the angels shall come forth, and sever the wicked from among the just**, And shall cast them into the furnace of fire: there shall be wailing and gnashing of teeth" (Matthew 13:47-50).

This passage again discusses the angels involved with the harvest at the end of the world. *Only at the end of the age is this parable applicable to the kingdom of heaven.* When Jesus returns, the "good" will be gathered for preservation. These are the saints of God, both wise and foolish. The "bad" will be cast away into the furnace of fire. Are saints gathered out of the kingdom of heaven because they aren't good enough? No. The wicked are gathered out of the earth and cast into hell. We will also revisit this passage later on.

REAPING THE EARTH

> And I looked, and behold a white cloud, and upon the cloud one sat like unto the Son of man, having on his head a golden crown, and in his hand a sharp sickle. And another angel came out of the temple, crying with a loud voice to him that sat on the cloud, Thrust in thy sickle, and reap: for the time is come for thee to reap; for the harvest of the earth is ripe. And he that sat on the cloud thrust in his sickle on the earth; and the earth was reaped. And another angel came out of the temple which is in heaven, he also having a sharp sickle. And another angel came out from the altar, which had power over fire; and cried with a loud cry to him that had the sharp sickle, saying, Thrust in thy sharp sickle, and gather the clusters of the vine of the earth; for her grapes are fully ripe. And the angel thrust in his sickle into the earth, and gathered the vine of the earth, and cast it into the great winepress of the wrath of God.
>
> (Revelation 14:14-19)

In this last parallel, we have slightly greater depth. The Son of man sits upon a cloud with a sharp sickle and reaps the earth. Those who are reaped are the righteous dead and the faithful saints who still remain. The saints are reaped into the sky where they receive glorified bodies, being fully manifested as the sons of God. The unrighteous are also reaped like in the first two parables. Where are they reaped? These are not reaped into heavenly bodies like the righteous, but are reaped into the winepress of God. What happens in the winepress of God? Simply put: death and destruction.

"And the winepress was trodden without the city [outside of the perimeter of Jerusalem], and blood came out of the winepress, even unto the horse bridles, by the space of a thousand and six hundred furlongs" (Revelation 14:20).

Thus, when Jesus refers to the harvest at the end of the age, we must understand that the earth is reaped twice. One reaping involves the catching away of the church. The other reaping involves the gathering of the unrighteous for punishment. Some of the unrighteous will be reaped into the valley of Megiddo, where the battle of Armageddon will shortly take place. Some will not, because not all of the unrighteous will be reaped into the winepress of God. There will be some who do survive the war campaign of Christ and are not present at the battle of Armageddon. As we will discuss later, these will stand at the judgment seat of Christ.

The Parable of the Fig Tree

We will now transition back into the discourse of Jesus on the Mount of Olives. Jesus stops the narrative to tell a parable. This parable helps us to identify the generation in which all these things will take place. Most biblical scholars agree that according to the Bible, a generation can be any amount of time extending up to one hundred years or one hundred and twenty years.

Now learn a parable of the fig tree; When his branch is yet tender, and putteth forth leaves, ye know that summer is nigh: So likewise ye, when ye see these things come to pass, know ye that the kingdom of God is nigh at hand. Verily I say unto you, This generation shall not pass away, till all be fulfilled. Heaven and earth shall pass away, but my words shall not pass away.

Some have suggested that the fig tree is to be interpreted as the restoration of the nation of Israel, or the restoration of the city of Jerusalem to Israel. It follows that its budding is the sign of the generation in which all these things will come to pass. If this were true, the countdown for the generation that would see the return of Christ began in 1948 AD (when an

Israeli state was formed) or 1967 AD (when Jerusalem was fully restored to Israel). This may be true considering passages like Luke 13:1-9.

Others have used this passage to argue a preterist position, basically stating that this is proof that Jesus mystically returned at the destruction of the temple in 70 AD. These individuals would say that the same people that heard these words were the ones that were alive to watch the fulfillment of this prophecy. On the surface, this admittedly seems to be an excellent explanation of the phrase "this generation shall not pass away, till all be fulfilled." However, the number of problems that arise from this position regarding other texts are numerous, forcing most biblical literalists to eventually discard it. The easiest problem to point out is the issue of the millennial reign of Christ, which according to this view either ended in 1070 AD or has to be spiritualized and redefined to mean an ongoing, indeterminable amount of time that extends through the present day. In my opinion, both of these options are unacceptable.

I personally approach this from another standpoint, which I believe is by far the most logical. The fig tree putting forward its leaves is the *sign* that summer is near. Thus, the events that Jesus has described are the signs that his coming and the end of the age are at hand. Regardless of whether or not the fig tree is defined as present-day Israel, as we recognize the signs, we will know that the time is at hand. In this way we avoid the trap of setting false dates that only serve to discredit the faith.

What are we to do with the use of the term *generation* in this passage if we are not dogmatic about the fig tree representing Israel? Dr. Bill Hamon gives us great perspective on this in his book *Prophetic Scriptures yet to be Fulfilled: During the Third and Final Church Reformation.*

As an example, take the word **generation**. In man's way of thinking that would be the generation alive at the time of the statement or a period of time of 40 to 100 years. Let us look at a biblical prophetic application of a *generation*. In Psalm 22, David made some prophetic statements about the suffering, praise, and posterity of the coming Messiah. Then after describing all the Messiah would do and accomplish, he made a prophetic statement: *"A **seed** shall serve Him; it shall be accounted to the Lord for a **generation**"* (Psalm 22:30 KJV). Apostle Paul declared that the promise to Abraham was to his *seed*, by which he revealed that prophetically God was not just speaking of Isaac but of Christ Jesus. He then stated that we the Church are the promised seed of Abraham by being the seed of Christ by being born of His Holy Spirit... Matthew 1:17 says there are 14 generations from Abraham to David and 14 generations from David to the Babylonian captivity, and so there are 14 listed. Then he states that there are 14 generations from Babylonian captivity until Christ, but when you list all the names, there are only 13 generations. That is not a mistake because the one Body of Christ is the 14th generation. The Church is that seed that the Lord counts as one generation.

Apostle Peter declared that the Church is a *chosen generation* and a holy nation (see 1 Peter 2:9)."[36]

Jesus tells us that the generation he is speaking of will not pass away until all is fulfilled. Jesus then reaffirms the authority of what he is telling the disciples by commenting that the very words he is speaking hold more permanence than heaven and earth themselves. It is a very sobering reminder that he was the Word who become flesh and dwelt among us.

The Day and Hour

> But of that day and that hour knoweth no man, no, not the angels which are in heaven, neither the Son, but the Father. And take heed to yourselves, lest at any time your hearts be overcharged with surfeiting, and drunkenness, and cares of this life, and so that day come upon you unawares. For as a snare shall it come on all them that dwell on the face of the whole earth.

Jesus tells us that the day and hour of his coming are unknown. He doesn't know, the angels do not know, and the saints do not know. The day is only known to the Father, but the season should be known by those who are faithful and diligent. Jesus tells us to take heed, or else that day will come upon us while we are unaware. This means that *the goal is to be aware* when the day is approaching. Paul clarifies this statement in his letter to the Thessalonians.

"For yourselves know perfectly that the day of the Lord so cometh as a thief in the night. For when they shall say, Peace and safety; then sudden destruction cometh upon them, as travail upon a woman with child; and they shall not escape. **But ye, brethren, are not in darkness, that that day should overtake you as a thief**" (1 Thessalonians 5:2–4).

Only for those who are in darkness is there a threat that the day of the Lord will come at a time they do not expect; the Lord overtaking them as a thief in the night. To those who are in the light, we are told the signs, and the time. Although we may not know the day or hour, we will probably know the week, and the month, and certainly the year once Daniel's seventieth week has commenced. All of those who are left upon the earth will be in a snare, unable to escape the kingdom that Jesus is manifesting in its fullness.

THE DAYS OF NOAH

But as the days of [Noah] were, so shall also the coming of the Son of man be. For as in the days that were before the flood they were eating and drinking, marrying and giving in marriage, until the day that [Noah] entered into the ark, And knew not until the flood came, and took them all away; so shall also the coming of the Son of man be.

For those of you who read my first book *Noah's Ark and the End of Days*, you will understand when I say that an entire volume could be written on this one passage. For this study, we will only touch on it briefly. Suffice it to say that what occurred at the time of Noah will be occurring in the days and years leading up to the return of Christ. As we already discussed, once the restrainer is removed, the earth will return to this state for a minimum of seven prophetic years. There will be an integration of fallen angels and Nephilim into society, and they will rule over men. Those that align themselves with the antichrist will not expect the judgment and victory of Jesus. The church will be gathered into the "ark" of the last days and will rise as the wrath of God strikes. Jesus specifically mentions marriage, eating, and drinking will continue, which are activities that all cultures practice.

The destruction and final judgment in Noah's day did not happen until after Noah was sealed into the ark. It took Noah seven days to get all of the animals onto the ark before he boarded and was sealed in. This is significant, because it is a shadow of the purpose of the number seven in the end times.

"There went in two and two unto Noah into the ark, the male and the female, as God had commanded Noah. And it came to pass **after seven days**, that the waters of the flood were upon the earth" (Genesis 7:9-10).

It will take the Holy Spirit seven prophetic years to gather the body of Christ worldwide and cause us to finish the final works. Upon completion, we will be sealed for all eternity as the bride of Christ. Consider that the final works have to be finished in order for heaven to release Jesus to return. For example, the final works will lead to the restitution of all things. This is what Peter tells us in the book of Acts:

"And he shall send Jesus Christ, which before was preached unto you: **Whom the heaven must receive until the times of restitution of all things**, which God hath spoken by the mouth of all his holy prophets since the world began" (Acts 3:20-21).

Contrary to certain points of view on the return of Jesus, he <u>cannot</u> return until the restitution of all things as spoken by the mouth of God's holy prophets. The church must finish what God has prophesied before heaven will release Jesus. This means moving the church into a posture of the measure of the stature of the fullness of Christ corporately (Ephesians 4:13). Until then, we aren't going anywhere. However, at this point the Scripture will be fulfilled which says:

"That in the dispensation of the fulness of times he might gather together in one all things in Christ, both which are in heaven, and which are on earth; even in him" (Ephesians 1:10).

The dead saints that are in heaven will be gathered together with the surviving saints on earth in Christ at the time of his coming. After Jesus initially returns and gathers his church, the world will be judged by fire. This contrasts with the days of Noah, when the world was judged by water.

"Whereby the world that then was, being overflowed with water, perished: But the heavens and the earth, which are now, by the same word are kept in store, reserved unto fire against the day of judgment and perdition of ungodly men" (2 Peter 3:6-7).

Those who are in darkness will not know what is coming until Jesus returns. In Noah's day, the inhabitants of the earth did not expect the flood, and by this judgment were swept away into damnation. It will be similar at the coming of Christ. The world will not expect the Word of God to be fulfilled.

The Catching Away

Then shall two be in the field; the one shall be taken, and the other left. Two women shall be grinding at the mill; the one shall be taken, and the other left. Watch ye therefore, and pray always, that ye may be accounted worthy to escape all these things that shall come to pass, and to stand before the Son of man: for ye know not what hour your Lord doth come.

The remainder of this narrative discusses the rapture in more detail. It says that two will be in the field, one taken and the other left. In the days of Noah, Noah and the animals were delivered from the flood that destroyed those who remained. Their deliverance came in the form of the ark that rose above the waters of judgment. At the end of the age, people are literally going to be removed from their geographical locations to meet the Lord in the air (1 Thessalonians 4:15-17).

I must address a point of confusion here. It has been said that those "taken" from the field and the mill are being "taken" by the "flood of judgment." In other words, being taken is a bad thing. Those who believe this say that the ones that are taken are not actually being caught up to meet the Lord in the air. Instead, they are being judged, and as faithful believers it should be our desire to be "left." This is because of the following phrasing, "…and knew it not until the *flood came, and took* them all away…then shall two be in the field; the one shall be _taken_, and the other left" (Matthew 24:39-40).

In order to understand that we _want_ to be taken, we have to understand the Greek phrasing here. The word _took_ in reference to the flood has a different connotation in the Greek language than the word translated "taken," when referring to those in the field and at the mill. They actually have opposite meanings. The word _took_ in verse 39 of Matthew 24 comes from the word _airo_ and means to take up or away, to put away, or to remove. Think of picking up some trash from the floor and putting it in the garbage. In contrast the word _taken_ in verses 40 and 41 of Matthew 24 comes from the Greek word _paralambano_ and means to receive near, associate oneself with (in any familiar or intimate act or relation), and to take unto. Think of picking up a cherished child and holding him or her close to your chest as you comfort them. This means that while the flood is going to put away wickedness, God is going to bring those counted worthy near to him. In short, I want to be taken!

Referencing the Coming Sheep Nations

Additionally, it is the author's conviction that when Jesus acknowledges that there will be mills and fields it is a _direct reference_ to the sheep nations that will arise to house and protect the people of God in the last days. This is a very new idea for many, but not for Scripture. Rest assured there will be more to come later in this book. Suffice it to say for now that there are many Scriptures that speak to God's provision in the midst of tribulation, not the least of which involves what God did for the Israelites in Goshen while he poured out judgments upon Egypt.

"And I will sever in that day the land of Goshen, in which my people dwell, that no swarms of flies shall be there; to the end thou mayest know that I am the LORD in the midst of the earth" (Exodus 8:22).

"Only in the land of Goshen, where the children of Israel were, was there no hail" (Exodus 9:26).

"And the blood shall be to you for a token upon the houses where ye are: and when I see the blood, I will pass over you, and the plague shall not be upon you to destroy you, when I smite the land of Egypt" (Exodus 12:13).

In addition, Psalm 91 contains a wealth of promises regarding the provision of God against all of the tribulation the enemy would try to vault at us. Consider the following caption:

"I will say of the LORD, He is my refuge and my fortress: my God; in him will I trust. Surely he shall deliver thee from the snare of the fowler, and from the noisome pestilence" (Psalm 91:2-3).

Jesus also tells us to pray, not that we will be taken, but to pray *so that* when he returns we are counted worthy to escape all these things. We are commanded to be filled with the Spirit, the connation meaning continually filled all of the time. Our prayer is not only intended to be for petition and supplication, but for the very infilling of the glory of God.

"And be not drunk with wine, wherein is excess; but be filled with the Spirit" (Ephesians 5:18).

This is the end of the harmonized Olivet discourse. What will follow will be an analysis of one of the most difficult and sobering messages in all of scripture: the judgment seat of Christ.

PART 5

CHAPTER 20

The Context of Parables

Now that we have harmonized the three accounts of the Olivet discourse, we will discuss the rest of what Jesus shared. After Jesus finished describing the catching away of the church, he began to explain how everything would work from that point forward. Primarily taken from Matthew, this part of the narrative has proven to be elusive to the church for generations. The problem has been that these parables can only be understood within the context of the eschatological view that the interpreter holds. Understandably, few have ever recorded interpretations that follow a kingdom paradigm.

As we begin to tackle these parables, I will not waste time attempting to debunk other views. I will simply interpret these parables according to the paradigm that we have developed, and allow the Scriptures to stand for themselves. The first parable is about the goodman at the coming of Jesus, and we'll be looking at it in both Matthew's account and Mark's account. This parable is only a few verses long, but serves as an introduction for the parables to come. This parable is a warning, which is a fitting introduction:

THOSE APPOINTED TO WATCH

"For the Son of Man is as a man taking a far journey, who left his house, and gave authority to his servants, and to every man his work, and commanded the porter to watch. Watch ye therefore: for ye know not when the master of the house cometh, at even, or at midnight, or at the cockcrowing, or in the morning: Lest coming suddenly he find you sleeping. And what I say unto you I say unto all, Watch" (Mark 13:34-37).

"But know this, that if the goodman of the house had known in what watch the thief would come, he would have watched, and would not have suffered his house to be broken up. Therefore be ye also ready: for in such an hour as ye think not the Son of man cometh" (Matthew 24:43-44).

Let us begin by defining the parabolic elements of these statements. In Mark, the Son of Man leaves his servants, which are the saints, to do their appointed work. He sets a porter over the house to watch over the saints, thus the porter represents the five-fold ministry that Jesus has appointed to watch over his flock. In Matthew, the goodman of the house represents the five-fold ministry that Jesus has appointed to watch over his people. This can be harmonized with the porter in Mark's account. They represent the shepherds of the flock.

The thief in Matthew's account is not Jesus. Although Jesus comes like a thief in the night to the unbelievers and the unprepared, *he never refers to himself as a thief*. There is a big difference between calling oneself a thief, and simply using the word to describe the actions that one is carrying out. Jesus is the Master of the house. The thief is none other than the accuser of the brethren, Satan himself. The house represents the house of God.

"The thief [Satan] cometh not, but for to steal, and to kill, and to destroy: I [Jesus] am come that they might have life, and that they might have it more abundantly" (John 10:10).

A NOTABLE WARNING

Jesus gives a warning in the parable. He warns those who have been delegated leadership over the house of God. Jesus is going to hold the shepherds responsible for their spheres of influence at his coming. If they do not watch, the house that they are set over will be broken up by the efforts of Satan. Jesus reminds us that he is coming at an hour (not month, or year) that we are not expecting. Mark makes this inarguably clear when he writes, "For ye know not when the master of the house cometh, at even, or at midnight, or at the cockcrowing, or in the morning."

Now, we will analyze the parallel that these particular passages find in Old Testament law. This parable is based upon a law of the Mosaic Covenant.

If a man shall deliver unto his neighbour money or stuff to keep, and it be stolen out of the man's house; if the thief be found, let him pay double. If the thief be not found, then the master of the house shall be brought unto the judges, to see whether he have put his hand unto his neighbour's goods. For all manner of trespass, whether it be for ox, for ass, for sheep, for raiment, or for any manner of lost thing which another challengeth to be his, the cause of both parties shall come before the judges; and whom the judges shall condemn, he shall pay double unto his neighbour.

(Exodus 22:7-9)

How does this all come together? Jesus is like the man who has delivered up goods (members of his flock) to his neighbor (meaning his officer/leader/goodman/porter). If the thief attempts to steal the goods but is caught, the thief must pay double. This is the restoration and increase of God that is continually granted to the ministry of the faithful and watchful leaders in the body of Christ. This is also reflected in the restoration of first love within backslidden and lukewarm groups of believers. In the following passage, God is calling to repentance those who had lost their first love:

"Nevertheless I have somewhat against thee, because thou hast left thy first love. Remember therefore from whence thou art fallen, and repent, and do the first works; or else I will come unto thee quickly, and will remove thy candlestick out of his place, except thou repent" (Revelation 2:4-5).

If the thief is not found, the neighbor is taken before the judges, that there may be a judgment made between the parties. Jesus cannot have judgment made against him since he is also the Judge, and so in the parallel, any leader found with a broken house will be guilty. God does not appreciate it when the saints are lost due to unwatchful stewards. In the end, many of these will be the leaders of the "virgins" who are not found worthy to be taken. We'll be looking more at this later, but suffice it to say that there will be justice.

Setting a Timeframe

This parable is pretty straightforward. However, the passages to come are extremely difficult, and contain some of the most difficult truths in the Bible. Unfortunately, what Jesus is communicating is far too often lost in translation. We must establish the parabolic context. In other words, before we begin we must understand the events that are providing context for the parables. These events involve the second coming of Jesus, the resurrection of the dead, the judgment seat of Christ, and the setting up of the millennial kingdom. The parables will actually describe what takes place in the seventy-five day period following the end of Daniel's seventieth week, according to Daniel 12:11-12.

"And from the time that the daily sacrifice shall be taken away, and the abomination that maketh desolate set up, there shall be a thousand two hundred and ninety days. Blessed is he that waiteth, and cometh to the thousand three hundred and five and thirty days [1,335 days – 1,260 days = 75 days]" (Daniel 12:11-12).

THE JUDGMENT SEAT OF CHRIST

We have already set the foundation for understanding the second coming of Jesus and the rapture, but what is the judgment seat of Christ, and what does it have to do with these parables? The term "judgment seat of Christ" is coined by the apostle Paul and used on only two occasions in the Bible. He uses it to explain a time when the saints will have to stand before Jesus and give an account of all they did, being judged for the things done in the flesh. Some people believe that once we are saved we simply die and go to heaven, this being the end of the matter. This theory could not be further from the truth.

"But why dost thou judge thy brother? or why dost thou set at nought thy brother? for we shall all stand before the **judgment seat of Christ**" (Romans 14:10).

"For we must all appear before the **judgment seat of Christ**; that every one may receive the things done in his body, according to that he hath done, whether it be good or bad" (2 Corinthians 5:10).

Could the Bible be any more straightforward? When the saints stand before the judgment seat of Christ we will receive judgment for the things done in our body, whether *good or bad*. This understanding is foundational for the coming parables. However, before moving forward, we are going to discuss the difference between the two judgments of God. This will eliminate any confusion. The first is the judgment seat of Christ, which will occur shortly after the battle of Armageddon. It will actually occur on Mount Zion in Jerusalem, where thrones are set up after the battle of Armageddon. Here, Jesus will be the Judge because he is the Christ.

THE GREAT WHITE THRONE

The second judgment is the Great White Throne Judgment which occurs at the end of the millennial rule. The millennial rule is the thousand-year period during which Jesus rules with a rod of iron. This occurs after he redeems earth. Thus, the judgment seat of Christ and the Great White Throne Judgment are separated by a one-thousand-year interval. Jesus judges the saints and those who survive Armageddon at the judgment seat of Christ. God the Father judges the rest of the dead at the Great White Throne Judgment. At this judgment, the nations of the earth that come into being during the millennium will be dealt with as well.

Beginning with the Seventh Trumpet

With this said, let us continue to establish context for the coming parables. We will begin our journey at the seventh trumpet. This is what is written:

> And the seventh angel sounded; and there were great voices in heaven, saying, The kingdoms of this world are become the kingdoms of our Lord, and of his Christ; and he shall reign for ever and ever. And the four and twenty elders, which sat before God on their seats, fell upon their faces, and worshipped God, Saying, We give thee thanks, O Lord God Almighty, which art, and wast, and art to come; because thou hast taken to thee thy great power, and hast reigned. And the nations were angry, and thy wrath is come, and the time of the dead, that they should be judged, and that thou shouldest give reward unto thy servants the prophets, and to the saints, and them that fear thy name, small and great; and shouldest destroy them which destroy the earth.
>
> (Revelation 11:15-18)

When the seventh angel sounds Jesus comes to finish the work of transforming the kingdoms of this world into his kingdom. He is the stone cut without hands that strikes the fifth world power and sets up an ever-lasting kingdom (Daniel 2:44). This work of transforming the kingdoms of the world begins with the church, as they herald the gospel of the kingdom as a witness to all nations. Jesus comes to finish the job. In this passage, the impending wrath of God refers to the bowls (or vials) of wrath that will be poured out according to Revelation 16.

Another important aspect of this passage is when it speaks of, "the time of the dead, that they should be judged, and that thou shouldest give reward unto thy servants the prophets, and to the saints, and them that fear thy name, small and great; and shouldest destroy them which destroy the earth." Pay close attention to this. Firstly, there is a reference to the resurrection of the dead which occurs at the coming of Christ, immediately preceding the rapture. Secondly, there is a reference to the judgment seat of Christ which will shortly take place. Rewards are given to the prophets (those who lived before Jesus came), the saints, and those who fear the name of Jesus. Three groups receive reward. There is a difference between those who fear the name of Jesus and the saints. Then there is another group that is destroyed. Who is this group that is destroyed at the judgment seat of Christ? This will be answered later in the book.

JERUSALEM AT THE RETURN OF JESUS

The judgment seat of Christ occurs after the second coming of Jesus. Is there any further information that we can gather about its timing? For instance, can we know if it occurs before or after the battle of Armageddon?

In Zechariah chapter 14, we learn that Jerusalem will be under siege by the time Jesus arrives during his war campaign. His war campaign takes place after he has already returned, meaning after the seventh trumpet. This is the record:

"Behold, the day of the LORD cometh, and thy spoil shall be divided in the midst of thee. For I will gather all nations against Jerusalem to battle; and the city shall be taken, and the houses rifled, and the women ravished; and half of the city shall go forth into captivity, and the residue of the people shall not be cut off from the city. Then shall the LORD go forth, and fight against those nations, as when he fought in the day of battle" (Zechariah 14:1-3).

During the day of the Lord, the nations are gathered together against Jerusalem to battle. The antichrist establishes his throne in the midst of Jerusalem (possibly in the temple) at the midpoint of Daniel's seventieth week, but he has left by the time the day of the Lord arrives. In my first book, I pointed out that he is probably motivated to leave because of the revival that erupts when the two witnesses are raised to life at the end of the great tribulation.

And after three days and an half the spirit of life from God entered into them [the two witnesses], and they stood upon their feet; and great fear fell upon them which saw them. And they heard a great voice from heaven saying unto them, Come up hither. And they ascended up to heaven in a cloud; and their enemies beheld them. And the same hour was there a great earthquake, and the tenth part of the city fell, and in the earthquake were slain of men seven thousand: **and the remnant were affrighted, and gave glory to the God of heaven.**

(Revelation 11:11-13)

When the antichrist leaves Jerusalem, it would make sense that he is wrathful and immediately begins to execute vengeance. Regardless of the mechanism, Jerusalem is under siege when Jesus arrives to set the Jewish remnant free. This is when he stands on the Mount of Olives, causing it to split so that the inhabitants can flee. As the passage continues below, we find that the saints are also with Jesus. This is a reference to us operating as the army of God during the day of the Lord. Jesus prophesied in Matthew 23:39 that Jerusalem would not see him again until the inhabitants said, "Blessed is He who comes in the name of the Lord." This will certainly be true on this day.

And his feet shall stand in that day upon the mount of Olives, which is before Jerusalem on the east, and the mount of Olives shall cleave in the midst thereof toward the east and toward the west, and there shall be a very great valley; and half of the mountain shall remove toward the north, and half of it toward the south. And ye shall flee to the valley of the mountains; for the valley of the mountains shall reach unto Azal: yea, ye shall flee, like as ye fled from before the earthquake in the days of Uzziah king of Judah: and the LORD my God shall come, and all the saints with thee.

(Zechariah 14:4-5)

TRANSLATING TO ARMAGEDDON

After setting the captives free, the army of God proceeds north to the valley of Megiddo, from where the siege has been mounted. The end-time kings have been gathered here, along with their armies, according to the events associated with the sixth bowl.

And the sixth angel poured out his vial upon the great river Euphrates; and the water thereof was dried up, that the way of the kings of the east might be prepared. And I saw three unclean spirits like frogs come out of the mouth of the dragon, and out of the mouth of the beast, and out of the mouth of the false prophet. For they are the spirits of devils, working miracles, which go forth unto the kings of the earth and of the whole world, to gather them to the battle of that great day of God Almighty. Behold, I come as a thief. Blessed is he that watcheth, and keepeth his garments, lest he walk naked, and they see his shame. And he gathered them together into a place called in the Hebrew tongue Armageddon.

(Revelation 16:12-16)

Traveling across land is a thing of the past at this point. The valley of Megiddo is a few miles north of Jerusalem. Jesus simply opens up a dimensional portal to translate us there. By using the word *translate* I am describing the transfer of individuals from one time-space to another by removal into the spirit realm and reinsertion into the natural realm. Heaven opens onto the field where the battle of Armageddon is appointed to take place. The army of God steps through this portal, and the slaughter begins:

And I **<u>saw heaven opened</u>**, and behold a white horse; and he that sat upon him was called Faithful and True, and in righteousness he doth judge and make war. His eyes were as a flame of fire, and on his head were many crowns; and he had a name written, that no man knew, but he himself. And he was clothed with a vesture dipped in blood: and his name is called The Word of God. And the armies which were in heaven followed him upon white horses, clothed in fine linen, white and clean. And out of his mouth goeth a sharp sword, that with it he should smite the nations: and he shall rule them with a rod of iron: and he treadeth the winepress of the fierceness and wrath of Almighty God. And he hath on his vesture and on his thigh a name written, KING OF KINGS, AND LORD OF LORDS. And I saw an angel standing in the sun; and he cried with a loud voice, saying to all the fowls that fly in the midst of heaven, Come and gather yourselves together unto the supper of the great God; That ye may eat the flesh of kings, and the flesh of captains, and the flesh of mighty men, and the flesh of horses, and of them that sit on them, and the flesh of all men, both free and bond, both small and great. And I saw the beast, and the kings of the earth, and their armies, gathered together to make war against him that sat on the horse, and against his army. And the beast was taken, and with him the false prophet that wrought miracles before him, with which he deceived them that had received the mark of the beast, and them that worshipped his image. These both were cast alive into a lake of fire burning with brimstone. And the remnant were slain with the sword of him that sat upon the horse, which sword proceeded out of his mouth: and all the fowls were filled with their flesh.

(Revelation 19:11-21)

At the battle of Armageddon, the beast and false prophet are taken and cast alive into the lake of fire. Everyone is destroyed by the two-edged sword that comes out of the mouth of Jesus. Afterwards, the fowls of the air eat up the remains of the dead. It is truly a gruesome picture. We can pick up the story in the book of Isaiah.

BACK TO JERUSALEM

"And it shall come to pass in that day, that the LORD shall punish the host of the high ones that are on high, and the kings of the earth upon the earth. And they shall be gathered together, as prisoners are gathered in the pit, and shall be shut up in the prison, and after many days shall they be visited. Then the moon shall be confounded, and the sun ashamed, when the LORD of hosts shall reign in mount Zion, and in Jerusalem, and before his ancients gloriously" (Isaiah 24:21-23).

It is apparent from this passage that God cleans out Jerusalem in order to reign in it. As a matter of fact, it appears as though God moves the antichrist out so that he can move in. Then God sets up his throne upon the earth, in Mount Zion and in Jerusalem. This will happen at some point after Armageddon. It is at this point that the judgment seat of Christ begins. We find a reference to this event in the book of Daniel.

I beheld till the thrones were cast down, and the Ancient of days did sit, whose garment was white as snow, and the hair of his head like the pure wool: his throne was like the fiery flame, and his wheels as burning fire. A fiery stream issued and came forth from before him: thousand thousands ministered unto him, and ten thousand times ten thousand stood before him: the judgment was set, and the books were opened... I saw in the night visions, and, behold, one like the Son of man came with the clouds of heaven, and came to the Ancient of days, and they brought him near before him. And there was given him dominion, and glory, and a kingdom, that all people, nations, and languages, should serve him: his dominion is an everlasting dominion, which shall not pass away, and his kingdom that which shall not be destroyed.

(Daniel 7:9-10, 13-14)

God has crushed Satan under our feet at Armageddon, punished the host of the high ones that are on high, punished the kings of the earth, delivered the remnant, set up his thrones, and opened the books. Why are books being opened in Daniel 7:10? *This is the beginning of the judgment seat of Christ*, occurring after the battle of Armageddon upon Mount Zion in Jerusalem. As we observe from the text, Jesus (described as one like the Son of man) is brought to the Ancient of Days and dominion is given to him.

FROM THE JUDGMENT SEAT OF CHRIST TO THE GREAT WHITE THRONE

Returning to the book of Revelation, we are going to finish off the story leading up to the Great White Throne Judgment. Fortunately, this story is more or less a straightforward narrative, whereas the judgment seat of Christ is somewhat obscure. The rest of the story begins where we left off in the book of Revelation. It begins with yet another reference to the judgment seat of Christ, because it discusses that judgment is given to the saints. Afterwards, it will discuss the millennial rule of Christ, which is followed by the Great White Throne Judgment.

And I saw an angel come down from heaven, having the key of the bottomless pit and a great chain in his hand. And he laid hold on the dragon, that old serpent, which is the Devil, and Satan, and bound him a thousand years, And cast him into the bottomless pit, and shut him up, and set a seal upon him, that he should deceive the nations no more, till the thousand years should be fulfilled: and after that he must be loosed a little season. **And I saw thrones, and they sat upon them [the thrones], and judgment was given unto them [the saints]:** and I saw the souls of them that were beheaded for the witness of Jesus, and for the word of God, and which had not worshipped the beast, neither his image, neither had received his mark upon their foreheads, or in their hands; and they lived and reigned with Christ a thousand years. But the rest of the dead lived not again until the thousand years were finished. This is the first resurrection. Blessed and holy is he that hath part in the first resurrection: on such the second death hath no power, but they shall be priests of God and of Christ, and shall reign with him a thousand years. And when the thousand years are expired, Satan shall be loosed out of his prison, And shall go out to deceive the nations which are in the four quarters of the earth, Gog, and Magog, to gather them together to battle: the number of whom is as the sand of the sea. And they went up on the breadth of the earth, and compassed the camp of the saints about, and the beloved city: and fire came down from God out of heaven, and devoured them. And the devil that deceived them was cast into the lake of fire and brimstone, where the beast and the false prophet are, and shall be tormented day and night for ever and ever. **And I saw a great white throne**, and him that sat on it, from whose face the earth and the heaven fled away; and there was found no place for them. And I saw the dead, small and great, stand before God; and the books were opened: and another book was opened, which is the book of life: and the dead were judged out of those things which were written in the books, according to their works. And the sea gave up the dead which were in it; and death and hell delivered up the dead which were in them: and they were judged every man according to their works. And death and hell were cast into the lake of fire. This is the second death. And whosoever was not found written in the book of life was cast into the lake of fire.

(Revelation 20)

It is clear that the two judgments are separated by a one-thousand-year interval. After Armageddon, only the antichrist and the false prophet are cast into the lake of fire. The fallen spirit beings, including Satan, "the host of the high ones on high" and the kings of the earth are all locked in the pit according to the Bible (Isaiah 24:21-22, Revelation 20:1-3). Jesus does not deal with them during his judgment. He judges the prophets, the saints, those who fear God, and those who destroy the earth. The fallen spirit beings, along with Satan, will be cast into the lake of fire immediately before the Great White Throne Judgment. This will only occur after Satan is loosed at the end of the millennial reign. Afterwards, whoever is not found written in the Book of Life at the Great White Throne Judgment will also be cast into the lake of fire.

The understanding of the judgment seat of Christ is pivotal for understanding the coming parables. With the proper foundation, we can effectively continue.

CHAPTER 21

The Parable of the Faithful and Wicked Servants

Who then is a faithful and wise servant, whom his lord hath made ruler over his household, to give them meat in due season? Blessed is that servant, whom his lord when he cometh shall find so doing. Verily I say unto you, That he shall make him ruler over all his goods. But and if that evil servant shall say in his heart, My lord delayeth his coming; And shall begin to smite his fellowservants, and to eat and drink with the drunken; The lord of that servant shall come in a day when he looketh not for him, and in an hour that he is not aware of, And shall cut him asunder, and appoint him his portion with the hypocrites: there shall be weeping and gnashing of teeth.

(Matthew 24:45-51)

Two Kinds of Servants

The very first thing we must understand is that there are two kinds of servants. Jesus declares this from the outset of this parable. He reveals that there are faithful and wise servants, and there are evil servants. Both are servants of God. In order to be a servant of God under the New Covenant, one must be saved by grace through faith in Jesus Christ (Ephesians 2:8). Both groups of servants are individuals that have received Jesus as Lord, but their obedience determines their status.

This parable is a continuation of the former parable regarding the goodman set over the house of God. As we will find, each of the following parables builds on the revelation revealed in the former parables. A cursory reading of this parable and the three parables of Matthew chapter 25 can appear to describe the same event. The truth is that they progressively reveal different events that occur during and after the return of Jesus Christ.

Faithful and Wise Servants

In this parable, God questions who is a wise and faithful servant. The Lord of the house is Jesus Christ. The meat is the solid food of the word that has been appointed to be given to the people of God in due season.

"But **strong meat** belongeth to them that are of full age, even those who by reason of use have their senses exercised to discern both good and evil" (Hebrews 5:14).

God wants the servants set over his house to ensure that those in his body are brought to maturity. The servants are appointed to give meat in due season. God commands a blessing upon those who are involved in this ministry at his coming. Remember that this parable deals with the time of Jesus' return. Those who are not involved in this activity at his coming have failed him, because his coming requires the manifestation of a bride who has "come in the unity of the faith, and of the knowledge of the Son of God, unto a perfect man, unto the measure of the stature of the fulness of Christ" (Ephesians 4:13).

The parable continues to define the blessing that God commands upon the faithful and wise servants at his coming. They are promised rulership over all the Lord's "goods." The rewards of God are not material, but positional. This will become more apparent as we move forward.

Evil Servants

The remainder of this particular parable deals strictly with the wicked servants. These are synonymous with the goodmen over the house that the thief breaks up. They fail to watch, and the Son of Man returns at an hour that they do not expect. This parable explains that these leaders conclude that Jesus has delayed his coming. This means that they believe that Jesus should have already come, and doubt him because he has not come yet.

For this reason they begin to smite their fellow servants. This prophecy describes the falling away of leaders in the body of Christ during the time of the end. These leaders not only fall away, but turn on the faithful leaders and attack them. They will give themselves over to wickedness in order to make war within the body of Christ. They will be driven by feelings of betrayal, as they will assume that God has abandoned them. It goes on to explain that they will fall into sin, as they will eat and drink with the drunken. They will not have what it takes to lead under the circumstances that are to be revealed.

The parable concludes that the Lord will come at an hour that the evil servants do not expect. They will be cut asunder and have a portion appointed with the hypocrites. What does this mean? The phrase "cut asunder" comes from the Greek word *dichotomeo,* and literally means to bisect, and by extension, to flog severely. The evil servants will suffer severe punishment.

CHAPTER 22

Clarifying Kingdom Terminology

The parable of the ten virgins contains the next paradigm-shaking revelation from the Olivet discourse. However, before we tackle that parable, we must make a distinction. Both of the forthcoming parables (the parable of the ten virgins and the parable of the talents) will utilize the phrase "the kingdom of heaven." This book is unashamedly centered on the message of God's kingdom. However, we cannot truly understand what the kingdom message is until we address the question: Is the *kingdom of heaven* the same thing as the *kingdom of God*?

ESTABLISHING THE FALSE PREMISE

It has been suggested by many theologians that a distinction is to be made between these two kingdoms. For instance, the Scofield Reference Bible has this theological approach written right into the footnotes. It has been said that the *kingdom of heaven* includes the sphere of Christian profession (both saved and unsaved) while the *kingdom of God* specifically deals with the true believers. This chapter will establish that this is a false premise. It will prove that we can conclude the matter as follows: ONE KINGDOM, ONE KING.

In order to prove this we are going to systematically compare and contrast passages from the synoptic gospels that interchange these terms. This is extremely important because if we allow ourselves to fall into the trap of defining the *kingdom of heaven* and *the kingdom of God* as separate kingdoms, we will ultimately lose the power of the kingdom message. Furthermore, it will become impossible to properly address the parables dealing with the kingdom, because we will approach them out of a wrong paradigm. Wrong paradigms will almost always lead to wrong conclusions.

JOHN THE BAPTIST, JESUS, AND THE KINGDOM

We will begin our journey with John the Baptist. John was the forerunner of Jesus Christ. He went forth to proclaim the coming of the Messiah. His message was straightforward and to the point. This is what he said:

"Repent ye: for the **kingdom of heaven** is at hand" (Matthew 3:2).

John the Baptist was, in essence, preaching the message of the kingdom. Isn't it interesting that he wasn't preaching the gospel of Jesus Christ? He said that the reason for repentance was to make way for the coming of

God's kingdom. We find that this was also the message that Jesus preached. Jesus didn't preach the gospel of Jesus Christ; he preached the kingdom.

"From that time on Jesus began to preach, Repent, for the **kingdom of heaven** is near"(Matthew 4:17).

This is where we will find our first harmonization of terms. In the exact same depiction of Jesus, Mark explains the message that Jesus preached:

"Now after that John was put in prison, Jesus came into Galilee, preaching the gospel of the kingdom of God, And saying, The time is fulfilled, and the **kingdom of God** is at hand: repent ye, and believe the gospel" (Mark 1:14-15).

If we are to believe that the *kingdom of heaven* and *the kingdom of God* are two different kingdoms, we run into a problem. In essence, the question forcibly arises: Which kingdom did Jesus preach? Did he preach *the kingdom of heaven* or *the kingdom of God*? Furthermore, which kingdom was near? If they were both "near" or "at hand," where does the Bible explain the mechanics of how Jesus separately manifested two kingdoms through his ministry? Of course, when we understand them to be the same kingdom, these questions disappear and we are left with one simple truth: ONE KINGDOM, ONE KING. Let us look at the next example.

The Poor and the Kingdom

"Blessed are the poor in spirit, for theirs is **the kingdom of heaven**" (Matthew 5:3).

"And he lifted up his eyes on his disciples, and said, Blessed be ye poor: for yours is **the kingdom of God**" (Luke 6:20).

During the famous Sermon on the Mount, Jesus set out to change the way the world thought. This monologue is full of many of the most profound sayings ever recorded in history. In the midst of everything that Jesus explains, he says that the poor are blessed because "theirs is the kingdom." In Matthew's account, the poor inherit *the kingdom of heaven*. In Luke's account, the poor inherit *the kingdom of God*. If the kingdoms are different, which kingdom do the poor inherit? The synoptic gospels have again blurred the distinction between *the kingdom of God* and *the kingdom of heaven*. Why? The fact of the matter is that they are the same kingdom: ONE KINGDOM, ONE KING.

The Patriarchs and the Kingdom

Consider this question: which kingdom did Abraham, Isaac and Jacob retire to, *the kingdom of God* or *the kingdom of heaven*?

"I tell you, many will come from east and west, and will sit at table with **Abraham, Isaac and Jacob in the kingdom of heaven**"(Matthew 8:11 AMP).

"There shall be weeping and gnashing of teeth, when ye shall see **Abraham, and Isaac, and Jacob**, and all the prophets, **in the kingdom of God**, and you yourselves thrust out. And they shall come from the east, and from the west, and from the north, and from the south, and shall sit down in the kingdom of God" (Luke 13:28-29).

Do Abraham, Isaac and Jacob have the burden of being eternally caught between two kingdoms? No. Again, we see that the same kingdom is being referred to as both *the kingdom of heaven* and *the kingdom of God*. The synoptic gospel writers do not maintain a consistent division between these two terms. Instead they treat *the kingdom of God* and *the kingdom of heaven* as the same thing: ONE KINGDOM, ONE KING.

THE DISCIPLES PREACH THE KINGDOM

After three examples, an undeniable pattern begins to arise. However, there are many more instances of the overlapping of kingdom terminology throughout the synoptic gospels. For instance, when Jesus sent out his disciples, he commissioned them to preach the kingdom.

"And as ye go, preach, saying, **The kingdom of heaven** is at hand. Heal the sick, cleanse the lepers, raise the dead, cast out devils: freely ye have received, freely give."(Matthew 10:7-8).

"Then he called his twelve disciples together, and gave them power and authority over all devils, and to cure diseases. And he sent them to preach **the kingdom of God**, and to heal the sick" (Luke 9:1-2).

As we can straightforwardly see, Jesus is depicted in the same scene by both gospel writers. They are not writing about two different people named Jesus who said two different things at two different times. They are telling the same story, which is the reason why these gospels are called synoptic. In this scene, the terms *kingdom of God* and *kingdom of heaven* are interchanged because as far as the gospels are concerned, both terms are referring to the same kingdom. ONE KINGDOM, ONE KING.

MANY MORE EXAMPLES

To avoid being overly repetitive the following table will illustrate additional passages that harmonize the terms *kingdom of heaven* and *kingdom of God*.

Kingdom of Heaven	Kingdom of God
Matthew 11:11-12	Luke 7:28
Matthew 13:11	Mark 4:11, Luke 8:10
Matthew 18:3-4, Matthew 19:14	Mark 10:14-15, Luke 18:16-17
Matthew 19:23	Matthew 19:24, Mark 10:23-25, Luke 18:24-25
Matthew 13:31	Mark 4:30

THE KINGDOM OF THE SON

Now that we have established that *the kingdom of God* and *the kingdom of heaven* are two terminologies describing the same kingdom, we can touch on a few other potential difficulties. Besides being referred to as the *kingdom of God* and the *kingdom of heaven*, we also find terms such as *the kingdom of the Son* and *the kingdom of the Father*. Are these additional terms describing the same kingdom as well? Consider the following passages:

"For the Son of man shall come in the glory of his Father with his angels; and then he shall reward every man according to his works. Verily I say unto you, There be some standing here, which shall not taste of death, till they see **the Son of man coming in his kingdom**" (Matthew 16:27-28).

"For whosoever shall be ashamed of me and of my words, of him shall the Son of man be ashamed, when he shall come in his own glory, and in his Father's, and of the holy angels. But I tell you of a truth, there be some standing here, which shall not taste of death, till they see **the kingdom of God**" (Luke 9:26-27).

These two passages give us the evidence that we need to accurately conclude that *the kingdom of God* is synonymous with *the kingdom of the Son*. Moreover, since the case has been made that the *kingdom of God* is synonymous with the *kingdom of heaven*, it follows that *the kingdom of the Son* is synonymous with *the kingdom of heaven*. In short: ONE KINGDOM, ONE KING. This is very important, because the whole message of the kingdom hinges on the proper understanding of *the kingdom of the Son*.

"Who hath delivered us from the power of darkness, and hath translated us into **the kingdom of his dear Son**" (Colossians 1:13).

When we understand that the only way into the *kingdom of the Son* is through spiritual translation, we set the parameters necessary for properly interpreting kingdom parables. The only kingdom parables that aren't exclusive to the true born-again church deal with the time frame after the return of Jesus Christ. It will be at that time that the kingdoms of this world have already become God's kingdoms according to Revelation 11:15. Therefore, the wicked will have to be cast out of the world. The only parables that require this understanding are the *parable of the wheat and the tares* and *the parable of the net*, both found in Matthew 13.

THE KINGDOM OF THE FATHER

In any case, in order to address *the kingdom of the Father* we must keep something in mind. The fact of the matter is that as Christians, we serve the triune God. We do not have three Gods, we have one, and Jesus makes this blatantly clear.

"I and my Father are one" (John 10:30).

When we try to differentiate *the kingdom of the Father* from *the kingdom of the Son*, we will run into problems, because they are the same God. Nonetheless, certain passages seem to hint at the idea that the Father and the Son have different kingdoms. It can be deduced from these passages that the Son's kingdom comes first, and the Father's kingdom comes second.

"Then cometh the end, **when he [Jesus] shall have delivered up the kingdom to God, even the Father**; when he shall have put down all rule and all authority and power. **For he must reign, till he hath put all enemies under his feet. The last enemy that shall be destroyed is death**" (1 Corinthians 15:24-26).

According to this passage, Jesus must reign in his kingdom until death has been destroyed. According to Revelation 20:14 death isn't destroyed until the end of the millennial reign, which is the thousand-year period during which Jesus rules the earth with a rod of iron (Revelation 19:15). Therefore, it has been concluded that Jesus brings his kingdom first, and then his Father's kingdom comes after the millennial reign is over. However, the fact of the matter is that the Father and the Son are one. Moreover, *the kingdom of the Father* is actually made synonymous with *the kingdom of God* by the gospel writers.

"For this is my blood of the new testament, which is shed for many for the remission of sins. But I say unto you, I will not drink henceforth of this fruit of the vine, until that day when I drink it new with you in **my Father's kingdom**"(Matthew 26:28-29).

"Verily I say unto you, I will drink no more of the fruit of the vine, until that day that I drink it new in **the kingdom of God**"(Mark 14:25).

ONE KINGDOM, ONE KING

Since the gospel writers clearly exchange the term *the Father's kingdom* for *the kingdom of God*; and since it's been proven that *the kingdom of God* is synonymous with both *the kingdom of heaven* and *the kingdom of the Son,* we are back to our original conclusion: ONE KINGDOM, ONE KING. In order to solve the potential issue created by 1 Corinthians 15, we can simply conclude that the primary person of the Godhead manifesting as King will shift. The kingdom stays the same, and the members of it are also the same.

CHAPTER 23

Thy Kingdom Came

Now that we have established that *the kingdom of God* and *the king-dom of heaven* are the same thing, we must address an equally important question, namely, "How did the kingdom arrive?" I dealt with this topic thoroughly in my book *Noah's Ark and the End of Days*. The rest of this chapter will be an adapted reprint of this teaching.

We must understand that before there was the gospel of Jesus Christ, there was the gospel of the kingdom. It is the gospel of the king-dom that Jesus preached before he was crucified.

"And Jesus went about all the cities and villages, teaching in their synagogues, and preaching **the gospel of the kingdom**, and healing every sickness and every disease among the people" (Matthew 9:35).

No Jesus, No Kingdom

There is no kingdom gospel without Jesus Christ. The kingdom exists *within us* when we receive Jesus Christ as our Lord and Savior. The kingdom of God is the culture of heaven infiltrating the earth through his people. It is his kingdom, and he is the King.

Nebuchadnezzar's Dream

When did this kingdom arrive? We will begin our story in the book of Daniel, when Daniel is giving the interpretation of Babylonian King Nebuchadnezzar's dream:

> Thou, O king, sawest, and behold a great image. This great image, whose brightness was excellent, stood before thee; and the form thereof was terrible. This image's head was of fine gold, his breast and his arms of silver, his belly and his thighs of brass, His legs of iron, his feet part of iron and part of clay. Thou sawest till that a stone was cut out without hands, which smote the image upon his feet that were of iron and clay, and brake them to pieces. Then was the iron, the clay, the brass, the silver, and the gold, broken to pieces together, and became like the chaff of the summer threshingfloors; and the wind carried them away, that no place was found for them: and the stone

that smote the image became a great mountain, and filled the whole earth.

(Daniel 2:31–35)

The interpretation of this dream explained that there would be five major world powers. From top to bottom the statue represented the chronological sequence in which they would occur. The first was the head of gold, representing the Babylonian kingdom of Nebuchadnezzar. Media-Persia was represented by the arms of silver. This world power was initially ruled by Cyrus. Greece was the world power represented by the belly and thighs of brass. Then came Rome, represented by the legs of iron. Since the fall of Rome there has never been another world power. Therefore, there is still one last kingdom to come, during which the "Stone" will "smite the image" and become a great mountain and fill the whole earth. Jesus is the Stone cut without hands (Ephesians 2:20).

We must begin by understanding that the implementation of the kingdom of God is not a singular event. Some have considered passages like the one in Daniel, and concluded that the kingdom does not come until Jesus actually returns. This simply isn't true. First of all, the Pharisees had some form of access to the kingdom (that they apparently did not use) prior to the coming of Jesus.

"But woe to you, scribes and Pharisees, pretenders (hypocrites)! For you shut the kingdom of heaven in men's faces; **for you neither enter**

yourselves, nor do you allow those who are about to go in to do so"
(Matthew 23:13 AMP).

This being said, the next major aspect of its implementation was accomplished during the first coming of Jesus at his death, burial, and resurrection. The final part of its implementation will occur at the second coming of Jesus Christ. It was during the Roman Empire that the kingdom was given spiritually to the people of God. It will be during the coming fifth world power that the kingdom of God will *literally* overtake every kingdom on earth.

THE WAR IN HEAVEN

This conversation brings us to a notable war that occurred in heaven. Prior to this war, Satan had free access to the throne of God.

"Now there was a day when the sons of God came to present themselves before the LORD [in heaven], and Satan came also among them" (Job 1:6).

This fact was changed after the war. It all begins with John the Baptist—the greatest prophet under the Old Covenant.

"Verily I say unto you, Among them that are born of women there hath not risen a greater than John the Baptist: notwithstanding he that is least in the kingdom of heaven is greater than he. **And from the days of John the Baptist until now the kingdom of heaven suffereth violence, and the violent take it by force**. For all the prophets and the law prophesied until John. And if ye will receive it, this is Elias, which was for to come. He that hath ears to hear, let him hear" (Matthew 11:11–15).

I have heard it said that *we* must take the kingdom of heaven by force, but in the context of this verse, the interpretation falls short of explaining all of the implications. It seems as though the kingdom of heaven was actually suffering violence. When Jesus said "now," he was not referring to "today," but referencing the actual day that he was speaking. This day was between the time when John the Baptist began his preaching and the three-day period involving the death, burial, and resurrection of Jesus. What violence could be brought to the kingdom of heaven? The Bible gives us a most incredible answer. A war broke out it heaven.

"And there was war in heaven: Michael and his angels fought against the dragon; and the dragon fought and his angels, And prevailed not; neither was their place found any more in heaven. And the great dragon was cast out, that old serpent, called the Devil, and Satan, which deceiveth the whole world: he was cast out into the earth, and his angels were cast out with him" (Revelation 12:7–9).

When John the Baptist began to preach, he fulfilled prophecy, becoming the forerunner of the Messiah according to Isaiah.

"The voice of him that crieth in the wilderness, Prepare ye the way of the LORD, make straight in the desert a highway for our God. Every valley shall be exalted, and every mountain and hill shall be made low: and the crooked shall be made straight, and the rough places plain: And the glory of the LORD shall be revealed, and all flesh shall see it together: for the mouth of the LORD hath spoken it" (Isaiah 40:3–5).

"In those days came John the Baptist, preaching in the wilderness of Judaea, And saying, Repent ye: for the kingdom of heaven is at hand. For this is he that was spoken of by the prophet Esaias [Isaiah], saying, The voice of one crying in the wilderness, Prepare ye the way of the Lord, make his paths straight" (Matthew 3:1–3).

This was the alarm that alerted the whole spirit realm that God was preparing to bring salvation, redeem his people, and usher in his kingdom. This is why Jesus went about preaching, "Repent! For the kingdom of heaven is at hand" (Matthew 4:17). Satan took this opportunity to begin a war in heaven that would last several years according to our time. How do we know that this passage in Revelation is in fact referring to a war that happened at that time? Why would the conclusion be drawn that Jesus is making reference to this war when he says the kingdom of heaven suffers violence? It is because of the *results* of the war.

The Results of the War

And I heard a loud voice saying in heaven, **Now is come salvation, and strength, and the kingdom of our God, and the power of his Christ**: for the accuser of our brethren is cast down, which accused them before our God day and night. And they overcame him by the blood of the Lamb, and by the word of their testimony; and they loved not their lives unto the death. Therefore rejoice, ye heavens, and ye that dwell in them. Woe to the inhabiters of the earth and of the sea! for the devil is come down unto you, having great wrath, because he knoweth that he hath but a short time.

(Revelation 12:10–12)

As it is easy to see, the results of the war are the very promises that we receive when we accept Jesus as Lord and enter into Christianity.

Salvation: "That if thou shalt confess with thy mouth the Lord Jesus, and shalt believe in thine heart that God hath raised him from the dead, thou shalt be saved. For with the heart man believeth unto righteousness; and with the mouth confession is made unto **salvation**" (Romans 10:9–10).

Strength: "And he said unto me, My grace is sufficient for thee: for my **strength** is made perfect in weakness. Most gladly therefore will I rather glory in my infirmities, that the power of Christ may rest upon me" (2 Corinthians 12:9).

"I can do all things through Christ which **strengtheneth** me" (Philippians 4:13).

Kingdom: "I John, who also am your brother, and companion in tribulation, and in the **kingdom** and patience of Jesus Christ, was in the isle that is called Patmos, for the word of God, and for the testimony of Jesus Christ" (Revelation 1:9).

"Who hath delivered us from the power of darkness, and hath translated us into the **kingdom** of his dear Son" (Colossians 1:13).

Power of His Christ: "Believe me that I am in the Father, and the Father in me: or else believe me for the very works' sake. Verily, verily, I say unto you, He that believeth on me, the works that I do shall he do also; and **greater works** than these shall he do; because I go unto my Father. And whatsoever ye shall ask in my name, that will I do, that the Father may be glorified in the Son" (John 14:11–13).

"And my speech and my preaching was not with enticing words of man's wisdom, but in demonstration of the Spirit and of **power**" (1 Corinthians 2:4).

"And he said unto me, My grace is sufficient for thee: for my strength is made perfect in weakness. Most gladly therefore will I rather glory in my infirmities, that **the power of Christ** may rest upon me" (2 Corinthians 12:9).

The Power of the Blood

Moreover, it was after this war that the saints overcame the dragon "by the blood of the Lamb and the word of their testimony" (Revelation 12:11). If we pause to consider when this became true of God-fearing individuals, it reinforces the point. The Old Testament saints did not have the blood of Christ available to them. Moreover, we don't have to wait until some future point in time to overcome the enemy by the power of the blood of the Lamb. Christians have been overcoming by the blood of the Lamb and the word of their testimony since the resurrection of Jesus! The overcoming power of the blood of Jesus continues through this day, as its power is not bound by time or space. The early church overcame by the blood of the Lamb; we overcome by the blood of the Lamb, and our children will continue to overcome by the blood of the Lamb. There is power in the blood!

"In whom we have redemption through his blood, even the forgiveness of sins" (Colossians 1:14).

THE WORK AT CALVARY

In addition to the clear fulfillment of all of these results of the war, consider the work that Jesus accomplished at Cavalry.

"And Jesus came and spake unto them, saying, **All power is given unto me** in heaven and in earth" (Matthew 28:18).

"I am he that liveth, and was dead; and, behold, I am alive for evermore, Amen; and have the **keys of hell and of death**" (Revelation 1:18).

"Blotting out the handwriting of ordinances that was against us, which was contrary to us, and took it out of the way, nailing it to his cross; **And having spoiled principalities and powers, he [Jesus] made a shew of them openly, triumphing over them in it**" (Colossians 2:14–15).

"The like figure whereunto even baptism doth also now save us (not the putting away of the filth of the flesh, but the answer of a good conscience toward God,) by the resurrection of **Jesus Christ: Who is gone into heaven, and is on the right hand of God; angels and authorities and powers being made subject unto him**" (1 Peter 3:21–22).

In the process of gaining salvation for the whole world, Jesus also did something else. He ended the war in heaven and sealed the victory. He made it so that Satan would never again have access to heaven to accuse us. An overview of the whole of Scripture reveals that the kingdom of God is here. We partake of it spiritually after we receive salvation. The final implementation will be in judgment when Jesus the "Stone" strikes the fifth world power as we see in the book of Daniel.

THE JOB MENTALITY

This is very important, because many people have a "Job" mentality. They think that Satan is constantly before God, reminding him of all the wrong that they have done. They even think that God grants Satan permission to destroy our lives when we are bad. Unfortunately, until we understand the work of the cross, we are forced to believe this. It is clearly in Scripture.

Now there was a day when the sons of God came to present themselves before the LORD, and Satan came also among them. And the LORD said unto Satan, Whence comest thou? Then Satan answered the LORD, and said, From going to and fro in the earth, and from walking up and down in it. And the LORD said unto Satan, Hast thou considered my servant Job, that there is none like him in the earth, a perfect and an upright man, one that feareth God, and escheweth evil? Then Satan answered the LORD, and said, Doth Job fear God for nought? Hast not thou made an hedge about him, and about his house, and about all that he hath on every side? thou hast blessed the work of his hands, and his substance is increased in the land. But put forth thine hand now, and touch all that he hath, and he will curse thee to thy face. **And the Lord said unto Satan, Behold, all that he hath is in thy power**; only upon himself put not forth thine hand. So Satan went forth from the presence of the Lord.

(Job 1:6–12)

The Lord himself delivered Job into the hands of Satan when Satan came before his throne. However, when we understand the cross, we can understand that Satan has absolutely no access to heaven anymore. Even after Satan was cast from heaven the first time, he still retained a degree of access. After tempting Eve in the garden, he was still coming before the throne of God thousands of years later in Job. *Jesus changed this fact.* In Revelation 12:7-8 (AMP) it says, "The dragon and his angels fought. But they were defeated, **and there was no room found for them in heaven any longer.**" Now Satan has no access to (the third) heaven; only we do. He lost every last bit of access after the victory of Jesus. Now that we have received the kingdom, *God no longer delegates power to Satan over us. God delegates power to us over Satan.*

More Power, More Authority

When we understand the power and purpose of Jesus bringing the kingdom, we can begin to operate differently. We can begin to operate with more power, authority, and expectation of God's blessings. However, we also come to the understanding that the kingdom of heaven is exclusive to the saints. Only those born again through Jesus Christ can interact with it in this age. As we proceed to the parable of the ten virgins, we will be keeping this in mind.

PART 6

CHAPTER 24

The Parable of the Ten Virgins

Then shall the kingdom of heaven be likened unto ten virgins, which took their lamps, and went forth to meet the bridegroom. And five of them were wise, and five were foolish. They that were foolish took their lamps, and took no oil with them: But the wise took oil in their vessels with their lamps. While the bridegroom tarried, they all slumbered and slept. And at midnight there was a cry made, Behold, the bridegroom cometh; go ye out to meet him. Then all those virgins arose, and trimmed their lamps. And the foolish said unto the wise, Give us of your oil; for our lamps are gone out. But the wise answered, saying, Not so; lest there be not enough for us and you: but go ye rather to them that sell, and buy for yourselves. And while they went to buy, the bridegroom came; and they that were ready went in with him to the marriage: and the door was shut. Afterward came also the other virgins, saying, Lord, Lord, open to us. But he answered and said, Verily I say unto

you, I know you not. Watch therefore, for ye know neither the
day nor the hour wherein the Son of man cometh.

(Matthew 25:1-13)

INTRODUCING THE PARABLE

In this parable, we are again at the time of the return of Jesus. It discusses the time leading up the appearing of Jesus, and then the actual catching away of the church. The kingdom of heaven is compared to virgins. Scripture reveals that the kingdom of God and the kingdom of heaven are synonymous. Remember that we cannot partake of the kingdom of God without spiritual interaction with the Holy Spirit. When we receive Jesus, the Holy Spirit becomes one with our spirit, and through this interaction we gain access to the kingdom of God. It is impossible to partake of the kingdom of God in this life if we have rejected Jesus as our Lord and Savior. This entire parable is about the saints, and by no means can any other foundation for interpreting the parable be considered.

THE VIRGINS

Jesus describes the kingdom as fifty percent wise and fifty percent foolish. Jesus has moved on from discussing the fate of his leaders at his coming. Now he is discussing individuals within his body and representing them as virgins. As we begin our exegesis, we must acknowledge that they are all called virgins—there are no whores or prostitutes. In the Bible, virgins are symbolic of purity and devotion. It must also be pointed out that the virgins are described as *wise and foolish*. Contrast this with the servants who were formerly described as faithful (and wise), or evil (Matthew 24:45-51). The words *evil* and *foolish* are very different. God holds leaders to a higher standard, but those virgins who are foolish enough to follow evil leaders will still suffer great loss.

"My brethren, be not many masters, knowing that we shall receive the greater condemnation" (James 3:1).

THE LAMPS

In this parable, the bridegroom is Jesus Christ. The kingdom of heaven, represented by virgins, goes forth to meet him. Note that all of the virgins go forth to meet Him. This is additional evidence that these are all born-again believers. If they were not, they would not be going forward to meet their bridegroom. The virgins have lamps with them, and these lamps represent the Word of God. They have received the Word of God (Jesus Christ) and it causes them to have light.

"Thy word is a lamp unto my feet, and a light unto my path" (Psalm 119:105).

THE OIL

Inside of the lamps there is oil. Oil represents the blood of Jesus, the Holy Spirit and the anointing of God. When Jesus called himself the anointed one, it was because the Holy Spirit had descended upon him.

"The Spirit of the Lord is upon me, because he hath anointed me to preach the gospel to the poor; he hath sent me to heal the brokenhearted, to preach deliverance to the captives, and recovering of sight to the blind, to set at liberty them that are bruised" (Luke 4:18).

"Thou hast loved righteousness, and hated iniquity; therefore God, even thy God, hath **anointed thee with the oil of gladness** above thy fellows" (Hebrews 1:9).

In this parable, all of the virgins began with the same oil. They all received the Holy Spirit at salvation. If the foolish virgins didn't have oil to begin with, their lamps would not "go out," because they wouldn't have been able to burn in the first place. Therefore, we understand that the wise virgins took an *additional* amount of oil with them so that when the oil in their lamps ran low, they would have sufficient reserves to keep the lamps burning. This additional oil was stored in "vessels" by the wise virgins. What does this mean? On one level, we receive power when we receive the baptism of the Holy Spirit, an event that usually occurs after salvation.

"But ye shall receive power, after that the Holy Ghost is come upon you: and ye shall be witnesses unto me both in Jerusalem, and in all Judaea, and in Samaria, and unto the uttermost part of the earth" (Acts 1:8).

However, this in and of itself is not enough. The Bible goes on to instruct us to be filled with all of the fullness of God (Ephesians 3:19). This means that we must remain an open conduit for the passage of the glory of God into the earth. In other words, to be filled with the fullness of God in a sinful world requires a continual flow of his Spirit not only to us, but through us. No amount of filling is sufficient. The filling must be perpetual, and it must continue throughout our lives.

"And be not drunk with wine, wherein is excess; but be filled with the Spirit" (Ephesians 5:18).

The use of the phrase "be filled" in this passage implies being *continually filled*. It could be read "keep being continually filled with the Spirit." This means that we are called to live a life of perpetual communion with the Holy Spirit. Being filled with the Holy Spirit is not a one-time event. He wants to continually pour into us, making us windows that reveal heaven into the earth. This is a lifestyle that the end of time will demand of the faithful. However, it is something that God has called all Christians to throughout history. We must be perpetually filled with all of the fullness of God if we are to corporately attain the level of a bride who has made herself ready.

"Let us be glad and rejoice, and give honour to him: for the marriage of the Lamb is come, and **his wife hath made herself ready**" (Revelation 19:7).

THE VIRGINS FALL ASLEEP

In this parable, the bridegroom does not come immediately. Instead, he tarries. The bridegroom takes his time and as a result, the virgins fall asleep. The fifth verse says of the virgins that "they all slumbered and slept." When the Greek translation of this phrase is considered, it basically states that they all "nodded off and fell asleep." It creates a picture that suggests that the virgins attempted to stay awake, but they simply dozed off because of the time it took the bridegroom. It wasn't just the foolish virgins, but *all* of the virgins that fell asleep.

The question that immediately arises is this: why do both the wise and the foolish virgins fall asleep? Scripture acknowledges the existence of a spiritual sleep, which is inherently bad. For instance, Assyria was rebuked for having "sleeping shepherds."

"Thy shepherds slumber, O king of Assyria: thy nobles shall dwell in the dust: thy people is scattered upon the mountains, and no man gathereth them" (Nahum 3:18).

However, it makes no sense to interpret the sleep of the virgins as spiritual slumber because if it were, the wise virgins wouldn't be participating. Moreover, spiritual slumber is not accidental. It is a purposeful decision. The slumber that is described is not blamed on the virgins. It is apologized for by the mention of the bridegroom's delay, and described as involuntary on the part of the virgins. Also, *all* of the virgins are pictured as sleeping. Some have concluded that the sleep of the virgins represents the state of the living church leading up to the last days. Yet, can it legitimately be concluded that one hundred percent of the church was spiritually asleep at any point in history? I don't believe so. Furthermore, if we are to conclude that the virgins represent the living church, we would have to accept that one hundred percent of the church will sleep until Jesus is *in the process of arriving*. This makes no sense at all, considering that God is returning for a bride without spot or wrinkle, which will take time (Ephesians 5:27). Considering these things, is there an alternative explanation that can we derive from Scripture?

The Bible repeatedly describes those who have died as those who have "fallen asleep." The fact of the matter is that people do not live forever. Those who are faithfully awaiting the Lord's coming, should he fail to come in their lifetimes, will die. Those who are *not* faithfully awaiting the Lord's return will also die. In this way, the same type of "sleep" creates two camps of believers. Paul tells us in 1 Thessalonians 4:14 that "if we believe that Jesus died and rose again, even so **them also which sleep** in Jesus will God bring with him." This falls in line with the Greek phraseology that they "nodded off and fell asleep." It wasn't as though it was some form of purposeful rebellion on the part of the virgins. Their "sleep" was the result of the extensive wait imposed upon them by the bridegroom.

It's about the Resurrection of the Dead

It is clear that at the coming of Christ, the dead will have to be raised. This is because according to the Bible we will live together in Christ whether we "wake or sleep."

"For God hath not appointed us to wrath, but to obtain salvation by our Lord Jesus Christ, Who died for us, that, whether we wake or sleep, we should live together with him" (1 Thessalonians 5:9-10).

This parable has often been used to teach the rapture of the living church at the time of Christ's coming. However, the populations addressed in the parable have *all* fallen asleep. Since we understand that the sleep cannot be described away as spiritual slumber, and that it must be understood as death, this parable is actually describing the resurrection of the dead. The only way that the virgins can include those that are alive at the second coming is if some of the virgins do not fall asleep. Understanding this is essential to understanding the full implications of the parable.

In this parable, the dead in Christ are awakened by the cry that goes forth to signify the approach of the bridegroom at the midnight hour. What is this cry? At the coming of Christ, a shout is described as going forth. This is obviously the cry that Jesus describes in the parable.

"For this we say unto you by the word of the Lord, that we which are alive and remain unto the coming of the Lord shall not prevent them which are asleep. **For the Lord himself shall descend from heaven with a shout**, with the voice of the archangel, and with the trump of God: and the dead in Christ shall rise first" (1 Thessalonians 4:15-16).

FURTHER CLARIFYING THE CONCEPT

A common misconception is that the dead are resurrected directly into the sky during this event. This is not what the Bible says. It says that this shout will go forth as the Lord is approaching. The voice of the archangel and the seventh trumpet will go forth as well. Then it says that the dead in Christ shall rise first. However, the Bible doesn't say that they rise into the sky. Instead, it implies that they arise into the earth. They are actually alive and walking on the earth again. Afterwards, the rapture occurs, taking both the resurrected dead and the living church into the sky together. In other words, both groups are caught up at the same time. Those who are alive will be "caught up together with those" that have been raised from the dead.

"Then we which are alive and remain shall be caught up **together with them** in the clouds, to meet the Lord in the air: and so shall we ever be with the Lord" (1 Thessalonians 4:17).

This should come as no surprise, since this exact same thing happened when Jesus died. The following passage has been a source of confusion for many. The gospel author described that after Jesus was resurrected, Old Testament saints came out of their graves and were seen by many people. There was a certain amount of time during which those that had died in centuries past were permitted to walk the earth and interact with the earth's inhabitants. What came of them is not explained. However, through Christ's work, the dead were resurrected into their bodies and permitted to again interact with those on the earth. I believe that this is a shadow of things to come.

"And, behold, the veil of the temple was rent in twain from the top to the bottom; and the earth did quake, and the rocks rent; And the graves were opened; and many bodies of the saints which slept arose, And came out of the graves after his resurrection, and went into the holy city, and appeared unto many" (Matthew 27:51-53).

Taking this into account, the parable of the virgins describes the dead in Christ as being raised to life while Jesus is approaching. His approach is his second advent. They will be awakened and caused to "go out to meet him." Where are they going out of? They are going out of their graves.

To avoid any possible confusion at this point, let me make it clear that this very limited resurrection of certain dead upon the resurrection of Jesus <u>does not</u> fulfill biblical prophecy of the last day resurrection of the dead. Some have said that it does. I have heard this view taught on at least one occasion, and I want to take a moment to point out the absolute falsity of this perspective.

Writing many years after the resurrection of Jesus, Paul made it clear that two certain individuals were leading some away from the faith. How? They were teaching that the resurrection had already come. In other words, they were probably pointing to the event I have just described in order to argue that the resurrection of the dead had already been fulfilled. Paul said of them that they had erred concerning the truth. In light of this, it is easy to conclude that anyone coming to similar conclusions has also erred. While the event at Jesus' resurrection can serve as a shadow to help us understand the nature of the final resurrection of the dead, it is by no means intended to be interpreted as its fulfillment.

"And their word will eat as doth a canker: of whom is Hymenaeus and Philetus; **Who concerning the truth have <u>erred</u>, saying that the resurrection is past already**; and overthrow the faith of some" (2 Timothy 2:17-18).

The Midnight Hour

The midnight hour represents the end of the time frame required for the return of the bridegroom. It signifies the transition from one day to the next, and by prophetic implication, from one age to the next. In the parable, God's plan is for the virgins to go out and meet the bridegroom. In order to do this, their lamps have to burn long enough to make it outside to meet him.

The lamps that Jesus refers to use a wick dipped in oil. As fire burns on the wick, carbon accumulates. When there is too much carbon, one can trim the wick by removing the carbon at the top of it. When there is plenty of oil in the lamp, this is very effective, and the flame will burn significantly brighter. This is the case with the wise virgins. When there is no oil in the lamp, it makes little sense to trim the wick. The fire has nothing to burn and will quickly go out. This is the case with the foolish virgins.

To Every Seed His Own Body

In order to continue, we must establish the fact that there are three groups in this parable: the virgins, the bridegroom, and those who sell. After the foolish virgins awake to realize they do not have enough oil (or we could say spiritual power) to be prepared, they request some from the wise virgins. Where does this spiritual power come from? It comes from the lives they sowed into death. The Bible is clear that our natural body is sown as a seed, and that the seed sown will determine the harvest that is reaped. In other words, if we fail to receive continual infilling of the Spirit during our lives, we will reap accordingly at the resurrection. In the case of the foolish virgins, when they are resurrected they will find that their "oil" has run out.

"And that which thou sowest, thou sowest not that body that shall be, but bare grain, it may chance of wheat, or of some other grain: But God giveth it a body as it hath pleased him, and **to every seed his own body**" (1 Corinthians 15:37-38).

THOSE WHO SELL

The foolish virgins are told to go and *buy from those who sell* when they ask the wise virgins for their extra oil. This is not a rebuke by the wise virgins, but a possible solution. It is interesting that the response of the wise virgins seems to acknowledge the possibility that the oil could be given. However, because of the fact that the oil will not be enough for both populations, the foolish virgins are told to go and buy from those who sell. Since we understand that this is describing the state of those who have experienced the resurrection of the dead, the context is the very brief time frame between this event and the actual arrival of Jesus Christ. This aligns with the parable perfectly, because the cry goes forth as the bridegroom is approaching. This could be minutes, hours, or at most, a few days.

Those who sell are the leaders in the body of Christ. They are also present on the earth, because the whole group of believers that will experience rapture will do so at the same time. Although the virgins correlate specifically to those participating in the resurrection of the dead, those that sell do not. It doesn't say of "those that sell" that they ever fell asleep. They are leaders that are alive during the second coming of Jesus. The question is: how can a leader "sell" the Holy Spirit?

This is parabolic and not literal. It is biblically wrong to "sell" the anointing. Peter illustrates this when he rebukes Simon the sorcerer after Simon offers money for the apostles' power (Acts 8:18-24). To "buy" means that the people of God are called to submit to the leadership of those who are faithful and will feed them "with meat in due season." In other words, the additional oil comes from the price we pay in seeking God according to paths that will yield maturity in our lives and the continual filling of his Spirit. These paths require submission to spiritual authority, but not in foolishness. Maturity in Christ comes at a high price.

The Nature of His Coming

"And whosoever doth not bear his cross, and come after me, cannot be my disciple. For which of you, intending to build a tower, sitteth not down first, and counteth the cost, whether he have sufficient to finish it? Lest haply, after he hath laid the foundation, and is not able to finish it, all that behold it begin to mock him" (Luke 14:27-29).

The wise virgins have already purchased additional oil. They purchased it and brought it with them because of the lives they lived before they died. Their lives were sown as seeds, just like the lives of the foolish virgins, but upon resurrection, the wise virgins have sufficient "oil" to go out and meet the bridegroom. The foolish virgins are denied the oil of the others and are told to go and buy. Unfortunately, there is not enough time. In a frail attempt to go through the long and arduous process of maturing in Christ at the last minute and achieving a complete spiritual filling, they are not present for the arrival of the bridegroom. The bridegroom returns while they go to buy. Those who were ready went with the bridegroom to the marriage and the door was shut.

This is a parabolic picture of the rapture, the bridal procession, and the arrival at the wedding supper of the Lamb. Only the portion of the church that is ready will participate in the bridal procession, becoming the army of God that will conquer at Armageddon. The rest are left. We will _all be changed_ (1 Corinthians 15:51) but Scripture does not require that we _all_ meet with Jesus in the air (1 Thessalonians 4:15-17). Some will remain with the evil leaders from the former parable. The evil leaders were appointed their portion with the hypocritical saints, although they will still inherit incorruption and eternal life (1 Corinthians 15:53).

A Difficult Warning

As the parable closes out, the foolish virgins are pictured as crying out, "Lord, Lord, open to us!" What follows is a peculiar comment that can cause difficulty with the passage.

God responds by saying, "Verily I say unto you, I know you not." The problem is: how can God not know them when they participated in the kingdom, and even received the salvation of Jesus? We will return to the Greek for a proper answer. In this response, the word *know* in the Greek language is the word *eido*. This word primarily means "to see." It becomes "know" when it is used in the perfect tense—*have seen*. God is saying, "I have not seen you." This makes complete sense because the foolish virgins weren't present when the bridegroom arrived. Figuratively, how can we see someone who isn't there?

Furthermore, this is to be differentiated from a statement made by Jesus that sounds almost the same.

"And then will I profess unto them, **I never knew you**: depart from me, ye that work iniquity" (Matthew 7:23).

Jesus does not say that he "never" knew the virgins. In the above passage he is actually talking about false prophets that were never saved. The virgins represent the church, both wise and foolish. This is also why, after explaining to the five foolish virgins that he hadn't seen them, he does not tell them to depart. There is no judgment passed against them, either. Conversely, he will emphatically tell the false prophets to depart from him because they are workers of iniquity. The comments, though seemingly similar, are quite different indeed, both in their implications and in the populations they address.

The parable of the virgins concludes with a warning.

"Watch therefore, for ye know neither the day nor the hour wherein the Son of man cometh" (Matthew 25:13).

CHAPTER 25

Wedding Supper of the Lamb

The difficulty that the parable of the virgins presents is significantly clarified when the wedding supper of the Lamb is properly understood. The wedding supper of the Lamb is a prophetic event prophesied in the book of Revelation. The only problem is that the actual timing and location is not given. This is the passage that prophetically identifies this coming event.

"Let us be glad and rejoice, and give honour to him: for the marriage of the Lamb is come, and his wife hath made herself ready. And to her was granted that she should be arrayed in fine linen, clean and white: for the fine linen is the righteousness of saints. And he saith unto me, Write, **Blessed are they which are called unto the marriage supper of the Lamb**. And he saith unto me, These are the true sayings of God" (Revelation 19:7-9).

Searching for More Information

Although the marriage supper of the Lamb is mentioned, a description is not to be found. Instead, we find that the passage continues on to describe Jesus walking out into the battle of Armageddon with his army. He destroys the antichrist and his troops with the sword that comes out of his mouth. Afterwards, the fowls of the air are gathered to eat the dead flesh. This is called the supper of the Great God. Are we to assume that this is synonymous with the marriage supper of the Lamb?

"And I saw an angel standing in the sun; and he cried with a loud voice, saying to all the fowls that fly in the midst of heaven, Come and gather yourselves together unto **the supper of the great God**; That ye may eat the flesh of kings, and the flesh of captains, and the flesh of mighty men, and the flesh of horses, and of them that sit on them, and the flesh of all men, both free and bond, both small and great" (Revelation 19:17-18).

When addressing this question, we must articulate that two different terminologies are employed. The wedding supper of the Lamb and the supper of the Great God are separate terminologies, and nowhere in Scripture are we given a reason to identify them as the same thing. However, if the supper of the Great God is not the wedding supper of the Lamb: what is the wedding supper of the Lamb? Furthermore, how will it help us to understand the parable of the virgins? It will surprise many to find out that the wedding supper of the Lamb is described by the prophet Isaiah. Although he doesn't tell us the title of the event, he does tell us that its location is Mount Zion. He even gives us a menu.

"Then the moon shall be confounded, and the sun ashamed, **when the Lord of hosts shall reign in mount Zion, and in Jerusalem, and before his ancients gloriously**…Thou shalt bring down the noise of strangers, as the heat in a dry place; even the heat with the shadow of a cloud: **the branch of the terrible ones shall be brought low. And in this mountain shall the Lord of hosts make unto all people a feast of fat things, a feast of wines on the lees, of fat things full of marrow, of wines on the lees well refined**" (Isaiah 24:23, 25:5-6).

PLACING THE EVENT

It is impossible to bring this into context until we understand the order of events involved in the second coming of Christ. However, since we have already established a clear understanding of these things, I will briefly review them here. There will be a period of great tribulation, which ends upon the return of Jesus. He returns only once, and it is at this time that the resurrection of the dead and the rapture occur. There is a procession of Jesus with his saints, during which every eye will see Jesus. A war campaign will commence at some point during this period that will climax at the battle of Armageddon (which may very well correspond with the Day of

Atonement). After this battle there will be a procession back to Jerusalem, where the judgment seat of Christ will occur. However, before the judgment seat of Christ occurs, something else must happen first—the marriage supper of the Lamb.

The Jewish Wedding Custom

In order to understand this parable and the wedding supper of the Lamb, it becomes necessary to have some familiarity with Jewish wedding custom. In Jewish wedding custom, the bridegroom would pay the bride's father a determined price. After the covenant was established, he would leave the bride at her father's house and go to prepare his own house. Only after his own house was prepared would he go forth to take his bride. During the time that it took the bridegroom to prepare, the bride would patiently wait for him while doing some preparation herself.

It was customary for the bride to have no idea when the bridegroom would arrive, and often the arrival was at night. The bridegroom would come with male escorts in a torchlight procession. When he arrived in the town, a shout would signify to the expectant bride that the bridegroom was coming. Within minutes he would be at her door, and she along with female escorts would make the procession back to the bridegroom's father's house.

Shortly after returning to the groom's home, the bridegroom and bride would enter into the bridal chamber where the marriage was physically consummated. This bridal chamber was called a *huppah*. After the consummation of the marriage was finished, the bridegroom would make an announcement to those waiting outside of the huppah, and these attendants would then make the announcement to all of the wedding guests. This would begin a seven-day celebration.

Integrating Custom into Prophecy

When we consider the procession, Jesus returns to earth with his holy angels (Matthew 24:31). He gathers his church, but cuts some of the evil leaders asunder and appoints them their portion with the hypocrites (Matthew 24:51). Of those virgins that are taken to complete the procession back to the father's house, only those that are ready are taken. This procession is a bridal procession, although during this procession the glorified saints will also be fulfilling their role as the army of God (Jude 1:14-15, and possibly Joel 2:1-11). According to the biblical scenario, it will last several days, climaxing in the battle of Armageddon. The procession will then finalize by entering into Mount Zion in Jerusalem. Mount Zion is the location of the wedding supper of the Lamb.

When we consider the mountain where the marriage supper of the Lamb will take place, only those who are _in_ the mountain will participate. There will be those outside of the mountain that don't get in. They don't get in because they don't arrive until after the "door is shut." They will remain outside while the wedding supper of the Lamb involves those _in_ the mountain. This comes out ever so clearly in the interlinear translation.[37]

"And Jehovah of hosts shall make a feast of fat things **for all the peoples in this mountain**; a feast of wine on the lees, of fat things full of marrow, refined win on the lees" (Isaiah 25:6 INT).

In other words, when the foolish virgins are pictured as standing at the door, they will probably be literally standing at Mount Zion, where the marriage is taking place. This is after the battle of Armageddon. After the marriage is consummated, I assume that there will be a literal seven-day feast (as opposed to a seven-year feast, as some have erroneously concluded). This may very well align with the first Feast of Tabernacles following the return of the Lord. However, since the foolish virgins were not ready for the procession to take place, they were late. They will not be allowed into the wedding supper of the Lamb, but it doesn't mean that they are going to hell. It simply means that they have missed out. Like the rest of the saints, they will still be judged at the judgment seat of Christ, which will be described in the parable of the talents, and thus will be the next prophetic event after the marriage and wedding supper of the Lamb. However, before continuing further, we are going to spend some more time discussing the doctrine of the resurrection of the dead.

CHAPTER 26

The Resurrection of the Dead

The parable of the ten virgins reveals an extremely difficult concept for many of us. First of all, it raises the bar considerably. It places a sobering spin on the consequences of our life choices. Second of all, it is difficult to consider the rapture and the resurrection of the dead taking place at the end of a tribulation period. It is much easier to believe that the rapture is a great evacuation that allows us to avoid difficult circumstances.

However, it is impossible to argue that all of this is not true, if we are frank with ourselves and accept Scripture at face value. Nonetheless, the parable of the virgins does not provide enough evidence in and of itself to allow us to fully understand the resurrection of the dead. This is why we are going to go through the doctrine of the resurrection of the dead verse by verse. It is interesting to note that according to the writer of Hebrews, the resurrection of the dead and its implications should be foundational knowledge.

The Doctrine of Christ

"Therefore leaving the principles of the doctrine of Christ, let us go on unto perfection; not laying again the foundation of repentance from dead works, and of faith toward God, Of the doctrine of baptisms, and of laying on of hands, **and of resurrection of the dead**, and of eternal judgment" (Hebrews 6:1-2).

Contained within the principles of the doctrine of Christ are six foundational doctrines. These are:

1. Repentance from dead works.

2. Faith towards God.

3. Doctrine of baptisms.

4. Laying on of hands.

5. Resurrection of the dead.

6. Eternal judgment.

The doctrines actually break down into three sets. The first two doctrines (repentance from dead works and faith towards God) address our relationship with God. The second two doctrines (doctrine of baptisms and the laying on of hands) deal with ministry on earth. The last two doctrines (resurrection of the dead and eternal judgment) are for the purpose of establishing sobriety, holy fear, and a serious attitude regarding our approach to faith. When we do not understand the last two doctrines, it makes it difficult to take our faith seriously. *It takes an eternal perspective to motivate us beyond the limitations and challenges of the moment.*

Defining the Resurrection of the Dead

The first concept we must establish is a definition. When I am speaking about the resurrection of the dead, I am talking about the global event that is prophesied to occur at the return of Jesus. There is another type of resurrection of the dead. This is the miracle of raising a single person from the dead by the power of Jesus. This concept is established when Jesus explained to Martha why Lazarus would be raised from the dead.

"Martha saith unto him, I know that he shall rise again in the resurrection at the last day. Jesus said unto her, **I am the resurrection**, and the life: he that believeth in me, though he were dead, yet shall he live: And whosoever liveth and believeth in me shall never die. Believest thou this" (John 11:24-26)?

Isaiah Prophesies the Resurrection of the Dead

We can raise the dead because Jesus is the resurrection. Having said that, let us continue to establish an understanding of the *event* of the resurrection of the dead. Martha is quoted as saying that Lazarus will rise again in the resurrection of the last day. How did she know this? There are several Old Testament references to this event. Let's take a look at two of these.

"Thy dead men shall live, together with my dead body shall they arise. Awake and sing, ye that dwell in dust: for thy dew is as the dew of herbs, and the earth shall cast out the dead" (Isaiah 26:19).

In this passage, Isaiah is prophesying about a future event when the earth will cast out its dead. He says, "thy dead _men_ shall live." Animals will not participate in the resurrection of the dead. This event is specifically for humans. He says, "awake and sing." Those that are raised with him, meaning those who participate in the first resurrection, are to rejoice. The reason is that they will be entering the kingdom age with Jesus. As established in the book of Revelation, those who participate in the resurrection of the dead at that time are not under the power of the second death. This is a good thing, something to rejoice about!

"Blessed and holy is he that hath part in the first resurrection: on such the second death hath no power, but they shall be priests of God and of Christ, and shall reign with him a thousand years" (Revelation 20:6).

Daniel Prophesies the Resurrection of the Dead

The second Old Testament verse that we will look at comes from the book of Daniel. Chapters 11 and 12 of Daniel come from a dissertation given to him by the heavenly being that is sent to him (Daniel 10:11). Daniel is not prophesying, but writing down what he is being told. Everything is told to him in chronological order. When reading Daniel 11 and 12, we are reading a recitation of the time of the end. Unlike other prophetic portions of the Bible, there is little effort on the part of the interpreter to place the portions of the prophecy in their correct order. Daniel is told about the beginning of the final antichrist's campaign (Daniel 11:21-30), his defilement of the temple (Daniel 11:31), his persecution of the saints (Daniel 11:32-35), his self-magnification (Daniel 11:36-39), his wars (Daniel 11:40-44), and his eventual encampment in "between the seas in the glorious holy mountain" (Daniel 11:45).

Once all of this has been explained, the heavenly being goes on to say that after the antichrist encamps "between the seas in the glorious holy mountain" Michael the archangel will stand up and there will be a time of trouble. At this time, the resurrection of the dead is explained.

And at that time shall Michael stand up, the great prince which standeth for the children of thy people: and there shall be a time of trouble, such as never was since there was a nation even to that same time: and at that time thy people shall be delivered, every one that shall be found written in the book. **And many of them that sleep in the dust of the earth shall awake**, some to everlasting life, and some to shame and everlasting contempt. And they that be wise shall shine as the brightness of the firmament; and they that turn many to righteousness as the stars for ever and ever.

(Daniel 12:1-3)

It is explained that many of them that sleep in the dust of the earth shall awake. This is the resurrection of the righteous dead at the return of Jesus. It goes on to say that some will awake to everlasting life, and some to everlasting shame and contempt. I used to believe that those awaking to shame and contempt were solely those who received a resurrection specifically for the White Throne Judgment at the end of the millennium. However, although those being sent to the lake of fire will certainly be full of shame and contempt, this also has application to the first resurrection. The fact of the matter is that the words *shame* and *everlasting contempt* do not mean everlasting condemnation, everlasting judgment, hell, or any other word used to describe the destiny of unrepentant sinners. *They are descriptive of emotions.*

The passage goes on to say that those who are wise will shine with the brightness of the firmament, and those who turn many to righteousness like the stars forever. The brightness of the firmament means the brightness of the sky. Sometimes it can be so bright outside that we have to squint.

The brightness of the stars, however, is another order of magnitude entirely. Their brilliance can been seen many light-years away. The prophet documents that there are at least two different types of brilliance in the resurrection. Regarding the use of the word *wise*, we find a correlation between this passage and the parable of the virgins. The only virgins taken are those that are described as wise.

"Then shall the kingdom of heaven be likened unto ten virgins, which took their lamps, and went forth to meet the bridegroom. And **five of them were wise**, and five were foolish" (Matthew 25:1-2).

From this passage in Daniel, not only do we find a prophecy regarding the resurrection of the dead, but also details about its timing and implications. These two passages from Daniel and Isaiah would most certainly have been the foundation for Martha's comment to Jesus.

THE RESURRECTION OF THE DEAD IS NOT UNIFORM

Strictly considering Old Testament perspectives, it is clear that the resurrection of the dead will not be uniform, as some have supposed. For example, when Henry Ford developed the Model T, he had vision for this to be the only car that would ever need to be designed or driven. He felt that it was the perfect car. Obviously, history did not work out as he had hoped.

When we get on the highway today we find that there are many different types of cars. Some are beautiful, some are decent, and some show signs of contempt. The fact of the matter is that not everyone receives the same car.

The way many Christians understand the resurrection of the dead is similar to the way that Ford envisioned the future of the Model T. They view the resurrection of the dead as a uniform event. The thought is that everyone will get the same kind of glorified body in the resurrection. However, in the same way that we see many different types of cars on the highway, we will also see many different types of bodies in the resurrection. Some will have one type of glory, others another type of glory, and some will be resurrected to everlasting shame and contempt.

New Testament, Same Doctrine

Let us begin to look further into the doctrine of the resurrection of the dead in the New Testament.

"Women received their dead raised to life again: and others were tortured, not accepting deliverance; that they might obtain a **better resurrection**" (Hebrews 11:35).

This scripture comes from a passage in Hebrews discussing the various ways those that have gone before us suffered for their faith. The passage is specifically making mention of those who died for their faith under the

Old Covenant. Notice that it says in this portion of Scripture that "others were tortured, not accepting deliverance; that they might obtain a *better* resurrection." The fact of the matter is that if there is a better resurrection, there is also a worse resurrection. If God is a God of justice, it becomes impossible to expect a uniform judgment and reward for all saints. There is no justice in uniformity. There will be a better resurrection for some than for others.

A CHALLENGING QUOTE

"That I may know him, and the power of his resurrection, and the fellowship of his sufferings, being made conformable unto his death; **If by any means I might attain unto the resurrection of the dead. Not as though I had already attained**, either were already perfect: but I follow after, if that I may apprehend that for which also I am apprehended of Christ Jesus" (Philippians 3:10-12).

Here we find another reference to the resurrection of the dead. Paul makes a challenging comment, declaring that it was not as though he had already attained the resurrection of the dead. What does this mean? Will some of the dead in Christ not receive a resurrection? Could this be what Paul is communicating when he says, "If by any means I *might* attain unto the resurrection of the dead"? Is there a point of faithfulness that we must attain in order to be counted worthy to participate in this resurrection? If so, how high would the standard be, considering that this comment was made by the apostle Paul himself!

In truth, the apostle is communicating that he was not already glorified. At least this was his intent with the words "not as though I had <u>already</u> <u>attained</u>." Keep in mind that he had formerly been stoned to death (in all practicality), but shortly thereafter was healed and continued preaching.

"But some Jews arrived there from Antioch and Iconium; and having persuaded the people and won them over, they stoned Paul and [afterward] dragged him out of the town, thinking that he was dead.But the disciples formed a circle about him, and he got up and went back into the town; and on the morrow he went on with Barnabas to Derbe" (Acts 14:19-20 AMP).

By saying "If by any means I might attain unto the resurrection of the dead" still seems to create a problem though. While he knew he had not already been glorified in resurrection, could he have been entertaining the idea that he may not? The good news is that this conclusion it is invalidated by a proper understanding of the judgment seat of Christ. *All* Christians must stand before the judgment seat of Christ, and without a resurrection, some would not be able to participate. Therefore, *all* of the righteous dead must be resurrected at the return of Jesus, because immediately after the battle of Armageddon, Jesus sits in the temple in Jerusalem. It will most likely be immediately after the wedding supper of the Lamb that the judgment seat of Christ begins.

"**For we must all appear** before the judgment seat of Christ; that every one may receive the things done in his body, according to that he hath done, whether it be good or bad" (2 Corinthians 5:10).

In light of our understanding of the judgment seat of Christ, the understanding of Paul's comment regarding the resurrection of the dead in Philippians takes on a different connotation. In effect, he was communicating that since he was still not at the end of his life, he still had time to turn away from Jesus. He understood that at the level of the faith he had attained, if he were to fall away, it would be impossible for him to be renewed to repentance, and that he could no longer have a part in the resurrection. Praise God he stayed faithful!

THE QUALIFICATIONS OF IMPOSSIBILITY

"For it is **impossible** for those who were once enlightened, and have tasted of the heavenly gift, and were made partakers of the Holy Ghost, And have tasted the good word of God, and the powers of the world to come, If they shall fall away, to renew them again unto repentance; seeing they crucify to themselves the Son of God afresh, and put him to an open shame" (Hebrews 6:4-6).

On this note, understand that sin can never separate us from God. Falling away requires a quality heart decision, just like receiving Jesus as Lord requires a quality heart decision. As we discussed, the heart refers to our subconscious. Furthermore, should people fall away, most can be renewed to repentance. The only ones that cannot be renewed unto repentance are those who fulfill every requirement of this passage. These requirements are: (1) they were enlightened, (2) they tasted of the heavenly gift, (3) were made partakers of the Holy Spirit, (4) have tasted of the good word of God, (5) have tasted of the powers of the age to come. The grace comes primarily on the last requirement. Until individuals have walked out into operation in deep realms of the power of God, they still qualify for renewal unto repentance. This is the purpose of rededication for those who have backslidden.

SHOWING THE MYSTERY

The next passage that we will look at comes from 1 Corinthians.

"Behold, I shew you a mystery; We shall not all sleep, but we shall all be changed, In a moment, in the twinkling of an eye, at the last trump: for the trumpet shall sound, and the dead shall be raised incorruptible, and we shall be changed" (1 Corinthians 15:51-52).

In this passage, Paul explains that not all saints will sleep (meaning die), but we shall all be changed. Clearly, it is impossible to be a saint and not participate in the resurrection of the dead. Paul says that we will *all* be changed. The word all comes from the Greek word *pas*, and means any, every, and the whole. In addition, the resurrection results in those resurrected becoming incorruptible. This is also important. The bodies of the resurrected, no matter what their glory, will be immortal bodies. Lastly, according to this passage, the dead are raised before the saints who are alive begin to be changed or "raptured." Going back to the parable of the virgins, those who do not go into the marriage will still be changed, but they will not partake of the "better" resurrection. This is all based on the principle of God's justice.

SETTING THE RECORD STRAIGHT

When it comes to 1 Corinthians 15:51-52, many of us are familiar with this passage, but unfamiliar with all that precedes it. Beginning early in that chapter, Paul begins a long discourse on the resurrection of the dead. In that time period, an entire sect of the Jews, called Sadducees, taught that there was no resurrection of the dead. In the book of Acts, the temple high priest was from this sect, revealing the influence that this approach to interpretation used to hold (Acts 5:17). This was a popular debate and Paul began to set the record straight.

"Now if Christ be preached that he rose from the dead, how say some among you that there is no resurrection of the dead? But if there be no resurrection of the dead, then is Christ not risen: And if Christ be not risen, then is our preaching vain, and your faith is also vain" (1 Corinthians 15:12-14).

If there was no resurrection of the dead, then Jesus had not risen. This would only make sense because Jesus told us that he is the resurrection. Thus, if there is no resurrection of the dead, then our faith is in vain. He goes on to explain that removing the eternal perspective from the faith is akin to removing the purpose for what we do. It removes the motivation to press into the faith with the abandon that God desires of us.

As Paul goes through this teaching on the meaning and purpose of the resurrection of the dead, he gets to a place where he begins to describe what we can expect to see at the resurrection of the dead.

"All flesh is not the same flesh: but there is one kind of flesh of men, another flesh of beasts, another of fishes, and another of birds. There are also celestial bodies, and bodies terrestrial: but the glory of the celestial is one, and the glory of the terrestrial is another. There is one glory of the sun, and another glory of the moon, and another glory of the stars: for one star differeth from another star in glory. **So also is the resurrection of the dead**. It is sown in corruption; it is raised in incorruption" (1 Corinthians 15:39-42).

Paul tells us that there are different kinds of flesh that live on the earth. In the animal kingdom there is a hierarchy. These are terrestrial bodies. He also explains that there are different kinds of bodies in the sky. These are celestial bodies. He explains that among the celestial bodies there are different glories. The sun has a glory, the moon has a glory, and the stars have different glories. After this explanation, he delivers the conclusion of the matter. He says that in the same way that there is a hierarchy of terrestrial bodies and a hierarchy of celestial bodies, so also will it be at the resurrection of the dead.

The Reality of Justice

There will be as many types of resurrections as there are lives that were lived by the saints. We will each be judged and rewarded based upon what we did with our faith. This is justice. Unfortunately, some will receive a resurrection that will cause them sorrow, like we saw explained in the book of Daniel. These will have to come to terms with the fact that this is their eternal inheritance. They will look upon the saints that shine like the stars and know that they have justly received the reward they chose with the life they lived. There will be weeping and gnashing of teeth! They will become inhabitants of the earth during the millennium; they are immortal and perfect, but they do not dwell on the earth as rulers over cities. This will make more sense in the next chapter.

Of course, others who paid the price for a better resurrection will find that they are glorified with a great glory. What a day it will be for those who sold out their whole lives to Jesus and receive the riches they have stored up in heaven! They will be exalted, given rulership, and a high rank in the hierarchy of not only the millennial rule, but on into the untold stories of eternity.

Further Elements for Comprehension

There are some further elements that are important for us to understand about the resurrection of the dead. Those who are resurrected from the dead will not be married or given in marriage. It only makes sense to presume that this will be true of those who are changed at the Lord's coming as well (1 Corinthians 15:51-52).

"Jesus answered and said unto them, Ye do err, not knowing the scriptures, nor the power of God. For in the resurrection they neither marry, nor are given in marriage, but are as the angels of God in heaven" (Matthew 22:29-30).

Another point regarding the resurrection of the dead pertains to the resurrection of the unjust dead. This is a different resurrection, and occurs at a different time. According to Revelation, the rest of the dead do not live again until the consummation of the millennial rule.

"But the rest of the dead lived not again until the thousand years were finished. This is the first resurrection" (Revelation 20:5).

The rest of the dead that this passage refers to are the unjust dead. These are the men that were the enemies of God during their lives. They rejected God, and they opposed his people. They died in their sin. Paul speaks to this resurrection of the unjust as a separate event from the resurrection of the just.

"But this I confess unto thee, that after the way which they call heresy, so worship I the God of my fathers, believing all things which are written in the law and in the prophets: And have hope toward God, which they themselves also allow, **that there shall be a resurrection of the dead, both of the just and unjust**. And herein do I exercise myself, to have always a conscience void to offence toward God, and toward men" (Acts 24:14-16).

The explanation of this resurrection is purely for the purpose of a final judgment. The rest of the account is described at the end of Revelation chapter 20. These dead do not appear before the judgment seat of Christ, but before the Great White Throne. They are judged according to their works and cast into the lake of fire, which is the location of eternal judgment. They will burn forever. The Book of Life is also present in this passage, because those who are born during the millennium will also be judged according to their works. Those who do not abandon righteousness when Satan is loosed from the pit (Revelation 20:7) will be granted entry with the saints into the next phase of God's plan. Those born during the millennial rule who align with Satan when he is released from the pit will join those of the resurrection of the unjust in eternal damnation.

And I saw a great white throne, and him that sat on it, from whose face the earth and the heaven fled away; and there was found no place for them. And I saw the dead, small and great, stand before God; and the books were opened: and another book was opened, which is the Book of Life: and the dead were judged out of those things which were written in the books, according to their works. And the sea gave up the dead which were in it; and death and hell delivered up the dead which were in them: and they were judged every man according to their works. And death and hell were cast into the lake of fire. This is the second death. And whosoever was not found written in the Book of Life was cast into the lake of fire.

(Revelation 20:11-15)

THE ARMY OF GOD

We must understand that our God is a God of justice. He has everything figured out. There is no way to "cheat the system." A last point of consideration involves the last-day army of God. Considering that there are different types of resurrections, and that not all of the saints will get caught up into the clouds, who exactly will participate in the army of God? Our answer comes from the following passage.

"These shall make war with the Lamb, and the Lamb shall overcome them: for he is Lord of lords, and King of kings: and **they that are with him are called, and chosen, and faithful**" (Revelation 17:14).

Notice that three qualifications are given for this company. These are not generalized characteristics for all Christians, but qualities that set apart this army of participants.

> Called: This means invited or appointed. All men are called to repentance, but only some will humble themselves and receive Jesus as their Lord and Savior.

> Chosen: This means selected. Jesus tells us that many are called, but few are chosen (Matthew 22:14). In the context of Matthew 22:14, we are chosen by our response and obedience to the righteous works that God calls us to perform.

> Faithful: This means trustworthy, sure, or true. This is in regard to follow-through. Paul explained to the Philippians that since his road was not over yet, he needed to be faithful and keep pressing towards the high calling. This describes those who finish strong.

CHAPTER 27

The Parable of the Talents

For the kingdom of heaven is as a man travelling into a far country, who called his own servants, and delivered unto them his goods. And unto one he gave five talents, to another two, and to another one; to every man according to his several ability; and straightway took his journey. Then he that had received the five talents went and traded with the same, and made them other five talents. And likewise he that had received two, he also gained other two. But he that had received one went and digged in the earth, and hid his lord's money. After a long time the lord of those servants cometh, and reckoneth with them. And so he that had received five talents came and brought other five talents, saying, Lord, thou deliveredst unto me five talents: behold, I have gained beside them five talents more. His lord said unto him, Well done, thou good and faithful servant: thou hast been faithful over a few things, I will make thee ruler over many things: enter thou into the joy of thy lord. He also that had received two talents came and said, Lord, thou deliveredst unto me two talents: behold, I have gained two other talents beside them. His lord said unto him, Well done, good and faithful servant; thou hast been faithful over a few things, I will make thee ruler over many things: enter thou into the joy of thy lord. Then he which had received the one talent came and said, Lord, I knew thee that thou art an hard man, reaping where thou hast not sown, and gathering where thou hast not strawed: And I was afraid, and went and hid thy talent in the earth: lo, there thou hast that is thine. His lord answered and said unto him, Thou wicked and slothful servant, thou knewest that I reap where I sowed not, and gather where I have not strawed: Thou oughtest therefore to have put my money to the exchangers, and then at my coming I should have received mine own with usury. Take therefore the talent from him, and give it unto him which hath ten talents. For unto every one that hath shall be given, and he shall have abundance: but from him that hath not shall be taken away even that which he hath. And cast ye the unprofitable servant into outer darkness: there shall be weeping and gnashing of teeth.

(Matthew 25:14-30)

Introducing the Parable

Jesus begins this parable with the words "for the kingdom of heaven is…" Just as I pointed out with the parable of the virgins, this means that the entire parable references those who are saved. This framework cannot be dismissed from our interpretation. Everyone in the parable has received Jesus because they partake of the kingdom of heaven. Only from this foundation can we build the correct interpretation.

The Servants and the Talents

The parable describes three servants. The man travelling to a far country is Jesus, and the servants are the saints. Note that everyone in the parable is called a "servant," there are no "enemies." To one servant he gave five talents, to another two talents, and to the third servant, one talent. The number of talents that the servants receive is in direct proportion to their ability.

"For unto whomsoever much is given, of him shall be much required: and to whom men have committed much, of him they will ask the more" (Luke 12:48).

The talents represent different starting conditions. It is a simple fact that because we live in a fallen world, some people begin with better circumstances than others. There are those born into wealth, and those that are born into abject poverty. There are those born with great intelligence, and those born with less. There are those born into influence, and those born under oppression. According to our ability, we are given talents. The amount of fruit produced through our lives is not measured by quantity, but by faithfulness to what we were appointed.

Immediately after delivering goods to his servants, the travelling man leaves. The servants then take the master's goods and begin to steward them. The first servant trades with his talents and gains another five talents. He produces a one hundred percent increase. The second servant trades with his two talents and gains another two talents. He also produces a one hundred percent increase. The third servant digs a hole and places his talent inside of it. He produces nothing.

Reckoning with the Servants

When the man returns, the Bible says that he "reckoneth" with his servants. This is vitally important. By reckoning with his servants, the Master is essentially judging their works. This parable actually references the second coming of Jesus, and then places us at the judgment seat of Christ. Whereas the first parables dealt with the circumstances surrounding the return of Christ, this parable has moved forward in time to describe how the saints will be judged. The saints are described as servants, and they receive according to the things done in their flesh, *whether good or bad*.

"For we must all appear before the judgment seat of Christ; that every one may receive the things done in his body, according to that he hath done, **whether it be good or bad**" (2 Corinthians 5:10).

The first servant stands before the judgment seat, bringing the original five talents, along with the increase. His Lord congratulates him. He is called a faithful servant, and the Lord says he will make him a ruler over many things. Again, at the judgment seat of Christ, our reward is positional, not material. His reward comes in the form of a designated sphere of rule.

"Blessed and holy is he that hath part in the first resurrection: on such the second death hath no power, but they shall be priests of God and of Christ, **and shall reign with him** a thousand years" (Revelation 20:6).

The Lord deals with the second servant in a similar way. When he stands before the judgment seat of Christ, he presents the original talents, along with the increase. The Lord sees the increase and calls him a faithful servant. The second servant is also made a ruler over many things. The fact that he receives the same reward as the first servant reveals that our reward is based on how we steward what we are given, not the quantity of what we actually produce.

THE WICKED AND SLOTHFUL SERVANT

Once we get to the third servant, the story changes. This servant began with an excuse. He did not present what he had, but began by making an appeal to the Lord. The excuse was fear! This servant was afraid to step out and do anything with what God gave him. After he made his excuses, he gave the talent back to the Lord. Thus, at the judgment seat of Christ, this servant represents the population of Christians who received Jesus, yet did nothing that God called them to do. The end is not good.

The Lord answered him, saying, "Thou wicked and slothful servant!" God was not pleased, and does not hide his frustration. Whereas the servant twists the character of the Lord into an excuse for not serving him, the Lord confronts the feeble excuse, explaining that his character *should have been* the servant's motivation to produce. He goes on to say that at the very least, the money should have been given to the exchangers so that the talent would gain usury (or interest).

THE MONEY EXCHANGERS

Who are the money exchangers, and what usury is Jesus referring to? Specifically, when we sow our finances into the ministries of others, we participate in their reward. Although we are called to do more than simply finance someone else, this simple act is one way to earn some reward. Paul makes this blatantly obvious. When the Philippians gave a monetary gift to him, they had fruit abound to their account as a result of what Paul did with their money.

"Now ye Philippians know also, that in the beginning of the gospel, when I departed from Macedonia, no church communicated with me as concerning giving and receiving, but ye only. For even in Thessalonica ye sent once and again unto my necessity. Not because I desire a gift: but **I desire fruit that may abound to your account**" (Philippians 4:15-17).

BURNING THE WORKS

This servant not only represents Christians who do nothing, but also those who are unwilling to release their finances into the works of God. He is wicked, slothful, and greedy! The result is unfavorable judgment. His talent is taken from him and given to the one who produced the most. This represents the fire that tries our works at the judgment seat of Christ.

"Now if any man build upon this foundation gold, silver, precious stones, wood, hay, stubble; Every man's work shall be made manifest: for the day shall declare it, because it shall be revealed by fire; and the fire shall try every man's work of what sort it is. If any man's work abide which he hath built thereupon, he shall receive a reward. If any man's work shall be burned, he shall suffer loss: but he himself shall be saved; yet so as by fire" (1 Corinthians 3:12-15).

This servant suffers great loss indeed, but he is still a servant. He enters heaven, but he enters without any reward. For this reason he will enter eternity with great grief. I can hardly fathom the grief that will be felt by those who must stand before a righteous and holy Savior—and present nothing. To look the Savior of our souls in his eyes, eyes that burn with the passion of eternity, and say, "I have failed you. I have wasted my entire life, and though you gave me everything, I gave you nothing." The sorrow and travail will be indescribable! For all eternity, their opportunity for reward is lost, because in this life, they failed Jesus.

DEFINING THE OUTER DARKNESS

This parable closes with a difficult passage:

"And cast ye the unprofitable servant into outer darkness: there shall be weeping and gnashing of teeth" (Matthew 25:30)

The main thing that we must understand is that this is still a servant of the Lord. Even though his works have been burned by the fire, he will still enter into eternity with Jesus. *Outer darkness does not represent hell, but a positional reality in the kingdom of heaven.* If he were going to hell, Jesus would have mentioned the "furnace of fire." Even though he still enters eternity with Jesus, there will be weeping and gnashing of teeth. In fact, this is the same phrase used to describe the sorrow of those who actually do enter hell.

"And shall cast them into a **furnace of fire**: there shall be **wailing and gnashing of teeth**" (Matthew 13:42).

The words "wailing" (Matthew 13:42) and "weeping" (Matthew 25:30) are actually the same word in Greek. It is a sobering thought to think that both those who are cast to hell, and those who lose their reward at the judgment seat of Christ, will experience the sorrow. This is mirrored in the parable of the uninvited wedding guest (Matthew 22:1-14). When a man is found at the wedding feast without his garments, he is also cast into outer darkness, but not hell, because there is no mention of a "furnace of fire" or "punishment." Our wedding garments are our righteous works (Revelation 19:8), which can be lost (Revelation 16:15) thereby causing us to walk naked to our shame.

"And he saith unto him, Friend, how camest thou in hither not having a wedding garment? And he was speechless. Then said the king to the servants, Bind him hand and foot, and take him away, and cast him into outer darkness, there shall be weeping and gnashing of teeth. For many are called, but few are chosen" (Matthew 22:12-14).

THE NEXT PHASE OF THE JUDGMENT SEAT OF CHRIST

Thus, at the end of this parable we are at the end of the first segment of the judgment seat of Christ. As we proceed forward into the last part of the Olivet discourse, we will find that Jesus is no longer speaking in parables at all. We will remain in the time frame of the judgment seat of Christ.

Jesus will now introduce the concept of sheep and goat nations at the judgment seat. Sheep nations are only mentioned by name in one location in the Bible, yet they are profoundly important to God's plan for the end of the age. Everything discussed in this book from the revelation of the heart, to the gospel of the kingdom, to the timeline and events of the end times, come together to yield sheep nations—their purpose, and their destiny.

PART 7

CHAPTER 28

What is a Sheep Nation?

"When the Son of man shall come in his glory, and all the holy angels with him, then shall he sit upon the throne of his glory: And before him shall be gathered all nations: and he shall separate them one from another, as a shepherd divideth his sheep from the goats: And he shall set the sheep on his right hand, but the goats on the left. Then shall the King say unto them on his right hand, Come, ye blessed of my Father, inherit the kingdom prepared for you from the foundation of the world" (Matthew 25:31-34).

From where do we derive the term "sheep nations"? In Matthew 25, Jesus declares that he will separate the nations as a shepherd divides his sheep from his goats. The nations that Jesus divides like sheep are what I refer to as "sheep nations." The nations that Jesus divides like goats are what I refer to as "goat nations." In the Bible, the right hand always denotes the hand of favor. The nations divided like sheep will be set on his right hand, and the nations divided like goats will be set on his left hand. Therefore, sheep nations are going to receive favorable judgment after the return of Jesus.

WE ARE STILL AT THE JUDGMENT SEAT OF CHRIST

Jesus returns in glory at the end of the great tribulation. This occurs at the sounding of the seventh trumpet. There is a short period of time during which the bowls of wrath are poured out on the earth. At this time, the church will fulfill her ministry as the literal army of God, fighting with Jesus in many battles climaxing at Armageddon (Jude 1:14-15, Isaiah 13:1-5, Habakkuk 3:15-16, and possibly Joel 2:1-11). After Armageddon, there is going to be a judging of nations. *This judgment will be at the judgment seat of Christ*. Matthew 25:14-46 gives us a fuller understanding of what takes place at the judgment seat of Christ, but Paul coins the term that we attach to this event.

"But why dost thou judge thy brother? or why dost thou set at nought thy brother? for we [the saints] shall all stand before **the judgment seat of Christ**" (Romans 14:10).

In order for Jesus to judge nations like sheep after his second coming, these nations must arise and be in operation on earth before his return. This means that during Daniel's seventieth week, and extending through the end of the great tribulation, sheep nations will exist. They will probably begin to arise even earlier than this. What will be their purpose? The primary purpose of sheep nations will be to herald the gospel of the kingdom of God to the whole world. They will house the glory of God waiting to be poured out in the last days. They will reveal kingdom government influencing entire geographies. In this, sheep nations will effectively preserve the people of God, feed and educate the people of God, and protect the people of God during the reign of the final antichrist.

Clarifying the Concept of Nations

In Matthew 25, the word "nations" is translated from the Greek word *ethnos*. This word indicates ethnic groups, and thus where we get our word "ethnic" from. However, this is not just indicating ethnicities such as Indian or Panamanian. The word *ethnos* is used to describe nations with geographic boundaries, as well as ethnic groups that transcend national boundaries. We must keep this in mind because we are not to become so concrete in our parameters of word use that we impose parameters of interpretation that are not etymologically founded.

When we are talking about nations at the judgment seat of Christ, we are in essence talking about two things. One, there will be representation of people groups that were living within geographically defined boundaries. There will also be representation of all ethnicities. We must also understand they are referred to in the plural. Sheep nations do not refer exclusively to the single holy nation composed of born-again believers at this judgment, but they will include born-again believers prior to the return of Christ. This will be further explained as we proceed.

"But ye are a chosen generation, a royal priesthood, **an holy nation (ethnic group)**, a peculiar people; that ye should shew forth the praises of him who hath called you out of darkness into his marvellous light" (1 Peter 2:9).

Those who have the salvation of Jesus Christ are considered to be a single, unique *ethnos*. God, through the work of Jesus Christ at Calvary, has created an entirely new ethnic group composed of all nations through the blood of Jesus. These nations are made one holy nation in him.

The judgment seat of Christ will have two phases. The first deals with rewards for the saints (pictured by the parable of the talents). The second phase is for the unregenerate nations that survive the return of Christ. It is at this time that God in his perfect justice and wisdom will select which among the nations will enter the millennium. During the second phase, we will stand as onlookers.

By saying that all nations will be gathered before him, Jesus is saying every *ethnos* will hold representation at the judgment seat of Christ. However, these are human or unredeemed Gentile nations as opposed to members of our single holy nation.

Then shall the King say unto them on his right hand [the sheep nations], Come, ye blessed of my Father, inherit the kingdom prepared for you from the foundation of the world: For I was an hungred, and ye gave me meat: I was thirsty, and ye gave me drink: I was a stranger, and ye took me in: Naked, and ye clothed me: I was sick, and ye visited me: I was in prison, and ye came unto me. Then shall the righteous answer him, saying, Lord, when saw we thee an hungred, and fed thee? or thirsty, and gave thee drink? When saw we thee a stranger, and took thee in? or naked, and clothed thee? Or when saw we thee sick, or in prison, and came unto thee? And the King shall answer and say unto them [the sheep nations], Verily I say unto you, **Inasmuch as ye have done it unto one of the least of these my brethren [the saints], ye have done it unto me**.

(Matthew 25:34-40)

THE THREE ASSEMBLIES

The two assemblies of nations that are gathered before Jesus at the judgment seat of Christ are referred to as sheep and goat nations. In addition, there is a third assembly. These are called the brethren of King. When the King refers to his brethren, he is specifically referring to the glorified saints. This is where the saints are pictured as onlookers during this judgment.

Only saints qualify to be called the brethren of God. When Jesus says, "As ye have done it unto one of the least of these my brethren," he is pointing out that the members of the sheep nations cooperated with the "brethren" during the last days. This group of "brethren" is comprised of those who received a reward (or judgment) in the previous parable. As we have seen, these parables have been a chronological explanation of the order of events after the Lord's return.

Jesus does the same thing he did in moving from the parable of the goodman to the parable of the virgins. In that case, he spoke about leaders in his body as the goodman/porter, afterwards making reference to them as "those who sell." In a similar fashion, Jesus spoke about the saints as "servants" in the previous parable (see last chapter), and now makes reference to them as the "brethren." Where else does God refer to the saints as his brethren?

"But he answered and said unto him that told him, Who is my mother? and who are my brethren? And he stretched forth his hand toward his disciples, and said, **Behold my mother and my brethren**" (Matthew 12:48-49)!

"Jesus saith unto her, Touch me not; for I am not yet ascended to my Father: **but go to my brethren**, and say unto them, I ascend unto my Father, and your Father; and to my God, and your God" (John 20:17).

"Have we not power to lead about a sister, a wife, as well as other apostles, and **as the brethren of the Lord**, and Cephas" (1 Corinthians 9:5)?

THE RIGHTEOUSNESS OF SHEEP NATIONS

Members of sheep nations will work together with the brethren in resisting the rule of the antichrist. However, as we begin to develop the concept of sheep nations, we run into a major issue. We have described the sheep nations at this judgment as the unregenerate nations that help the saints during the rule of the antichrist. The principle problem is that if the group judged as sheep nations includes those who are not saved, why does Jesus refer to them as righteous?

"Then shall **the righteous** answer him, saying, Lord, when saw we thee an hungred, and fed thee? or thirsty, and gave thee drink" (Matthew 25:37)?

The fact of the matter is that *in this age* there is no righteousness apart from salvation by grace through faith in Jesus Christ.

"As it is written, **There is none righteous**, no, not one" (Romans 3:10).

"For I say unto you, That except your righteousness shall exceed the righteousness of the scribes and Pharisees, ye shall in no case enter into the kingdom of heaven" (Matthew 5:20).

"But we are all as an unclean thing, and **all our righteousnesses are as filthy rags** [for cleaning menstrual blood]; and we all do fade as a leaf; and our iniquities, like the wind, have taken us away" (Isaiah 64:6).

Many would like to assume that in judgment there are simply saved and unsaved; that at the coming of Jesus it will either mean heaven or hell. Yet this cannot be entirely true because if it were, why are people getting judged as righteous sheep nations at the judgment seat of Christ? It's simply not black and white. What we will find—and it will shock many people—is that the righteousness of sheep nations will be established according to works. The principle thing we must understand is that *the age* that we are presently in will have ended by the time this judgment is taking place.

So, how are we to understand this? Let's begin by considering that there will be a remnant of Israel at the return of Christ. On this thought, it seems that there is a special exception for a remnant of the tribes of Israel in Jerusalem. It appears as though there may be an imputed righteousness, even though this would seem to break the rules. Notice that God is going to "call" those left in Zion and in Jerusalem holy.

"And it shall come to pass, that he that is left in Zion, and he that remaineth in Jerusalem, shall be called holy, even every one that is written among the living in Jerusalem" (Isaiah 4:3).

Those in Jerusalem are recorded as giving honor to God after the two witnesses of Revelation are resurrected from the dead and ascend to heaven (Revelation 11:13). However, even if we accept that those being judged as sheep nations correspond to a Jewish remnant mentioned in this passage, why are the nations referred to in the plural? Israel is considered a single nation. So how does this work?

Making the Transition

A major defining factor in properly understanding the judging of sheep nations comes from understanding that it occurs as the world transitions from one age to another. The age of the millennial rule will not be governed by the same standards as the age of the church. *In other words, once Jesus returns, the New Covenant is fulfilled.*

When we transition into the millennial reign, the Bible clearly states in at least two places that the law will be reinstated. During the millennium, the age of salvation by grace through faith in Jesus Christ *will have ended.*

"On the testimony of two or three witnesses shall a charge be established" (Deuteronomy 19:15 AMP).

"And many people shall go and say, Come ye, and let us go up to the mountain of the LORD, to the house of the God of Jacob; and he will teach us of his ways, and we will walk in his paths: **for out of Zion shall go forth the law**, and the word of the LORD from Jerusalem" (Isaiah 2:3).

"And many nations shall come, and say, Come, and let us go up to the mountain of the LORD, and to the house of the God of Jacob; and he will teach us of his ways, and we will walk in his paths: **for the law shall go forth of Zion**, and the word of the LORD from Jerusalem" (Micah 4:2).

Them That Fear Thy Name

This is where we return to a Scripture that was questioned several chapters back. Let us rehash this and see if we can't glean some additional insight.

"And the nations were angry, and thy wrath is come, and the time of the dead, that they should be judged, and that thou shouldest give reward unto **thy servants the prophets**, and to **the saints**, and **them that fear thy name**, small and great; and shouldest destroy **them which destroy the earth**" (Revelation 11:18).

Notice that there are four separate groups identified here.

1. The prophets.

2. The saints.

3. Them that fear thy name.

4. Those that destroy the earth.

Why are there four separate groups? This question can only be answered after we understand the way things pan out at the judgment seat of Christ. The judgment seat of Christ is the focal event necessary to transition the world from its present age and into the millennial rule. Jesus returns at the seventh trumpet and at that time "the kingdoms of this world have become the kingdoms of our Lord." Therefore, the purpose for the church age is essentially finished. Those who survive the return of Jesus and have not received him as their Lord and Savior will undergo judgment at the judgment seat of Christ. However, they will not be judged according to whether or not they made a quality decision to receive Jesus as their Lord and Savior. Remember that these people haven't died; they are simply involved in the transition from one age to the next. To put it as straightforwardly as possible, *the sheep nations in this parable are those being judged as righteous because of their affiliation with the agenda of the "brethren."* As the brethren, we stand as witnesses to their actions before the Lord.

According to Scripture, the definition of the group referred to as "prophets" is a reference to Old Testament prophets ending at John the Baptist (Matthew 11:13). The "saints" are those that have received salvation by grace through faith in Jesus Christ (Jude 3). This leaves the group described as "those that fear the name of the Lord" undefined. If they are not Old Testament prophets or New Testament saints, who are they? In short, I believe they are (or at the very least include) the unsaved *ethnos* that survived the return of Christ and were affiliated with sheep nations. They receive an imputed righteousness at the judgment seat of Christ after the saints (referred to as the "brethren") have received their rewards (or judgments). The sheep nations are permitted to enter into the millennial rule as citizens. It follows that the goat nations are defined as (or at the very least include) "those that destroy the earth." They will be judged as cursed, and not permitted to enter into the millennial rule.

The Judgment Seat of Christ is for the Purpose of Judging Works

It is important to comprehend that the judgment seat of Christ is a judging of works from beginning to end. It begins with a judging of the saints to determine what kind of reward we are to receive (2 Corinthians 5:10). This has nothing to do with salvation. When the judging of the saints is finished, Jesus will also judge the surviving *ethnos* of the world based upon their works. Jesus tells the sheep nations exactly why the sheep nations will enter the kingdom. He says, "For I was hungry and you gave me meat…" Giving someone meat is a work, it has nothing to do with receiving Jesus as Lord—yet this is exactly *why* they will enter the kingdom at this time. When we understand this, it increases our clarity many times over.

Making Sense of Loose Ends

There are very awkward passages that this understanding accounts for. For instance, in the book of Zechariah, the day of the Lord and the victory of Jesus Christ are pictured in the fourteenth chapter. It says that God brings all nations against Jerusalem to fight against them (Zechariah 14:2). Then it says that everyone who survives and is left of these nations will go up year by year to worship the Lord and to keep the Feast of Tabernacles.

"And it shall come to pass, that **every one that is left of all the nations which came against Jerusalem** shall even go up from year to year to worship the King, the LORD of hosts, and to keep the feast of tabernacles" (Zechariah 14:16).

This is not a parabolic statement. This will literally happen. This means that survivors whose *ethnos* were initially fighting against Jerusalem are permitted to enter into the millennial rule. How? By the time of the judgment seat of Christ, they fall into the category of "those that fear the name of the Lord." Interestingly enough, if they don't go up and keep the Feast of Tabernacles during the millennium, there will be consequences. It is news for many people to find out that the millennium is not the perfect state of existence once thought. There will be plagues and judgments still. Consider what Zechariah adds to his former statements:

"And it shall be, that whoso will not come up of all the families of the earth unto Jerusalem to worship the King, the LORD of hosts, even upon them shall be **no rain**. And if the family of Egypt go not up, and come not, that have no rain; there shall be **the plague**, wherewith the LORD will smite the heathen that come not up to keep the feast of tabernacles. This shall be **the punishment** of Egypt, and **the punishment of all nations** that come not up to keep the feast of tabernacles" (Zechariah 14:17-19).

Speaking of sheep nations, by siding with the passionate, wise and faithful saints, they will also submit themselves to a godly overhaul of the seven mountains society which are family, spirituality, business, government, arts, media, and education. Societal influence by the kingdom of God will ensure the continued blessing and preservation that God has appointed for the sheep nations. In these cases, virtually every area of life would be conformed to the principles of God. This is a major part of the heralding of the gospel of the kingdom that must take place "as a witness unto all nations" before the return of Christ (Matthew 24:14). This will occur as the kingdom of God, which exists outside of this dimension, enters into it through the hearts of the people of God. Remember how Jesus taught the disciples to pray:

"After this manner therefore pray ye: Our Father which art in heaven, Hallowed be thy name. **Thy kingdom come, Thy will be done in earth, as it is in heaven**" (Matthew 6:9-10).

Before the coming of Jesus, nations will bow the knee to his agenda. The greatest glory the world has ever witnessed is waiting to be revealed in the last days. God will draw nations to himself through the heralding of the gospel of the kingdom. *The gospel of Jesus Christ has the power to bring salvation to individuals, but the gospel of the kingdom has the power to bring salvation to nations.* The destiny of nations at the inception of the millennial rule will literally be determined on the basis of whether or not they chose to cooperate with the agenda of the kingdom of heaven. This is exciting.

The Facts Still Remain

Unfortunately, the existence of sheep nations does not mean all Christians (or unsaved members) will be protected. Many Christians will fall away before the end and will inevitably be destroyed. Others will refuse to participate in the final moves of God due to false doctrine and tradition. Many of these people will choose to reside outside of the realms of God's appointed provision, and will also be destroyed. Moreover, some of those having understanding will also be required to sacrifice their lives to bring the church into its final destination (Daniel 11:35). The road to Armageddon will inevitably be the bloodiest road history will ever reveal! As a result of the targeted execution, many Christians will die, many will go into captivity, and eventually even the power mentioned in Daniel 12:7, which I believe refers to the power of the sheep nations (since it cannot be the power of Christ), will be scattered.

"And they that understand among the people shall instruct many: yet they shall fall by the sword, and by flame, by captivity, and by spoil, many days. Now when they shall fall, they shall be holpen with a little help: but many shall cleave to them with flatteries. And some of them of understanding shall fall, to try them, and to purge, and to make them white, even to the time of the end: because it is yet for a time appointed" (Daniel 11:33-35).

"He that leadeth into captivity shall go into captivity: he that killeth with the sword must be killed with the sword. Here is the patience and the faith of the saints" (Revelation 13:10).

"And his [the antichrist's] power shall be mighty, but not by his own power [but by Satan's power]: and he shall destroy wonderfully, and shall prosper, and practise, and shall destroy the mighty and the holy people [the saints]" (Daniel 8:24).

"I beheld, and the same horn made war with the saints, and prevailed against them" (Daniel 7:21).

"And I heard the man [who was an angel] clothed in linen, which was upon the waters of the river, when he held up his right hand and his left hand unto heaven, and sware by him that liveth for ever that it shall be for a time, times, and an half [1260 days or the period of great tribulation]; and when he [the antichrist] shall have accomplished to scatter the power of the holy people [possibly by overcoming the earthly power of the sheep nations], all these things shall be finished [Jesus is returning]" (Daniel 12:7).

Leading up to the return of Jesus, sheep nations will provide the necessary circumstances to preserve enough Christians to fulfill the purposes of God throughout the great tribulation. They will also preserve the individuals who stand against the antichrist with the Christians. Ultimately, they will exist long enough to preserve those who will be involved in bringing the body of Christ to the measure of the stature of the fullness of Jesus Christ. This is also described as "the wife of the Lamb making herself ready" and "the bride being presented without spot or wrinkle or any such thing."

"Let us be glad and rejoice, and give honour to him: for the marriage of the Lamb is come, and **his wife hath made herself ready**" (Revelation 19:7).

"That he might sanctify and cleanse it with the washing of water by the word, That he might present it to himself **a glorious church, not having spot, or wrinkle, or any such thing**; but that it should be holy and without blemish" (Ephesians 5:26-27).

THE GOSHEN PRINCIPLE

Drawing from our original explanation of the heart, sheep nations are not limited by currently existing national borders. What does this mean? It is not as if in order to create a sheep nation Christians would have to target and invade a country and take over its religious system, government, and means of production. Remember that a kingdom exists within the hearts of people. Therefore, although sheep nations will occupy certain geographies, they will not necessarily need to take over existing national boundaries. The point is that certain geographies will come together to become sheep nations. Other ways of describing this coming phenomenon are "pockets of mercy" or "end-time Goshens." Those who are unsaved participants will come under the supernatural protection that God is providing to the geographic locations of sheep nations.

Else, if thou wilt not let my people go, behold, I will send swarms of flies upon thee, and upon thy servants, and upon thy people, and into thy houses: and the houses of the Egyptians shall be full of swarms of flies, and also the ground whereon they are. And I will sever in that day **the land of Goshen, in which my people dwell, that no swarms of flies shall be there**; to the end thou mayest know that I am the LORD in the midst of the earth. And **I will put a division between my people and thy people**: to morrow shall this sign be.

(Exodus 8:21-23)

After Joseph was raised to power in ancient Egypt, Pharaoh invited Jacob and his whole household to dwell in the land of Goshen. God greatly multiplied the Jews there until they numbered in the millions. Out of fear, the Egyptians enslaved them and murdered their male children. In God's timing, he sent Moses to deliver the Jewish people through a series of ten plagues. While Egypt was struck with plague after plague, Goshen, which borders right next to Egypt, saw not a single plague. Although the Israelites lived there, any foreigners would have been protected in this geography as well. God miraculously set this geography apart and protected it.

The coming sheep nations will exist under similar circumstances. Consider the fact that many of the trumpet judgments of Revelation correspond with plagues that were released against Egypt. For instance, the first trumpet (Revelation 8:7) correlates with the seventh plague (Exodus 9:22-25) in that trees and vegetation are destroyed. The third trumpet (Revelation

8:10-11) correlates with the first plague (Exodus 7:20-25) in that fresh water is made undrinkable. These are just two examples. If the judgments are similar (yet on a larger scale), it only makes sense to believe that God's provision will be similar (yet on a larger scale) as well. Furthermore, Scripture plainly says that God's plan is to perform works in the last days according to the works that he used to bring Israel out of Egypt.

"According to the days of thy coming out of the land of Egypt will I shew unto him marvellous things" (Micah 7:15).

To create balance, we must remember that God protected Goshen from *his judgments and plagues.* During this time, the Jews still had to cope with the oppression that came from the Egyptians. In the same way, even though there will be supernatural protection from the judgments of God, persecution will still exist. Mighty miracles will be wrought on behalf of the people of God and the sheep nations, but many will still die. This message does not contradict itself, but simply paints a full and accurate portrayal of what is to come.

THE WARS OF THE ANTICHRIST

The message of sheep and goat nations also makes sense regarding what we find in the book of Daniel chapter 11. Notice how the antichrist is continually at war. Who is he at war with?

Thus shall he [the final antichrist] do in the most strong holds with a strange god, whom he shall acknowledge and increase with glory: and he shall cause them to rule over many, and shall divide the land for gain. And at the time of the end shall **the king of the south push at him**: and **the king of the north shall come against him** like a whirlwind, with chariots, and with horsemen, and with many ships; and he shall enter into the countries, and shall overflow and pass over. He shall enter also into the glorious land, and many countries shall be overthrown: **but these shall escape out of his hand, even Edom, and Moab, and the chief of the children of Ammon**. He shall stretch forth his hand also upon the countries: and the land of Egypt shall not escape. But he shall have power over the treasures of gold and of silver, and over all the precious things of Egypt: and the Libyans and the Ethiopians shall be at his steps. But **tidings out of the east and out of the north shall trouble him**: therefore he shall go forth with great fury to destroy, and utterly to make away many. And he shall plant the tabernacles of his palace between the seas in the glorious holy mountain; yet he shall come to his end, and none shall help him.

(Daniel 11:39-45)

When I used to believe that the antichrist simply ruled the whole world because the church had been removed, the idea that he would continually be at war made no sense. The supernatural circumstances of his presence, and the fact that the kings that rule with him all have the same mind, seemed to rule out the possibility of a coup or conspiracy to be formed against him. The futurist notion of a "hive-mind" seems to be exactly what the Bible predicts for those allied with the antichrist.

"And the ten horns which thou sawest are ten kings, which have received no kingdom as yet; but receive power as kings one hour with the beast. **These have one mind**, and shall give their power and strength unto the beast" (Revelation 17:12-13).

In addition, the Bible says the final antichrist is given power over every nation, tongue and tribe, which describes the greatest degree of mind control ever wielded by any leader.

"And it was given unto him to make war with the saints, and to overcome them: and power was given him over all kindreds, and tongues, and nations" (Revelation 13:7).

The Bible goes so far as to say *all* whose names are not written in the Book of Life will worship him. The Book of Life is so important to understand that we will discuss it in the Epilogue. What you, as the reader, will discover is that this population "never written into the Book of Life" refers to the entire non-human/post-human/Nephilim population in the earth at that time. This actually helps our understanding quite a bit, because it means that not all non-Christian humans will be worshipping the beast.

"And all that dwell upon the earth shall worship him, **whose names are not written in the book of life of the Lamb** slain from the foundation of the world" (Revelation 13:8).

I used to question, who would be left to make war against the antichrist? However, now that I understand that he is at war with the saints because the rapture occurs at the end of Daniel's seventieth week (meaning the end of the great tribulation), and that sheep nations have risen up to reject his agenda and preserve the people of God, the passage formerly discussed in Daniel chapter 11 makes all the sense in the world. Goat nations have also risen up that will oppose the antichrist agenda out of mere human will. Unfortunately, these groups will reject the agenda of God at the same time. It is a fact that the groups represented by Edom and Moab in Daniel 11 are goat nations, because although they escape the antichrist's hand, they are still destroyed by Jesus at his coming. If they were sheep nations, this would not be so.

"The sword of the LORD is filled with blood, it is made fat with fatness, and with the blood of lambs and goats, with the fat of the kidneys of rams: for the LORD hath a sacrifice in Bozrah, and a great slaughter in the land of [**Edom**]" (Isaiah 34:6).

"I see Him, but not now; I behold Him, but He is not near. A star (Star) shall come forth out of Jacob, and a scepter (Scepter) shall rise out of Israel and shall crush all the corners of **Moab** and break down all the sons of Sheth [Moab's sons of tumult]" (Numbers 24:17 AMP).

SHEEP NATIONS, GOAT NATIONS, AND A NEW WORLD ORDER

As already discussed, when the Bible describes stars that fall from heaven, it is generally making reference to fallen angels (obviously in the case above the "Star" is actually describing Jesus). These fallen angels come to earth to assist the antichrist with his agenda after the restrainer has been removed. As far as the antichrist kingdom is concerned, the days of human government will have come to an end. It will be extremely difficult for human government to sufficiently sustain a population against what will be revealed. Although goat nations will exist apart from the antichrist kingdom, they won't have it easy. I will add that any members of the antichrist kingdom that take the mark of the beast and survive Armageddon will also find themselves among those at the left hand of Jesus at the judging of nations. There will be no hope for them.

"Then another angel, a third, followed them, saying with a mighty voice, Whoever pays homage to the beast and his statue and permits the [beast's] stamp (mark, inscription) to be put on his forehead or on his hand,

He too shall [have to] drink of the wine of God's indignation and wrath, poured undiluted into the cup of His anger; and he shall be tormented with fire and brimstone in the presence of the holy angels and in the presence of the Lamb" (Revelation 14:9-10 AMP).

Dissenters who reject the New World Order and the mark of the beast will find refuge in sheep and goat nations that have risen up. Sheep nations will be fortified by supernatural power from heaven to stand in the days of adversity. Those who are members of sheep nations at the return of Christ and are not saved by grace through faith (yet have not received the mark of the beast) will be granted entrance into the manifested kingdom of heaven on earth (the millennial rule of Jesus Christ). For those who are grouped as goat nations, they will be judged as cursed, even if they did not participate in the antichrist kingdom. *The judgment of sheep and goat nations is strictly to determine who among the Gentile nations will enter the millennial reign and who will not.* It has nothing to do with eternal life or salvation by grace through faith.

Another aspect that should be addressed is that the world as we see it today will not be the same at the time of the return of Jesus. The antichrist will attempt to rule the whole world, but he will fail. Nonetheless, the national boundaries that exist today will be nothing more than a memory at the return of Jesus. With national boundaries eliminated, sheep nations will probably not be current-day nations (although some of them may). They will be geographies of resistance, probably bordering geographies of conformance to a New World Order agenda and the totalitarian rule of the coming antichrist. The same will be true of goat nations.

CONCLUDING THE MATTER

In conclusion, in order to create a sheep nation in this age, the kingdom of God must rule in the hearts of influential people within a particular geography and/or people group. A sheep nation is a nation that is influenced by the kingdom of God reigning in and through the hearts of men. When God rules in the hearts of people within a particular geography and/or people group, and that nation is cooperating with and being actively influenced by God's people, God as King will be responsible to distinguish it. No other kingdom will be able rule over the members of a sheep nation, no matter how much they may try to impose their agenda.

"But I will sing of thy power; yea, I will sing aloud of thy mercy in the morning: for thou hast been my defence and refuge in the day of my trouble. Unto thee, O my strength, will I sing: for God is my defence, and the God of my mercy" (Psalm 59:16-17).

CHAPTER 29

Thy Kingdom Revealed

"And he said unto them, When ye pray, say, Our Father which art in heaven, Hallowed be thy name. Thy kingdom come. Thy will be done, as in heaven, so in earth" (Luke 11:2).

Jesus instructed us to pray that the kingdom would come so that God's will would be done. The purpose of this book has been to reveal the kingdom of God and its implications before and after the second coming of Christ. I pray that by this point you, as the reader, have an entirely new perspective of this verse. Before the second coming, the heralding of the gospel of the kingdom will result in the manifestation of sheep nations. After the second coming, this kingdom will fill the whole world, as Jesus rules gloriously before his saints in Jerusalem.

"Then the moon shall be confounded, and the sun ashamed, when the LORD of hosts shall reign in mount Zion, and in Jerusalem, and before his ancients gloriously" (Isaiah 24:23).

As we are approaching the end of this book, several questions may remain unanswered. The truth is that the kingdom of God cannot truly be understood until we have a solid grasp of the parables regarding the kingdom. These are among the most difficult parables in all of Scripture because they can seem problematic, and even contradictory. Some people have even questioned if there was a difference between the gospel that Jesus preached and the gospel that Paul preached because of these parables.

At this point, it is fitting to discuss the most important parables that Jesus used to describe the kingdom. Why save the best for last? These parables seal the revelation of the rest of the kingdom parables. By closing with them, my prayer is that all of the revelation that has been discussed in this book will be settled. We are progressively entering into the kingdom of God, and in doing so we are paving the way for the return of our Lord and Savior.

"Confirming the souls of the disciples, and exhorting them to continue in the faith, and that we must **through much tribulation enter into the kingdom of God**" (Acts 14:22).

The Parable of the Sower

The parable of the sower is a cornerstone in Christian teaching. The following is that passage taken from the book of Matthew:

The same day went Jesus out of the house, and sat by the sea side. And great multitudes were gathered together unto him, so that he went into a ship, and sat; and the whole multitude stood on the shore. And he spake many things unto them in parables, saying, Behold, a sower went forth to sow; And when he sowed, some seeds fell by the way side, and the fowls came and devoured them up: Some fell upon stony places, where they had not much earth: and forthwith they sprung up, because they had no deepness of earth: And when the sun was up, they were scorched; and because they had no root, they withered away. And some fell among thorns; and the thorns sprung up, and choked them: But other fell into good ground, and brought forth fruit, some an hundredfold, some sixtyfold, some thirtyfold. Who hath ears to hear, let him hear.

(Matthew 13:1-9)

The parable of the seed and the sower is infinitely important to our faith, but like anything else, if we approach the parable from the wrong premise, we miss the whole point. The fact of the matter is that *this parable pertains to the kingdom of God*. Note the clear reference to the hearing of the *word of the kingdom*.

"When any one heareth the **word of the kingdom**, and understandeth it not, then cometh the wicked one, and catcheth away that which was sown in his heart. This is he which received seed by the way side" (Matthew 13:19).

What does this mean? It means that everything about the parable must be interpreted from a kingdom perspective. Most teachings on this parable assume that Jesus is simply talking about evangelism, and this is very understandable. At the surface, the parable seems to be a great picture of how some will respond to the gospel of Jesus Christ while others will not. As we will see, this is an oversimplification. Beginning at this point, we will examine the parable.

The Types of Ground and the Seed

The nice thing about this parable is that Jesus explains it to us in the Bible. Before we look at the explanation, we will pick out the obvious things. From God's perspective, there are four kinds of ground upon which his seed can fall. These types of ground are wayside ground, stony ground, thorny ground and good ground. Since the ground where the sower is sowing is not assigned any parameters, we must accept that it represents the world. The types of ground describe the heart conditions of the people in the world. The sower is obviously Jesus, but what do his seeds represent?

"Now the parable is this: The seed is the word of God" (Luke 8:11).

"Being born again, not of corruptible seed, but of incorruptible, by the word of God, which liveth and abideth for ever" (1 Peter 1:23).

The seed that the sower sows is the incorruptible seed of the Word of God. This means that the seed is actually Jesus Christ himself, because John chapter 1 tells us that Jesus is the Word of God. Therefore, the parable portrays Jesus attempting to sow himself into the lives of people. The goal is not to simply get the seed into the ground, but to grow a harvest on each seed. The parable is not about how different people will get closer than others to receiving Jesus as Lord. The parable describes the kingdom, and what happens once the word of the kingdom has been sown into the hearts of people. Jesus wants to grow crops (meaning a people) that express *all* of his attributes.

THE PURPOSE FOR PARABLES

In Matthew 13, the narrative continues as the disciples ask Jesus why he speaks to them in parables. Jesus explains that parables are intended to conceal the truth from the spiritually deaf, but to reveal the truth to the saints. Parables reveal the mysteries of the kingdom of heaven. Jesus quotes Isaiah to explain that the ears of the Jewish people had grown cold, and that they would not understand. He comments that the prophets and righteous men of old desired to hear what the disciples were hearing. After this commentary, Jesus continues with the explanation of the parable:

Listen then to the [meaning of the] parable of the sower: **While anyone is hearing the Word of the kingdom and does not grasp *and* comprehend it, the evil one comes and snatches away what was sown in his heart.** This is what was sown along the roadside. As for what was sown on thin (rocky) soil, this is he who hears the Word and at once welcomes *and* accepts it with joy; Yet it has no real root in him, but is temporary (inconstant, lasts but a little while); and when affliction *or* trouble *or* persecution comes on account of the Word, at once he is caused to stumble [he is repelled and begins to distrust and desert Him Whom he ought to trust and obey] *and* he falls away. As for what was sown among thorns, this is he who hears the Word, but the cares of the world and the pleasure *and* delight *and* glamour *and* deceitfulness of riches choke *and* suffocate the Word, and it yields no fruit. As for what was sown on good soil, this is he who hears the Word and grasps *and* comprehends it; he indeed bears fruit and yields in one case a hundred times as much as was sown, in another sixty times as much, and in another thirty.

(Mathew 13:18-23 AMP)

Isn't it interesting that the first thing that Jesus says regarding the explanation is that it deals with hearing the *word of the kingdom*. Isn't it also interesting that the only ground that does not receive the seed is the wayside ground. Notice that the word of the kingdom is *not stolen from the minds* of those represented by the wayside ground. Satan steals it from within their hearts. This means that Satan steals this from the subconscious, where heavenly realities must be embraced before they can be revealed.

THE WORD OF THE KINGDOM

In all practicality, the easiest way to define the *word of the kingdom* is with the name of Jesus. The name of Jesus contains the authority to activate all of the realities, benefits and blessings of the kingdom of God. In other words, the Word of God (John 1) is also the Word of the kingdom. When we reject Jesus Christ we also reject his kingdom, because we cannot have one without receiving the other. Again, the gospel of the kingdom does not exist apart from the gospel of Jesus Christ.

THE MYSTERIES OF THE KINGDOM

"He answered and said unto them, Because it is given unto you to know the **mysteries of the kingdom** of heaven, but to them it is not given" (Matthew 13:11)

There are *mysteries of the kingdom* according to Matthew 13:11. The word "mysteries" comes from the Greek word *musterion*. These mysteries are the truths of God's kingdom being revealed through his people. These truths are beyond the reach of natural apprehension, and must be revealed by the Holy Spirit, who is our Teacher. This is why Jesus sent the Holy Spirit to guide us into all truth. The truths that the Holy Spirit guides us into don't just inform us, they transform us.

"Howbeit when he, the Spirit of truth, is come, he will guide you into all truth: for he shall not speak of himself; but whatsoever he shall hear, that shall he speak: and he will shew you things to come" (John 16:13).

Christianity is not just about embracing the gospel of Jesus Christ, but also about embracing the gospel of his kingdom. The gospel of Jesus Christ is the message that allows us to enter the kingdom. Once we receive Jesus, we become members of his kingdom. Thus, while the gospel of the kingdom includes the gospel of Jesus Christ, the gospel of the kingdom is much more than just the gospel of Jesus Christ. *This is where the parable begins.*

Remember that the seed is the incorruptible seed of Jesus himself. Jesus is trying to grow himself in us and express himself through us. This is why he will not return until the church is mature.

"Till we all come in the unity of the faith and of the knowledge of the Son of God, unto a perfect man, **unto the measure of the stature of the fulness of Christ**" (Ephesians 4:13).

Jesus is sowing his seed, and it is landing on the different types of ground in the world. The only ground that does not receive the seed is the wayside ground. This ground represents the entire percentage of people who do not receive Jesus (and thus his kingdom) when they hear the gospel. The word of God is sown into our hearts because our hearts perceive information that is both natural and spiritual. A thought can penetrate our heart, but if we reject that thought, and do not believe it or confess it, it will not affect us. We are only saved when we receive and believe the word of God in our hearts and confess it with our mouths.

"That if thou shalt confess with thy mouth the Lord Jesus, and shalt believe in thine heart that God hath raised him from the dead, thou shalt be saved. For with the heart man believeth unto righteousness; and with the mouth confession is made unto salvation" (Romans 10:9-10).

While Satan comes and immediately steals the message of the kingdom from the people represented by the wayside ground, the rest of the types of ground all represent saints. Why are the majority of these crops portrayed as dying? It is not that the individuals have not received the gospel of Jesus—notice that the seed takes root every time. The issue regards the kingdom. This is exactly what Jesus says. In the stony and thorny ground, it is the fruit of the seed that gets destroyed. Consider what would happen if Christians all over the world began to act in faith on things regarding the kingdom, like:

➢ Satan has no access to heaven, he cannot accuse us before God (Revelation 12:8-9)

➢ We are to express Jesus in his fullness (character and ministry) (Ephesians 4:15)

➢ We are recipients of wealth transfer (Proverbs 13:22)

➢ We are only sent because Jesus has all authority in heaven and on earth (Matthew 28:18-19)

➢ Kingdom government overtaking human institutions is possible (Matthew 6:10)

➢ Unity of the brethren is commanded (1 Peter 3:8, Ephesians 4:13)

➢ We are to cause heaven to manifest on earth (Luke 11:2)

This list is by no means all inclusive, but these are some of the mysteries of the kingdom. These are truths that are to be revealed to the world through the members of the kingdom of God. The mysteries of the kingdom are the truths of God's kingdom revealed through his people. This is what Satan is scared of! Unfortunately, these truths are the same things that the church fights against the hardest as well. It is as if many Christians are afraid to believe it. This is why such great increase describes the "good ground" while no lasting increase comes to any of the other "grounds."

A Closer Look at the Types of Ground

Regarding the wayside ground, these people immediately reject the message of the kingdom when they hear it. Needless to say, they do this by rejecting Jesus. They literally hand their incorruptible seed over to Satan, and are willing partakers in the theft of their promise. These do not receive eternal life.

Regarding the stony ground, these people receive the promise without counting the cost. They might enjoy the message, but when they face the attack of the enemy, they do not last. In my opinion, the lack of discipleship in the church has forced many into this camp. It is hard to play full-contact sports without a coach. Though they fail in their ministry to God and others, they still inherit eternal life.

The ground with thorns represents people who earnestly pursue the kingdom. However, when their pursuit of the kingdom leaves them in a position to choose faith or security, they default to safety and shy away from further pursuit of the kingdom. Their decisions circumvent the ability for the kingdom of God to be revealed through their lives. They care to further their career, please parents, and create their own identity more than to express their identity in Christ. They do little for God, although they are at least faithful in small things. These also inherit eternal life.

Those represented by the good ground will embrace Christ, and thereby allow him to produce his kingdom through their lives. They will bear much fruit. They will allow the incorruptible seed of Christ to not just take root, but to produce its intended yield in and through their lives. They will partake of the mysteries of the kingdom, not only being transformed personally, but also causing everything around them to be transformed.

The Way, the Truth, and the Life

When we truly understand who Jesus is to us, fully embracing him becomes more understandable. We gain our understanding of who Jesus is from the Bible—God's infallible source of truth. One passage that is particularly powerful regarding the revelation of Jesus is as follows:

"Jesus said to him, I am the Way, the Truth, and the Life; no one comes to the Father except by Me" (John 14:6 AMP).

We can only have access to eternal life and the Father through (salvation by grace through faith in) Jesus Christ. Jesus also explains that he is the way, the truth, and the life. These are key elements to embracing him and allowing his incorruptible seed to *mature* in our "ground." Our level of maturity is directly tied to our ability to establish God's kingdom on the earth. Only when the incorruptible seed is allowed to grow to maturity in our lives does it bring the desired crop.

Way: When Jesus refers to himself as the Way, he is inferring that he is the only doorway that leads us to God (John 10:9). If we are to enter in by him, we must be obedient to the things he commands of us. When we are obedient to what he tells us, we come to the Father. When we are not obedient to the things Jesus tells us (through the Bible, through prayer, through others, through dreams, through visions, etc.) we are not embracing Christ. *Since he is the Way, we must do things his way.* Disobedience to Christ causes us to not be "good ground."

Truth: When Jesus refers to himself as the Truth, he is inferring that we need to align the thoughts of our heart with the truth that is revealed in his Word. The more truth that we believe in our hearts (not our heads), the more like Christ we become. If we do not believe that we can do all things through Christ who strengthens us (Philippians 4:13), we are rejecting the seed of Christ in us. If we do not believe that we have been made free from sin and are now the servants of righteousness (Romans 6:18), we are rejecting the seed of Christ in us. If we do not believe that Jesus was talking about us when he said, "I assure you, most solemnly I tell you, if anyone steadfastly believes in Me, he will himself be able to do the things that I do; and he will do even greater things than these, because I go to the Father" (John 14:12 AMP), we are rejecting the seed of Christ in us. We are to conform our hearts to the truth of his Word pertaining to everything that is written in the Bible, even down to the issue of giants, demons, and the reality of the events discussed in the book of Revelation.

Life: When Jesus refers to himself as the Life, he is inferring that we are now entitled to live a supernatural life. We have access to supernatural health because we have already been healed by the stripes of Jesus (1 Peter 2:24). We are to live according to heavenly realities, and not earthly realities.

We are to express his character and do things the way he would do them. We are granted the very life of God. In this passage, the word translated "life" is the Greek word *zoe*. This word is always used in reference to eternal life and life associated with God.

When we are operating according to these three aspects of Christ, we will reveal the kingdom of heaven on the earth. It is inevitable. The whole point of Christianity is to grow up into all that Jesus has purchased for us, not to just get saved and baptized. Jesus has so much in store for us that it truly is beyond our comprehension, and actually requires the mind of Christ to receive. As it is written:

> But as it is written, **Eye hath not seen, nor ear heard, neither have entered into the heart of man, the things which God hath prepared for them that love him**. But God hath revealed them unto us by his Spirit: for the Spirit searcheth all things, yea, the deep things of God. For what man knoweth the things of a man, save the spirit of man which is in him? even so the things of God knoweth no man, but the Spirit of God. Now we have received, not the spirit of the world, but the spirit which is of God; that we might know the things that are freely given to us of God. Which things also we speak, not in the words which man's wisdom teacheth, but which the Holy Ghost teacheth; comparing spiritual things with spiritual. But the natural man receiveth not the things of the Spirit of God:

for they are foolishness unto him: neither can he know them, because they are spiritually discerned. But he that is spiritual judgeth all things, yet he himself is judged of no man. For who hath known the mind of the Lord, that he may instruct him? **But we have the mind of Christ**.

(1 Corinthians 2:9-16)

The Parable of the Wheat and the Tares

Jesus then describes a second parable based on the context of the first. It also deals with the kingdom, which is very important. Again, we have to realize that this parable regards the state of the kingdom of God, which we can only enter into through spiritual interaction with the Holy Spirit.

Another parable put he forth unto them, saying, The kingdom of heaven is likened unto a man which sowed good seed in his field: But while men slept, his enemy came and sowed tares among the wheat, and went his way. But when the blade was sprung up, and brought forth fruit, then appeared the tares also. So the servants of the householder came and said unto him, Sir, didst not thou sow good seed in thy field? from whence then hath it tares? He said unto them, An enemy hath done this. The servants said unto him, Wilt thou then that we go and gather them up? But he said, Nay; lest while ye gather up the tares, ye root up also the wheat with them. Let both grow together until the harvest: and in the time of harvest I will say to the reapers, Gather ye together first the tares, and bind them in bundles to burn them: but gather the wheat into my barn.

(Matthew 13:24-30)

The only population that bore a crop in the first parable were the saints. In the second parable, a new population is introduced. This is the population represented by the "tares." How can a new population be introduced into the kingdom of God that is not born of the seed of Jesus? We must ask this question because in the explanation, Jesus mentions that the tares are gathered "out of the kingdom" and removed (Matthew 13:40-41). They will be burned in the fire. In order to be removed from the kingdom, they would have to be "in" it to begin with. Furthermore, the tares are removed into the furnace of fire, which is a parabolic description of hell. Does this mean that some Christians go to hell? I ask this rhetorically, as we have already answered this question with a resounding no. However, there is still more to discuss on this point.

The Confusion Regarding the Gospel of the Kingdom

For this question and others like it, many have lowered the message of the kingdom parables. It has been said that these parables are simply dealing with the *profession* of the Christian faith. In other words, the kingdom of heaven somehow includes both saved and unsaved, even though Scripture is clear that entrance into God's kingdom requires a spiritual translation (Colossians 1:13). It follows that the tares that will be burned represent those who profess Christ but have not actually received Jesus as their personal Lord and Savior, even though they somehow belong to the kingdom. Frankly, to believe this removes the power of the gospel of the kingdom, because it assumes that anyone can partake of it at any time if they simply lie and profess the Christian faith. *This would also mean that the kingdom of heaven does not extend power from God's realm into ours, but that it is simply a collection of people!* Of course, by this point we understand that this conclusion is absolutely ridiculous.

The Tares at the End of the Age

The removal of the tares from the kingdom is an event that can only occur at the *end of the age.* Going back to the parable, we will continue with the explanation that Jesus gave:

He answered and said unto them, He that soweth the good seed is the Son of man; The field is the world; the good seed are the children of the kingdom; but the tares are the children of the wicked one; The enemy that sowed them is the devil; the harvest is the end of the world; and the reapers are the angels. As therefore the tares are gathered and burned in the fire; so shall it be in **the end of this world**. The Son of man shall send forth his angels, and they shall gather out of his kingdom all things that offend, and them which do iniquity; And shall cast them into a furnace of fire: there shall be wailing and gnashing of teeth. Then shall the righteous shine forth as the sun in the kingdom of their Father. Who hath ears to hear, let him hear.

(Matthew 13:37-43)

I have already alluded to this earlier in this book, but I am going to say it again. The burning of the tares occurs *at the end of the age,* after the kingdoms of the world have become the kingdoms of our Lord and his Christ. It is true that the tares represent a population that is not saved. However, they are not gathered out of the church, but out of the world. The church building may contain the spiritual seeds of Satan, because it is true that they can participate in church services. The true church, however, is comprised solely of born-again believers. Church is not a building, but the assembly of people that have been called out of the world by receiving Jesus as their personal Lord and Savior. This is God's perspective of the church, and it should be ours as well. When the end of the age is upon us, the seventh trumpet will sound. At the seventh trumpet, everything changes, because the kingdoms of the world become the kingdoms of God instantaneously (refer to Figure 5 in chapter 19).

"And the seventh angel sounded; and there were great voices in heaven, saying, **The kingdoms of this world are become the kingdoms of our Lord, and of his Christ**; and he shall reign for ever and ever" (Revelation 11:15).

The kingdom of heaven will open up onto the earth and consume it upon the sounding of the seventh trumpet. For this reason, the wicked must be removed. The whole world becomes the kingdom of God, and the tares must be taken out of it. The mystery of God is finished at the seventh trumpet, and the war campaign and subsequent activities are literally a formality. The glorification of the saints, causing us to fully manifest as the sons of God, is the completion of the mystery of God.

"But in the days of the voice of the seventh angel, when he shall begin to sound, the mystery of God should be finished, as he hath declared to his servants the prophets" (Revelation 10:7).

DEFINING THE PARABOLIC ELEMENTS

In the parable, Jesus is still the sower. The sower is not the one that falls asleep. There are a number of men that fall asleep while the tares are being sown. These men represent the leaders of the body of Christ. The field is not the kingdom but the world (Matthew 13:38). The enemy does not sow his seed into the kingdom of God, but into the world. The good seed represents the saints, whether they produce an increase or not. This comes from the first parable. The tares are the seed of the wicked one.

THE CHILDREN OF THE WICKED ONE

How are we to interpret the statement that the tares represent the "children of the wicked one?" I propose that it is two-fold. The enemy has sown both his spiritual nature and at times, physical offspring into the world. Both would be valid here. Both will burn in hell. Both exist and are clearly spoken of throughout scripture. An example of a person into whom Satan had sown his spiritual seed is found here:

"And when they had gone through the isle unto Paphos, they found a certain sorcerer, a false prophet, **a Jew**, whose name was Barjesus…Then Saul, (who also is called Paul,) filled with the Holy Ghost, set his eyes on him. And said, O full of all subtilty and all mischief, **thou child of the devil,** thou enemy of all righteousness, wilt thou not cease to pervert the right ways of the Lord" (Acts 13:6, 9-10)?

Clearly, this sorcerer was a man. I do not see any reason to interpret this passage as referring to anything other than a wicked person. Luke, the author of Acts, even makes the point of mentioning what kind of man this was—a Jew. In this case, the sorcerer had taken on the spiritual seed of Satan, and as a result became very wicked.

An example of a person into whom angelic seed had been literally sown is found here:

"And there was yet a battle in Gath, where was a man of great stature, that had on every hand six fingers, and on every foot six toes, four and twenty in number; and he also was born to the giant" (2 Samuel 21:20).

Resolving the Conflict

Both of these groups will be cast into the furnace at the end of the age. The world will be reaped by the angels. But how are we to deal with the fact that in this parable, the tares are gathered first?

"Let both grow together until the harvest: and in the time of harvest I will say to the reapers, **Gather ye together first the tares**, and bind them in bundles to burn them: but gather the wheat into my barn" (Matthew 13:30).

The problem is that there seems to be a conflict in the order of events. We have discovered that the church will be taken and glorified at the seventh trumpet. However, the battle of Armageddon will not occur for another number of days (according to my research). How can we fit into this order of events the children of the wicked one being gathered first? Consider that if the tares are gathered and burned first, the church would be gathered second. Apart from any other scripture, this could point to the thought that the wicked are destroyed before the saints are glorified. Does this make any sense when God uses his army of glorified saints to destroy the wicked?

"And I saw heaven opened, and behold a white horse; and he that sat upon him was called Faithful and True, and in righteousness he doth judge and make war... And the armies which were in heaven [the saints] followed him upon white horses, clothed in fine linen, white and clean" (Revelation 19:11, 14).

The key to understanding this rests in our ability to overlap scripture. While we have already touched on this issue, it is helpful to repeat the conclusions at this point. The fact of the matter is that the tares are simply gathered first. It does not say that they are gathered and burned first. The passage says that they are gathered first for the purpose of being burned later. This is a crucial element in our understanding. We now move to the book of Revelation to complete our understanding of this scenario.

And I heard a voice from heaven saying unto me, Write, Blessed are the dead which die in the Lord from henceforth: Yea, saith the Spirit, that they may rest from their labours; and their works do follow them. And I looked, and behold a white cloud, and upon the cloud one sat like unto the Son of man [Jesus], having on his head a golden crown, and in his hand a sharp sickle. And another angel came out of the temple, crying with a loud voice to him that sat on the cloud, Thrust in thy sickle, and reap: for the time is come for thee to reap; for the harvest of the earth is ripe. And he that sat on the cloud [Jesus] thrust in his sickle on the earth; and the earth was reaped. And another angel came out of the temple which is in heaven, he also having a sharp sickle. And another angel came out from the altar, which had power over fire; and cried with a loud cry to him that had the sharp sickle, saying, Thrust in thy sharp sickle, and gather the clusters of the vine of the earth; for her grapes are fully ripe. And the angel thrust in his sickle into the earth, and gathered the vine of the earth, and cast it into the great winepress of the wrath of God. And the winepress was trodden without the city, and blood came out of the winepress, even unto the horse bridles, by the space of a thousand and six hundred furlongs.

(Revelation 14:13-20)

Compare this to another reference of the end of the age and the appearing of Christ:

Immediately after the tribulation of those days shall the sun be darkened, and the moon shall not give her light, and the stars shall fall from heaven, and the powers of the heavens shall be shaken: And then shall appear the sign of the Son of man in heaven: and then shall all the tribes of the earth mourn, and they shall see the Son of man coming in the clouds of heaven with power and great glory. And he shall send his angels with a great sound of a trumpet, and they shall gather together his elect from the four winds, from one end of heaven to the other.

(Matthew 24:29-31)

It is clear from the passage in Revelation that an angel is reaping the tares (at least those classified as the clusters of the vine) into the battle of Armageddon. Prior to this, the angels that are released go out to gather the bodies of the elect that have died, thus causing the dead in Christ to rise. Jesus then uses his own sickle to rapture the worthy portion of the church—both the living and those that have been recently resurrected from the dead, as we discussed earlier in the book. When the reference is made to the wheat, we must accept that the "gathering into the barn" occurs after the tares are bundled. The barn refers to God's storage place for the saints, which will be the kingdom of Jesus Christ during the millennial rule.

Although the angels of the harvest are assigned to bundle the tares first in Matthew 13:30, this gathering and bundling is not spelled out. However it occurs, it is probably a quick work, and by no means are we to assume that the "burning" is performed immediately. In other words, the tares will be gathered, the church will be reaped, and the punishment of wickedness will occur precisely as described by the prophetic scriptures. In the end, all wickedness will be destroyed and burned.

A GLORIOUS FINALE

Thus we arrive at the conclusion of the matter. The gospel of the kingdom must go forth as a witness to all nations, and then the end will come. This gospel has the power to bring salvation to entire nations. It is the good news that the kingdom of God is here. Part of the result of the gospel of the kingdom going forth will be the establishment of sheep nations that oppose the agenda of the final antichrist. Sheep nations will occur as a result of the government of the kingdom of God ruling in and through the hearts of his people. This is the ultimate purpose of the mystery of the kingdom, which is the truth of God's kingdom being revealed through his church. When all of this comes together we will have *Kingdom Government and the Promise of Sheep Nations.*

The Book of Life

We have taken quite a journey, and I pray that God has opened hearts and minds to receive the things contained within this book. There is one final element that we have not yet discussed—the Book of Life.

THE SIMPLE PLAN OF SALVATION

Salvation is arguably both the simplest as well as the most confounding aspect of the Christian faith. Nearly any Christian professing faith in Jesus can explain God's plan for salvation: Jesus, being the express image and incarnation of God on earth, died for the sins of men. By his death and resurrection, he became an acceptable sacrifice for our sins, and now all who believe in him with their heart and confess with their mouth that Jesus is Lord will be saved. This salvation grants forgiveness and eternal life (Romans 10:9-10). The Bible goes on to say that he that believes and is baptized will be saved, but he who does not believe will be condemned (Mark 16:16).

The Hard Questions

After the simple plan of salvation, the issue becomes very difficult as we approach questions such as:

➤ Do stillborn and aborted babies go to hell?

➤ If God foreknew those who would be saved, why would he be so cruel as to create others and let them go to hell?

➤ Are certain people predestinated to go to heaven?

➤ Is predestination figurative, while the truth is that we have a choice?

➤ Can we lose our salvation?

➤ What is the Book of Life and how does it work?

Around these questions, entire denominations, and even entire perspectives of thought have been created. Is there really a right answer? Or do we simply have to settle for the Scripture that says:

"For as the heavens are higher than the earth, so are my ways higher than your ways, and my thoughts than your thoughts" (Isaiah 55:9).

The fundamental problem is that even when we "settle" for "settling that there are some things we will not understand," inevitably, there is some-one else demanding an answer for the questions. When we do not have the answers, they are frustrated, and so are we. What do we do?

Fortunately, God will give grace, and work through us even though we do not have all of the answers. However, this is no excuse for not seeking his truth. There is also no excuse for "settling" when God has put a desire in us for an answer to a spiritual question. He has given us the mind of Christ, and we are only in obedience as we continually seek illumination from the Holy Spirit concerning our questions. This chapter is intended to provide a framework through which all of these questions can be addressed.

Introducing the Book of Life

The Book of Life is among the least addressed topics in the Word of God. Many people, disciples, and theologians spend a lot of time debating the issues surrounding salvation, but when we understand the Book of Life, many of our questions become obsolete. What is the Book of Life? The Book of Life is a book in heaven that contains a record of those who have a right to salvation (Revelation 20:15). The book separates out three categories. The first category deals with those whose names are written in this Book of Life. There are also those whose names are blotted out of the Book of Life. These individuals form a second group. Thirdly, there is a group that is never writ-ten in the Book of Life.

Those whose names are still written in this book upon death have obtained the salvation of Jesus Christ. Glance over these Scriptures as they outline these basic conclusions:

"And I intreat thee also, true yokefellow, help those women which laboured with me in the gospel, with Clement also, and with other my fellowlabourers, **whose names are in the book of life**" (Philippians 4:3).

"He that overcometh, the same shall be clothed in white raiment; and **I will not blot out his name out of the book of life**, but I will confess his name before my Father, and before his angels" (Revelation 3:5).

"The beast that thou sawest was, and is not; and shall ascend out of the bottomless pit, and go into perdition: and they that dwell on the earth shall wonder, **whose names were not written in the book of life from the foundation of the world**, when they behold the beast that was, and is not, and yet is" (Revelation 17:8).

The apostle Paul, in the book of Philippians, explained that his fellow laborers had their names written in the Book of Life. He was not saying that only his fellow laborers were written in it while other Christians were not. He was exhorting his fellow laborers with the truth to encourage them.

In the second listed verse, Jesus builds upon this concept, explaining to the church of Sardis that if they overcome, their names will *not* be blotted out of the Book of Life. This meant that the names of those in the church were currently written in the Book of Life, but that their names *could* be blotted out. More specifically, if they did not overcome, their names *would* be blotted out.

The third group is found in Revelation 17:8. These individuals do not have their names written in the Book of Life at all. This leaves us with little room for debate. There are clearly three groups of people as far as the Book of Life is concerned. There is a group that has their names written in the Book of Life. There is another group that had their names written in the Book of Life at one point, but were then blotted out. Lastly, there is a group that *never* had their names written in the Book of Life.

Addressing the Issue of the Unborn

This is by no means enough information to settle the issue, but it is an inarguable point of origin. The Book of Life creates three categories of individuals. As we address questions regarding salvation, we will have to take into account all three groups. To remove one of these groups from the discussion creates an impossible theological scenario that can never be solved. Moving forward, the next question that must be answered is: What happens to unborn babies and children too young to receive Jesus as their personal savior?

Satan loves abortion! Could the reason for this be that the souls of unborn children go to hell because they cannot receive Jesus? When a person repeatedly has miscarriages, are those unfortunate souls lost to hell as well? The answer begins with the question: When does life begin? If life begins at birth, then unborn children do not actually exist from an eternal perspective. If life begins at conception, then unborn children must be accounted for in God's plan of salvation. This is what God said to Jeremiah:

"Before I formed thee in the belly I knew thee; and before thou camest forth out of the womb I sanctified thee, and I ordained thee a prophet unto the nations" (Jeremiah 1:5).

God knows humans before we are formed in the belly. Thus, our spirit is joined to our body upon conception. For this reason a fetus is *not* just a mishmash of cells. Since life *begins at conception*, the theology of salvation must account for the unborn as well as the mature adult.

Furthermore, it is not enough to simply say that life begins at conception, because this provides no information about where the non-physical nature of the human condition comes from—namely our soul and our spirit. Where is our spirit and soul formed? This question is answered in the following verse:

"For thou hast possessed my reins: thou hast covered me in my mother's womb. I will praise thee; for I am fearfully and wonderfully made: marvellous are thy works; and that my soul knoweth right well. **My substance was not hid from thee, when I was made in secret, and curiously wrought in the lowest parts of the earth**. Thine eyes did see my substance, yet being unperfect; and **in thy book all my members were written**, which in continuance were fashioned, when as yet there was none of them" (Psalm 139:13-16).

Here is the same verse in the Amplified Bible:

"For You did form my inward parts; You did knit me together in my mother's womb. I will confess and praise You for You are fearful and wonderful and for the awful wonder of my birth! Wonderful are Your works, and that my inner self knows right well. My frame was not hidden from You when I was being formed in secret [and] intricately and curiously wrought [as if embroidered with various colors] in the depths of the earth [a region of darkness and mystery]. Your eyes saw my unformed substance, and in Your book all the days [of my life] were written before ever they took shape, when as yet there was none of them" (Psalm 139:13-16 AMP).

Our substance is formed in the lowest parts of the earth. At this location there is some form of a "factory" where God produces the human substance. At conception, God knits our substance to our members in our mother's womb. This is how human life begins. In addition, this event is recorded in God's book. What is the mysterious book that this verse refers to? There is more than one book that God has. These include the seven-sealed book (Revelation 5), the book of remembrance (Malachi 3:16), and other books which are not necessarily described.

"And I saw the dead, small and great, stand before God; **and the books were opened**: and another book was opened, which is the book of life: and the dead were judged out of those things which were written in the books, according to their works" (Revelation 20:12).

According to this verse, the Book of Life stands apart from the rest of God's books. It is this book that the Bible refers to in Psalm 139. Upon conception, all humans are written into the Book of Life. This is one of the reasons why the Bible places such great emphasis on its importance. We are now going to consider the first reference to the Book of Life in the Bible:

"And Moses returned unto the LORD, and said, Oh, this people have sinned a great sin, and have made them gods of gold. Yet now, if thou wilt forgive their sin--; and if not, **blot me, I pray thee, out of thy book which thou hast written**. And the LORD said unto Moses, Whosoever hath sinned against me, him will I blot out of my book" (Exodus 32:31-33).

Is it more than coincidence that Moses refers to a book that contains names that can be blotted out? I believe so. I believe that before this book began to be called the Book of Life in the Bible, it was simply called God's book. In Psalm 69, this same book goes from being called God's book to the book of the living.

"Add iniquity unto their iniquity: and let them not come into thy righteousness. **Let them be blotted out of the book of the living**, and not be written with the righteous" (Psalm 69:27-28).

There is another hidden reference to the Book of Life that occurs in the book of Isaiah. The context of this passage is during the millennial rule of Jesus. Here, it is also being called the book of the living. It will be with Jesus in Jerusalem at that time.

"In that day shall the branch of the LORD [Jesus] be beautiful and glorious, and the fruit of the earth shall be excellent and comely for them that are escaped of Israel. And it shall come to pass, that he that is left in Zion, and he that remaineth in Jerusalem, shall be called holy, even every one that is **written among the living** in Jerusalem" (Isaiah 4:2-3).

Understanding this, we must realize that God must foreknow every human being that is born, because he is intimately involved in their existence. Not only does he foreknow every human being, but as it is written, he wrote us in his book though we were yet imperfect.

"Thine eyes did see my substance, **yet being unperfect**; and in thy book all my members were written…" (Psalms 139:16).

He knit each human substance to a body in the womb of a mother, and in order to do this, he cannot help but know every human. At this point we can answer the question: Do the unborn go to hell? The answer is no, because they are written in God's book, even though they are imperfect as they are conceived in sin.

"Behold, I was shapen in iniquity; and in sin did my mother conceive me" (Psalm 51:5).

David's Lost Child

This leads us to a story involving David. He committed adultery with a woman named Bathsheba, impregnating her. To avoid getting caught he had her husband killed. As a result, their first child was not permitted to live. David fasted and begged God for the life of the child, but to no avail. When the child died, this was his response:

"And he said, While the child was yet alive, I fasted and wept: for I said, Who can tell whether GOD will be gracious to me, that the child may live? But now he is dead, wherefore should I fast? can I bring him back again? I shall go to him, but he shall not return to me" (2 Samuel 12:22-23).

David knew that although he could not bring the child back into this world, he would be united with the child in paradise. David said, "I shall go to him." David knew that both he and the newborn child were written in the Book of Life. This pattern continues into the New Testament when Jesus brings the kingdom of heaven. *The only way to access the kingdom of heaven is through our spirit, and in order to be a part of the kingdom of heaven our spirit must have some form of interaction with the Holy Spirit.* This is what Jesus said of little children:

"But when Jesus saw it, he was much displeased, and said unto them, Suffer the little children to come unto me, and forbid them not: **for of such is the kingdom of God.** Verily I say unto you, Whosoever shall not receive the kingdom of God as a little child, he shall not enter therein" (Mark 10:14-15).

THE FOREKNOWLEDGE OF GOD

How does the foreknowledge of God fit into deciphering how salvation works? This is a very important question, because many verses make reference to God's foreknowledge of those appointed to salvation. For example, are certain individuals not written into the Book of Life if God foreknows that they will reject the gospel of Jesus Christ? Now that we have set a foundation based on understanding the Book of Life, we can correctly answer this question. The answer is no. By understanding the conception of humans, we *must* accept that God foreknows all humans. God writes every human into his book because he is involved in the conception of every human. Now we can move into this verse:

"For whom he did foreknow, he also did predestinate to be conformed to the image of his Son, that he might be the firstborn among many brethren. Moreover whom he did predestinate, them he also called: and whom he called, them he also justified: and whom he justified, them he also glorified" (Romans 8:29-30).

Who did God foreknow? God foreknew all humans. Which humans were predestined to be conformed to the likeness of Jesus? The answer is: the ones that God foreknew. What percentage of humans did God foreknow? He foreknew every single human that ever lived. If all humans are predestined, will all humans be saved and glorified? No. So, how do we reconcile that all of the humans that God foreknew will not go on to be glorified? The answer is that Jesus knew beforehand who would believe. Thus, in the preceding verse, the ones who are "foreknown" are qualified by the following verse as the ones Jesus knew would believe.

"But there are some of you that believe not. **For Jesus knew from the beginning who they were that believed not**, and who should betray him. And he said, Therefore said I unto you, that no man can come unto me, except it were given unto him of my Father" (John 6:64-65).

There is often confusion between the fact that God foreknows all humans and that God foreknows those who will believe. This is not a small distinction. This distinction allows everything to make sense. It is clear that God foreknows all humans, and that all unborn and newly born children are written in the Book of Life. It has also been established that God foreknows those who will not believe in him, separating adult people into two groups. Those that he foreknows will believe in him will be justified and glorified. Those who do not and will not believe in him will not be justified or glorified.

He is Not Willing that any should Perish

There is a difference between foreknowledge and calling. A calling is an appointment to a God-ordained purpose. A calling can be embraced or rejected. The following verse outlines that those who are called "might" receive the promise of eternal inheritance. This means that by the same token, those who are called "might not" receive the promise of eternal inheritance.

"And for this cause he is the mediator of the new testament, that by means of death, for the redemption of the transgressions that were under the first testament, **they which are called might receive the promise of eternal inheritance**" (Hebrews 9:15).

This does not eliminate the reality of choice. This is the reality of choice represented in the perspective of a mind that perceives eternity. God reserves a potential calling for every human born, and if everyone would believe, it would be his perfect will realized! The truth is that it is not the will of the Father that any should perish whatsoever. This is why all humans are written in the Book of Life upon conception.

"Even so it is not the will of your Father which is in heaven, that one of these little ones should perish" (Matthew 18:14).

"The Lord is not slack concerning his promise, as some men count slackness; but is longsuffering to us-ward, **not willing that any should perish**, but that all should come to repentance" (2 Peter 3:9).

The Chosen Ones

There are a large number of Scriptures referring to the fact that we have been "chosen." How do we reconcile being "chosen" if it is in our power to reject Jesus? Consider some of these verses declaring that the servants of God have been chosen by God, and not visa-versa. As you read, keep in mind that the word translated in some passages as "elect" is a derivative of the word translated "chosen." They both imply being selected.

"**Ye have not chosen me, but I have chosen you**, and ordained you, that ye should go and bring forth fruit, and that your fruit should remain: that whatsoever ye shall ask of the Father in my name, he may give it you" (John 15:16).

"If ye were of the world, the world would love his own: but because ye are not of the world, but **I have chosen you** out of the world, therefore the world hateth you" (John 15:19).

"Put on therefore, **as the elect [chosen] of God**, holy and beloved, bowels of mercies, kindness, humbleness of mind, meekness, longsuffering" (Colossians 3:12).

"Therefore I endure all things for the **elect's** sakes, that they may also obtain the salvation which is in Christ Jesus with eternal glory" (2 Timothy 2:10).

There are a multitude of Scriptures that carry a similar emphasis on the act of God choosing those who will follow him. They cannot be ignored for the sake of our perception of "fairness." The key to understanding why God chooses some is found in the fact that God calls more than he chooses. *He chooses those that he foreknows will respond.* He calls many, but he only chooses a few.

"For many are called, but few are chosen" (Matthew 22:14).

The Parable of the Wedding

This passage is the conclusion of a parable that Jesus spoke to address this issue. This is the parable:

And Jesus answered and spake unto them again by parables, and said, The kingdom of heaven is like unto a certain king, which made a marriage for his son, And sent forth his servants to call them that were bidden to the wedding: and they would not come. Again, he sent forth other servants, saying, Tell them which are bidden, Behold, I have prepared my dinner: my oxen and my fatlings are killed, and all things are ready: come unto the marriage. But they made light of it, and went their ways, one to his farm, another to his merchandise: And the remnant took his servants, and entreated them spitefully, and slew them. But when the king heard thereof, he was wroth: and he sent forth his armies, and destroyed those murderers, and burned up their city. Then saith he to his servants, The wedding is ready, but they which were bidden were not worthy. Go ye therefore into the highways, and as many as ye shall find, bid to the marriage. So those servants went out into the highways, and gathered together all as many as they found, both bad and good: and the wedding was furnished with guests. And when the king came in to see the guests, he saw there a man which had not on a wedding garment: And he saith unto him, Friend, how camest thou in hither not having a wedding garment? And he was speechless. Then said the king to the servants, Bind him hand and foot, and take him away, and cast him into outer darkness, there shall be weeping and gnashing of teeth. For many are called, but few are chosen.

(Matthew 22:1-14)

In this parable, the King is God the Father and his Son is Jesus. The marriage is the uniting of the church to Jesus in glorification. The first servants called to the wedding are the Jews. The Jews are called, but they reject the calling. When they continually reject the calling and even persecute the King's servants, the King becomes angry and destroys their city. This was a parabolic prophecy of the destruction of Jerusalem in 70 AD. Then the King tells his servants (the saints) to call all that they can to the wedding. Here God is pictured as making a call to the whole world. Jesus gave the great commission instructing us to preach the gospel to every creature. God proves his fairness in that the calling is not dependent upon his foreknowledge about us. However, he chooses vessels from among those that he foreknows will respond. This is modeled in Acts 9:15 when God says of the apostle Paul, "He is a *chosen vessel* unto me, to bear my name before the Gentiles, and kings, and the children of Israel."

Regarding the man found without wedding garments, he serves as our example of those who are chosen, but do not keep their wedding garments.

"Behold, I come as a thief. Blessed is he that watcheth, **and keepeth his garments**, lest he walk naked, and they see his shame" (Revelation 16:15).

The man was part of the kingdom; he was called to the wedding, and was even in attendance. However, since he did not keep his garments, he was not permitted to remain among those who had kept their wedding garments. In fact, the wedding garments are not simply the righteousness that God imputes to those covered by the blood of Jesus (2 Corinthians 5:21, Romans 5:17, Revelation 1:5). *The fine linens given to the bride of Christ are actually the righteous deeds or acts of the saints.* In the following verse, the Greek word translated "righteousness" is *dikaioma*, which means an equitable deed (or by implication a statute or decision). In contrast, when the Bible speaks of imputed righteousness through Christ, the Greek word *dikaiosune* is employed, which means equity of character and justification.

"Let us be glad and rejoice, and give honour to him: for the marriage of the Lamb is come, and his wife hath made herself ready. And to her was granted that she should be arrayed in fine linen, clean and white: for the fine linen is the righteousness [dikaioma] of saints. And he saith unto me, Write, Blessed are they which are called unto the marriage supper of the Lamb. And he saith unto me, These are the true sayings of God." (Revelation 19:7-9)

Losing the Reward

Righteous deeds are works that reveal our faith. They are done out of a pure heart in obedience to the will of God. In the parable, the man without these wedding garments serves as an example of those who lose their heavenly reward and are cast into outer darkness, where there is weeping and gnashing of teeth. Their works do not follow them because they are not righteous deeds, and for this reason they are not dressed properly (symbolically) for the wedding. They will not go into damnation where there is the "furnace of fire," but they will experience extreme and unbearable sorrow at the reality of the loss of their reward. As previously discussed, this man without wedding garments is the same as the unprofitable servant described in Matthew 25:24-30. God warns those who are the chosen and elect many times throughout Scripture that we *can* lose the reward by our actions. Salvation is not a reward, but a gift. The reward is the sphere of rulership we are granted by Jesus at the judgment seat of Christ in addition to the type of body we reap in the resurrection.

"Look to yourselves, that we **lose not** those things which we have wrought, but that we receive a full reward" (2 John 1:8).

In Review

To quickly review, God is intimately involved in every human conception. He foreknows all humans because he knits us together in our mother's womb, but he also knows those who will respond to his call. All human children that are conceived are written into his Book of Life. His perfect will would be for all to be saved, but this will not happen. For this reason he chooses those that he foreknows will respond. He uses the chosen as his instruments on the earth. The chosen will enter into the works; "before ordained" and finished from the foundation of the world.

"For we which have believed do enter into rest, as he said, As I have sworn in my wrath, if they shall enter into my rest: although the works were finished from the foundation of the world" (Hebrews 4:3).

"For we are his workmanship, created in Christ Jesus unto good works, which God hath before ordained that we should walk in them" (Ephesians 2:10).

Preparing Vessels

Having established these things, it is possible to understand why God prepares certain vessels for wrath, hardens hearts, and makes a distinction between his people and those who are not his people. The issue is not God's character, but those that he foreknows will reject him. Since God foreknows those who will reject him, he can and does use them to further his glory anyway. Many times, these methods appear contrary to the people themselves (such as the Egyptian Pharaoh in the book of Exodus), but from an eternal perspective, God remains righteous and just in these things. This is the foundation that is necessary to understand the following passage out of Romans 9:

And not only this; but when Rebecca also had conceived by one, even by our father Isaac; (For the children being not yet born, neither having done any good or evil, that the purpose of God according to election might stand, not of works, but of him that calleth;) It was said unto her, The elder shall serve the younger. As it is written, Jacob have I loved, but Esau have I hated. What shall we say then? Is there unrighteousness with God? God forbid. For he saith to Moses, I will have mercy on whom I will have mercy, and I will have compassion on whom I will have compassion. So then it is not of him that willeth, nor of him that runneth, but of God that sheweth mercy. For the scripture saith unto Pharaoh, Even for this same purpose have I raised thee up, that I might shew my power in thee, and that my name might be declared throughout all the earth. Therefore hath he mercy on whom he will have mercy, and whom he will he hardeneth. Thou wilt say then unto me, Why doth he yet find fault? For who hath resisted his will? Nay but, O man, who art thou that repliest against God? Shall the thing formed say to him that formed it, Why hast thou made me thus? Hath not the potter power over the clay, of the same lump to make one vessel unto honour, and another unto dishonour? What if God, willing to shew his wrath, and to make his power known, endured with much longsuffering the vessels of wrath fitted to destruction: And that he might make known the riches of his glory on the vessels of mercy, which he had afore prepared unto glory, Even us, whom he hath called, not of the Jews only, but also of the Gentiles?

(Romans 9:10-24)

Blotting Names out of the Book

As far as I have concluded, it appears as though no one is blotted from the Book of Life until death. The only exception would be those who have either known Christ and forsaken their salvation, or "taken away" from the words of the prophecy of God. These groups seem to immediately get blotted out during their lifetime—left without hope.

"For **it is impossible** for those who were once enlightened, and have tasted of the heavenly gift, and were made partakers of the Holy Ghost, And have tasted the good word of God, and the powers of the world to come, If they shall fall away, to renew them again unto repentance; seeing they crucify to themselves the Son of God afresh, and put him to an open shame" (Hebrews 6:4-6).

"And if any man shall take away from the words of the book of this prophecy, God shall take away his part out of the book of life, and out of the holy city, and from the things which are written in this book" (Revelation 22:19).

We are all written into the Book of Life at conception, and there is never mention of being "un-blotted." For this reason, it would follow that we are not blotted out until we are at a point when there can no longer be a decision made in favor of Christ. It is important to make the distinction that the Book of Life is not an entrance into the kingdom of God, because Jesus is the only door. Our name in the Book of Life simply means there is still provision for our entrance into the kingdom of heaven. Having said this, very young children appear to have additional provision for salvation—should they die—because Jesus stated that *of such is the kingdom of God* (Mark 10:14-15).

DISMISSING A TRADITIONAL PERSPECTIVE OF PREDESTINATION

Some have tried to argue that because the Bible describes us as being "chosen" and "pre-destined" that there is a limit to the reach of the sacrifice that Jesus made on the cross. In other words, Jesus truly died for the elect because only the elect will be saved. I hope that by this point I have answered enough questions and provided enough background to easily make my next point.

The idea that Jesus' death was only for the elect becomes the foundation for a more traditional "predestination" approach to salvation. This perspective, however, requires that the adherent embrace what is known as "limited atonement." Behind this idea is the concept that the sacrifice of Jesus was only sufficient for the chosen. In order to embrace this idea, the adherent must accept that all other humans were literally born for the purpose of being sent to hell.

This is a false paradigm and must be dismissed. The power of the death and resurrection of Jesus is not limited to the elect, but is sufficient in power to potentially redeem all mankind. This means that the provision has been made to redeem all mankind, both "chosen" and "not chosen."

"My little children, these things write I unto you, that ye sin not. And if any man sin, we have an advocate with the Father, Jesus Christ the righteous. **And he is the propitiation for our sins: and not for ours only, but also for the sins of the whole world**" (1 John 2:1-2).

THOSE NEVER WRITTEN INTO THE BOOK OF LIFE

At the end of all of this, there is still a question that remains. Who comprises the third group that is never written into the Book of Life? How can a group of people exist that are not written into the Book of Life when God foreknows all humans that are conceived? Is this a direct contradiction in Scripture? Or does this mean that this entire discussion is flawed?

There are only two verses in all of Scripture that mention individuals who are never written into the Book of Life, and both occur in the book of Revelation.

"And all that dwell upon the earth shall worship him, **whose names are not written in the book of life** of the Lamb slain from the foundation of the world" (Revelation 13:8).

"The beast that thou sawest was, and is not; and shall ascend out of the bottomless pit, and go into perdition: and they that dwell on the earth shall wonder, **whose names were not written in the book of life** from the foundation of the world, when they behold the beast that was, and is not, and yet is" (Revelation 17:8).

The fact of the matter is that there is only one conclusion available for us regarding these passages: *this particular population is not human at all.* It is simply impossible for a human to not be written into the Book of Life. Remember that God foreknows all humans that are born, and according to Psalm 139, we are all recorded in his Book of Life upon conception. Thus, with a revelation on the meaning and purpose of the Book of Life, we actually acquire a necessary key for understanding the end times. This key is a direct prophecy regarding the creation and existence of a post-human/

non-human/Nephilim population during the reign of the antichrist. This should come as no surprise, considering our thorough discussion regarding the removal of the restrainer and the truth about the coming New Age. This non-human population will be wholly and irrevocably dedicated to the satanic agenda without exception. All that are not written into the Lamb's Book of Life will worship the beast.

Whose agenda will you submit to?

Contact the author at www.bridemovement.com

ENDNOTES

1 "Final Frontier: The Crucifixion - Medical and Prophetic Aspects - Anatomy and Physiology of the Crucifixion of Jesus Christ, Bible Prophecy fulfilled, and Blood of Jesus Christ on the Mercy Seat." *Final Frontier: Home - Home - Free Christian teaching resources from Dr Richard Kent on Life after Death, NDE's, Creation, Evolution, Crucifixion, Shroud of Turin, Archaeology, Abortion, Rapture, Bible, Money, Miracles.* N.p., n.d. Web. 25 Aug. 2010. <http://www.finalfrontier.org.uk/index.php?main=5&sub=1&page=28>.

2 Hagin, Kenneth E. *The gifts of the Holy Spirit.* 3rd printing 2002. ed. Tulsa, OK: Faith Library Publications: 2002. Print.

3 Wallnau, Lance. "Module 9 Lesson 32: The Apostolic Mandate to Change Nations." *Lance Learning Group.* 7M University, n.d. Web. 25 Aug. 2010. <lancelearning.com/LinkClick.aspx?fileticket=V9dvThrwMt0%3D&tabid=251>.

4 Grant R. Jeffrey, *Countdown to the Apocalypse: Learn to Read the Signs That the Last Days Have Begun* (Colorado Springs: WaterBrook, 2008). Pages 126-128.

5 Ibid.

6 Eastman, Mark, and Chuck Missler. *Alien Encounters: The Secret Behind The Ufo Phenomenon.* Revised ed. Coeur d'Alene: Koinonia House, 2003. Print. Page 232.

7 Vine, W. E. Vine's Expository Dictionary of Old & New Testament Words. Nashville, Tenn.: T. Nelson Publishers, 2003. Print.

8 Radmacher, Earl D., Ronald Barclay Allen, and H. Wayne House. "Leviticus 23." *Nelson's NKJV study Bible: NKJV, New King James Version.* Nashville, TN: Nelson Bibles, 1997. 213. Print.

9 Ibid.

10 Ibid.

11 Ibid.

12 Ibid.

13 Bullinger, E. W. *Number in scripture*. New York: Cosimo Classics, 2005. Print.

14 Ibid.

15 *Interview with an Ex-Vampire*. Dir. Michael Relfe. Perf. Bill Schnoebelen, Stephanie Relfe. Mark 161718 Productions, 2005. DVD.

16 Springmeier, Fritz, and Cisco Wheeler. *The Illuminati formula used to create an undetectable total mind controlled slave*. Clackamas, Or.: Springmeier & Wheeler, 1996. Print.

17 Horn, Thomas R. *Nephilim Stargates and the Return of the Watchers*. United States of America: Anomalos Publishing Llc, 2007. Print.

18 Amos Emmanuel, Eni. *Delivered from the Powers of Darkness*. Ibadan, Nigeria: Scripture Union, 1987.

19 Nkuba, Babajika Muana. *Rescued from Hell* . Codognan, France: Parole de Vie, 1996. Print.

20 Amos Emmanuel, Eni. *Delivered from the Powers of Darkness*. Ibadan, Nigeria: Scripture Union, 1987.

21 Ibid.

22 "Emerald Tablets of Thoth - Preface." *Crystalinks Home Page*. N.p., n.d. Web. 22 Dec. 2010. <http://www.crystalinks.com/emeraldprefacebw>

23 Author's note: An excellent treatment on this viewpoint can be found in the following book: Skiba, Rob. *Archon Invasion: The Rise, Fall, and Return of the Nephilim*. United States of America: King's Gate Media, LLC, 2012. Print.

24 Quayle, Stephen. *Angel Wars: Past, Present, and Future - No Flesh Left Alive?* Bozeman, MT: End Time Thunder Publishers, 2011. Print.

25 Author's note: I believe that the leadership of the final kingdom will be a *combination* of fallen angels and their children since both could be defined as fallen spirit beings.

26 Horn, Thomas. *Forbidden gates: How Genetics, Robotics, Artificial Intelligence, Synthetic Biology, Nanotechnology, and Human Enhancement*

Herald The Dawn Of TechnoDimensional Spiritual Warfare. Crane, MO: Defender, 2010. Print.

27 "List of messiah claimants - Wikipedia, the free encyclopedia." *Wikipedia, the free encyclopedia.* N.p., n.d. Web. 6 May 2013. <http:// en.wikipedia.org/wiki/List_of_messiah_claimants>.

28 "List of people claimed to be Jesus - Wikipedia, the free encyclopedia." *Wikipedia, the free encyclopedia.* N.p., n.d. Web. 6 May 2013. <http:// en.wikipedia.org/wiki/List_of_people_claimed_to_be_Jesus>.

29 Horn, Thomas R. *Apollyon Rising 2012: the lost symbol found and the final mystery of the great seal revealed.* Crane, Mo.: Defender, 2009. Print.

30 Wilhelmsen, Jim. *Beyond Science Fiction.* Rev. date 12/05/08. ed. Bloomington, IN: iUniverse, 2008. Print.

31 "Reclaiming the 7 Mountains." *Reclaiming the 7 Mountains.* N.p., n.d. Web. 3 Sept. 2013. <http://www.reclaim7mountains.com/>.

32 Enlow, Johnny. *The Seven Mountain Prophecy.* Lake Mary, Fla.: Creation House, 2008. Print.

33 Hunt, Dave. *A Woman Rides the Beast*. Eugene, Or.: Harvest House Publishers, 1994. Print.

34 "List of cities claimed to be built on seven hills - Wikipedia, the free encyclopedia." *Wikipedia, the free encyclopedia.* N.p., n.d. Web. 3 Sept. 2013. <http://en.wikipedia.org/wiki/ List_of_cities_claimed_to_be_built_on_seven_hills>

35 "Jasher chapter 9." *Sacred-Texts.com*. N.p., n.d. Web. 12 Apr. 2013. <www.sacred-texts.com/chr/apo/jasher/9.htmhttp://>.

36 Hamon, Bill. "God's Times and Purposes."*Prophetic Scriptures yet to be Fulfilled: During the Third and Final Church Reformation*. Shippensburg, PA: Destiny Image Publishers, 2010. 32-33. Print.

37 Green, Jay P. The interlinear Hebrew/Greek English Bible . 4 v. ed. Wilmington, Del.: Associated Publishers and Authors, 1976. Print.